INDIA

THE GIANT AWAKENS!

INDIA

THE GIANT AWAKENS!

Manoher V. Sonalker

ATLANTIC

PUBLISHERS & DISTRIBUTORS (P) LTD

Published by
ATLANTIC
PUBLISHERS & DISTRIBUTORS (P) LTD
B-2, Vishal Enclave, Opp. Rajouri Garden,
New Delhi-110027
Phones : 25413460, 25429987, 25466842

Sales Office
7/22, Ansari Road, Darya Ganj,
New Delhi-110002
Phones : 23273880, 23275880, 23280451
Fax : 91-11-23285873
web : www.atlanticbooks.com
e-mail : info@atlanticbooks.com

ISBN 81-269-0769-X

Printed and bound in India at Syndicate Binders, Noida

Preface

India is a developing economy. Undoubtedly, the mainly agrarian economy that characterised the pre-independence Indian economy is giving place to rapid economic activity and higher levels of income. But will it be correct to say that India has succeeded in providing all its citizens a better quality of life? Has it built up a nation where even the poorest citizen can lead a life of simple dignity with at least his basic needs being satisfied? Has it been able to ensure that not a single citizen will remain hungry even for a day? Has it guaranteed an affordable shelter to all, and access to education to all its citizens? Has it instilled the spirit of unity and oneness among the millions of citizens of diverse caste, creed, community, religion or province? Has the government policy brought a significant improvement in the general lot or the people are still striving for their socio-economic rights? Numerous questions need to be answered to realise the steady progress of India in diverse fields in true spirit.

It is against this background that the present book has been written. I have not attempted to present an empirical study based on economic and statistical data or parameters. Rather, I have only sought to trace the quality of life as enjoyed by an average citizen of India after more than fifty years of Independence. Beginning with the pre-independence era, I have analytically studied India's steady progress in the diverse areas—Infrastructure, Agriculture, Education, Health, Development to name a few—in the light of progress made by countries like South Korea, Japan, China, Malaysia, Taiwan, etc., which judged by any standards are far ahead of India socio-economically. Besides, the profound question—is democracy losing ground—has been approached to from a different perspective. Thus, the present book is an humble attempt to provide the socio-economic scenario of India in its entirety, affirming the fact that the country is slowly awakening from the sleep extending over half a century and gradually taking its rightful place in the comity of nations.

It is hoped that the present book on socio-economics will appeal to all general readers concerned with the development of the Indian economy. Any penetrating comments and useful suggestions from esteemed readers in order to enhance the utility of the book will be gratefully acknowledged.

Manoher V. Sonalker

Contents

Introduction

For thousands of years, the landmass Eastwards of Makran Pass near Arabian Sea, along the mountain ranges Northwards to the Himalayas, and Eastwards towards the Arakan ranges (Burma/China) was known as Hindustan. The river Sindhu (now known as Indus) was the first major river encountered on coming down from the hilly regions of Afghanistan in the West through the Khyber Pass on to the vast plains stretching Eastwards/Southwards for thousands of kilometers.

But the name Hindustan was used to indicate the geographical location of landmass beyond the river Sindhu. It did not indicate a single nation known as Hindustan as it was inhabited for thousands of years by diverse people without a common language, culture, color, creed and religion. The term Hindustani merely identified the diverse people inhabiting the subcontinent.

For untold centuries, Hindustan (now known as Bharat/ India) was renowned for its fabulous wealth and attracted predators from all over the world. Despite widespread looting by numerous foreign invaders over the centuries, the wealth of Hindustan did not decrease. Not only was Hindustan renowned for its wealth in gold, silver, precious stones and jewellery, but also as center of learning where thousands of students would eagerly attend the famous centers of learning like Taxila, Nalanda. Arts, music, architecture, science, literature all flourished over the centuries. By and large the people including the peasantry from Kashmir in the North to Kanyakumari in the South, and from Sind and Baluchistan in the West to Megahalaya and Arunachal Pradesh in the East were reconciled to the occasional depredations of the invaders.

Numerous civilizations have emerged, flourished and disappeared leaving tantalizing relics scattered all over the world, spread over a period estimated at thousands of years. With coming of the new millennium in 2001 CE (as measured by the Common Era), one fervently hopes for a more prosperous, healthier and happier life for the entire world, particularly for billions of Indians, and fervently wishes that India takes its rightful place in the comity of nations, based not on its teeming population or ancient glory, but on achieving a healthy and prosperous nation with equitable distribution of wealth and a leader in the latest information and scientific technology, the benefits of which are shared by the people of India and also the world at large.

But is this only a pipe dream divorced from reality? Is this similar to the daydream of a young man endowed with wealth and all earthly advantages, but squanders his teens leading a selfish, comfortable life without bothering to utilize his advantages for building a future for himself and others? How far would it be appropriate to compare India of today with the young man described above? The achievements of a person or even a nation are a measure of the capabilities to plan, a course of action and strain every sinew to attain the targets, no matter what the obstacles.

But merely achieving targets does not necessarily give cause for celebration. Even if the targets are achieved, it could be due to the setting up of very low targets, or may be improper targets not resulting in sustained growth, or may be inequitable distribution of benefits on achieving targets. A comparison of achievements by countries within the same time frame, but with different resources and impediments, if any, at the starting point would give a better indication of the progress or the lack of it over the last 50 years.

It must be clarified that for economists GDP, GNP, per capita income, etc. are important indices of growth and numerical basis for measuring and comparing growth among nations. But here, the progress or lack of it is sought to be measured, not in theoretical terms, but in readily understandable practical terms.

The idea is to make an ordinary person, young or old, not conversant with economics, think in terms of achievement or lack of it, as seen in production/ distribution of goods/ services and in general the obvious quality of life as experienced by ordinary people.

Pre-Independence Era (Prior to 15 August 1947)

1

Before comparing the progress of over the last 50 years, it is necessary to go a bit further back in time so as to get a correct view of what India then was geographically and economically. For this purpose, January 1900 would be a good starting point.

Politically the Indian subcontinent, extending from Afghanistan border and the Himalayas in the North to not only Cape Comorin (now Kanyakumari) but also Ceylon (Now Sri Lanka) in the South, and Sind and Baluchistan in the West, to Chinese border in the East including Burma (now Myanmar), was for all practical purposes a part of the British Empire. Within this subcontinent there were almost 1000 states ruled by Maharajas, Nawabs, Rajas, etc. ranging in size from more than a 1,000 square miles like Baroda, Mysore, Hyderabad, Jaipur, etc. to tiny states of a few square miles, scattered all over the subcontinent. These Indian states, though having Indians as rulers, were for all practical purposes controlled by the British.

In due course, before 1947, Burma and Ceylon became independent. In August 1947, India was partitioned on religious grounds amidst horror, savagery and misery on a scale never experienced before and fervently hoping never to be repeated again. Sind, Western Punjab, and Baluchistan formed the Western wing of Pakistan. Punjabi Mussalmans constituted the majority of the population of Western Pakistan, while Bengali muslims formed the overwhelming population of the East Pakistan carved out of Bengal. Despite partition on religious grounds, millions of Muslims preferred to continue staying in India and constitute the second largest religious group in India. Today India has the largest Muslim population in the world – more even than the total population of Pakistan.

By 15 August 1947, the original Indian subcontinent (as of 1900) was fragmented as under:

	Approximate area in square miles
INDIA	1,175,000
WEST PAKISTAN	310,000
EAST PAKISTAN (BANGLADESH SINCE1971)	55,000
BURMA (MYANMAR)	262,800
CEYLON (SRI LANKA)	25,300

After partition all the former princely states lying in Indian territory, were merged into India, and today they are an integral part of the sovereign democratic republic of India.

2

Some Pre-Independence Commercial Links and Indian Entrepreneurship

The partition of the Indian subcontinent in 1947 resulted in the formation of India and Pakistan. Geographically, India lies between Latitude 15°N and 35°N and is roughly bisected by the Tropic of Cancer. Its location midway between Europe and Far East Asia has been an important factor in the development of trade links with the rest of the world over the centuries. It has always maintained trade and cultural links with the East as well as the West and also with countries North of the Himalayas. As such it has the rare benefit of cultural, social and commercial interaction with varied cultures over the centuries, unlike Japan which had no links with the rest of the world till the mid 19th century or China which believed in restricted trade and did not open the country for others.

But the advantage of international links also turned into serious disadvantage, as the wealth of India attracted invaders who looted the subcontinent over the centuries. The presence of natural resources, including gold mines and precious stones as also the skills of the artisans could more than replenish the looted treasures. Given the fact that over the centuries, the skills of the artisans and the guidance of the rulers could create new treasures, mainly jewellery crafted out of precious stones like diamonds, emeralds, rubies and metals like gold and silver to replace the looted ones.

However, with the advent of the Industrial Revolution in Europe, the foreigners were more interested in acquiring raw materials to meet the insatiable demands of their industries and markets for their manufactured goods, rather than treasures consisting of jewellery. In a way, the industrialized countries were now manufacturing products which were coveted by the non-industrialized countries. The demands for their products were also created by force by ensuring the death of the traditional industries. Countries like India paid a heavy price as they were ruled by foreigners. It was not only the industrial policy of preventing or discouraging Indian industries in every field, but also through manipulation of financial measures like the Sterling Pound/Rupee ratio.

But despite such adverse conditions, the Indian entrepreneur could not be kept down and tried to fight for establishment and growth of Indian enterprises against heavy odds. Scindia Steamship, Tata Iron & Steel Co., Punjab National Bank, Central Bank of India, Lakshmi Insurance Co., Hindustan Aeronautics, Indian Institute of Science, and a number of textile mills were some of the enterprises set up by Indians in the decades prior to 1947.

Thus it can be seen that Indian entrepreneurship has always been rising to meet the emerging challenges over the centuries and making the most of all the natural resources, including human resources. But one cannot help feeling that during the last few decades after attaining freedom, there has been a drastic underutilization/misutilisation of the resources resulting in inequitable growth and a fall in the living standards and quality of life, particularly the tribals and the rural poor.

Basic Infrastructure Before Independence

3

Before proceeding to look at the state of the nation today, it is worthwhile having a glance at the establishment of few important infrastructural facilities during the century preceding independence.

Transport & Communication: An appropriate transport and communication system was implemented in India with practically no delay in the development of new technologies, like steam engines for transport as well as for industrial use, telephones, telegraph, etc. in Europe.

The steam locomotive had just been invented and steam trains had been introduced in UK a few years earlier. Steam trains were also introduced in India in 1850s. By 1940 there was a well laid rail network all over India, which included not only British India but also the princely Indian states. The rail network was based not only on techno-economic feasibility, but also on strategic and commercial factors. Hence depending on the assessment of various factors in different regions, the rail network included not only broad gauge lines covering all arterial routes but also meter gauge and narrow gauge lines, the latter connecting the hill stations like Darjeeling, Ooty, etc. to the broad/meter gauge network. It may be noted that all the rail links were built and operated by private companies on commercial basis. By 1936 electrification of rail lines with electric locomotives had been implemented on some sections.

But merely laying down rail tracks and running trains was not enough. The tracks and rolling stocks had to be maintained. Railway workshops were set up throughout India for this purpose. And finally local staff had to be trained to run the trains and carry out maintenance and repairs.

Apart from the railways, a network of roads was also set up extending from the Northern most areas like North West Frontier Provinces to the Southern tip of Cape Comorin as also from West to East. Just like the railways, the road network also covered British India and the Princely States, and the basic consideration was strategic as well as commercial.

Full advantage was taken of the riverine network; Joint stock companies were set up to run regular steamer services carrying merchandise like tea and jute and also passengers particularly in Assam and undivided Bengal. The Ganges, flowing through the vast Indo Gangetic plain was also used commercially in a big way for riverine traffic. Coastal navigation was also not neglected, particularly on the West Coast. There were regular steamer services between Bombay and Goa, touching all minor ports in between. British companies ran regular cargo and passenger services to East Africa, Aden, Oman, the Trucial Coast (now UAE), etc. apart from regular services to UK, USA, Europe, Australia and the Far East. But in the early 20th century, Scindia Steam Navigation Co. Ltd., a 100% Indian Co. started regular passenger-cum-cargo services to UK, USA, etc. Other Indian shipping companies also started later on. Naturally, training institutes for development of maritime staff were also setup as also fully equipped workshops for repairs and maintenance of steamers.

As regards automobiles, full fledged production factories were setup after cessation of World War II in 1945, but assembly shops for vehicles imported in partly knocked down condition as also repair/services workshops were set up all over India by General Motors, Ford, Austin, etc. Birlas setup a factory in 1946 near Calcutta to manufacture cars, Tatas set up a plant at Jamshedpur to manufacture trucks. Factory to manufacture Leyland truck was set up at Madras. Tata also set up a plant to manufacture locomotives in this period.

Air travel was in its infancy in the world in the 1920s, but JRD Tata had started an air service in 1932 between Bombay and Karachi. After cessation of hostilities, Tata started an international air service between India and Europe by setting up a 100% Indian company called Air India International. But even design of aircraft was taken up before independence when Shri Walchand Hirachand set up Hindustan Aeronautics at Bangalore in erstwhile Mysore state.

(i) There was a regular telegraph service covering entire India with overseas cable links. Even a telegraph system had been installed in the major Indian cities within a decade of the Telephone being invented in England.

(ii) Educational institutions: a number of schools and colleges were set up in important towns for providing education to boys and girls, also establishment of institutes of science engaged in fundamental research in Physics, etc. leading to Nobel Prize in Physics being awarded to Dr. C. V. Raman doing research in India.

(iii) Medical services with hospitals and medical colleges being set up in important towns.

(iv) Municipal bodies to look after the health of the people.

(v) Museums and zoos, as also bird and animal sanctuaries (like the Kaziranga sanctuary, Assam, set up over a century ago in 1905).

(vi) Archeological Society of India to preserve India's heritage.

(vii) Establishment of observatories.

viii) Establishment of independent judiciary with courts at important towns and legal system based on the English System.

(ix) Establishment of armed forces, mainly Army, but also Navy and newly emerging Airforce (in 1930s).

Thus it can be seen that in the pre-independence periods the basic infrastructure for the nation's economy and defense to meet the normal requirements of the Indian subcontinent and incorporated the latest discoveries and inventions of the Western world.

4

World War II and Advent of Freedom

The World War II years from 1939-45 had an adverse effect on the industrial development of India. The cessation of World War II was followed by the terrible riots and ultimate partition of India in 1947, at a tremendous cost of human life and untold sufferings. Hence the progress of independent India can be said to have commenced from 1949-50.

Till 1947, Calcutta was the industrial and commercial hub of India. It was helped by its location on the Hooghly River where ocean going steamer could dock, as also the access to almost unlimited quantities of natural minerals like coal, manganese, mica, etc. within a radius of 100 miles. Similarly steel, was readily available with Tisco and IISCO plants nearby. Hence large industrial companies like Jeszops, Burns, Braithwaite, Andrew Yule, etc. were located at Calcutta. Apart from industry, Calcutta was the largest trading centre involved in the export of particularly plantations produce like tea, jute, etc.

But after partition, gradually the importance of Calcutta as an industrial and trading centre dwindled despite efforts of Dr B C Roy, the first Chief Minister of West Bengal, who even set up an industrial township, Durgapur, near Calcutta.

With the advent of freedom in 1947, India was free to plan for the rapid all round growth so as to ensure social equality and balanced growth in all sectors—industrial, agricultural, social, educational, health, etc.

Parliament, representing the will of the people of free India, decided to follow the Socialistic Pattern of Society, with detailed planning for all sectors, all over India, centralized in the Planning Commission, a body set up by Parliament.

The economic pattern thus designed, involved complete centralised control on the setting up and running of industrial units. The amount and type of capital, the location of the industrial unit, the item to be produced and quantity thereof, the import of machinery, raw material, strict labor legislation and even the sale of some items, in short all factors of production and even marketting were strictly controlled by the Government leaving practically no leeway for the entrepreneur to adjust for changing socio-economic and market factors.

Till 1939, i.e. till the outbreak of World War II, the infrastructure in the form of transport, power, communication, health services, educational facilities, judiciary, etc. were, more or less adequate to meet the needs of the populace. It may also be recalled that the 1930s saw the worst economic depression affecting the entire world. But with the outbreak of World War II in 1939, and entire Europe and North Africa being engaged in hostilities, India became an important centre for supply of goods and services to the allied forces. The pressure on infrastructure was further accentuated from 1943 by the Japanese aggression and victories in S.E. Asia and particularly after the fall of the most important bastion of Singapore. The Japanese forces did manage to reach the Indian border and staged attacks on Indian soil in N.E. India. This resulted in huge influx of allied forces in India and put a severe strain on the infrastructural facilities. Though the war ended in 1945, the period till 1947 saw civil unrest and massacres on an unprecedented scale.

The war years 1939-45 had put an unprecedented strain on the infrastructure. The political situation in India worsened and communal riots took place in widespread locations in India till ultimately the country was partitioned in 1947. But it was not only a geographical partition of a country, but the administrative services like the Armed Forces, Police, Judiciary, etc. also got divided with the Hindu population coming over to India from Pakistan, and part of the Muslims going over to Pakistan. It was a herculean task bringing a country back to normalcy, but thanks to strong political leadership and capable, sincere, dedicated and hard working administrators at all levels all over India, the country could be said to have achieved political and administrative stability by 1949 and could start on the path of national development as an independent nation.

Despite the enormous price paid in human sufferings and misery due to partition, there was negligible loss in physical assets like factories, workshops, commercial centers, etc. due to World War II or on account of partition. The Japanese did manage to carry out a few air raids on Calcutta in 1944, but no significant damage was caused. To that extent India could be considered lucky unlike, Europe, Japan and S.E. Asia which suffered practically complete destruction of ports, rail networks, bridges, communication networks, factories, towns, cities and more importantly heavy loss of life not only in the armed forces but also among the civilians as well. Having its major cities being destroyed by bombing by allied forces was bad enough for Japan, but for the first time in history, the US forces used atomic bombs over Hiroshima and Nagasaki which were completely destroyed. But what was worse, was the atomic contamination, a danger for generations unborn.

Though there was heavy loss of life and dislocation of all administrative services on account of partition, the basic infrastructure remained intact. In addition, financially India was much better of than any other country as Britain owed India, more than £ 50 million, a huge amount half a century ago, for goods and services supplied during the war years. By 1950, India had a stable democracy, an infrastructure which ranged from a good educational system with well organized schools and colleges, technical institutions, scientific research institutes, judicial system, administrative system, medical services, municipal bodies, transport and communication services indigenous as well as joint stock banking system and growing number of Indians well educated in all spheres, technical, social and other activities. One additional important factor was the fact that a large number of Indians were completely at home with the English language, which was a boon for proceeding to UK/USA for higher studies and acquiring technical expertise.

Thus at that point of time, not only India had a huge cash balance of more than £ 50 million in its favor, but also had a stable vibrant democarcy, an intelligent educated work force, capable, astute and experienced businessmen, distinguished scientists, technical personnal and also sincere and dedicated administrators at all levels. Considering all these factors, which seemed to be a strong foundation for success in a short time, it remains to be seen whether India has utilised the unusual strengths and strong foundation to even partly achieve, the potential existing half a century ago.

Opinion in India seems to be divided as to the extent to which the advantages existing half a century ago have been utilized to make India one of the leading nations in the world with a well developed growth in all sectors – agriculture, industrial, sciences, health, educational, etc. resulting in an equitable distribution of wealth created by the joint efforts of millions of Indians. It also needs to be seen whether the potential has been utilized to achieve internationally a reputation as producer of quality products – agricultural and industrial as also a trend-setter in all spheres of human endeavor including the latest technology for application in every sphere, whether it be agriculture, industrial, health, information dissemination, etc. and most importantly, has the potential existing half a century ago been utilized to ensure a better quality of life for its citizens living in urban or rural areas.

But a meaningful understanding of the nature and extent of progress or the lack of it in India during the half century commencing in 1950s can only be had by looking at the progress made by a few countries during the same period. The countries selected for comparison and the criteria adopted for such selection are indicated below. But the significant achievements in each of these countries will be described briefly in subsequent chapters.

The area of a country and its population has a bearing in making an effective comparison. Hence for the purpose of this study, the area of the country as also its population in 1975 is given. It may be clarified that 1975 has deliberately been chosen as the base year for comparison, as it is midway between 1950 and 2000, and this would give a better picture as in almost all cases the real process of commencement of growth started after cessation of World War II in 1945. Hence selection of 1975 as the base year above would be more appropriate than 1950.

	Country	Approx area (Sq miles)	Approx population (Millions)
1.	BANGLADESH	55,000	62.00
2.	CHINA	3,692,000	732.00
3.	FINLAND	130,000	5.00
4.	ISRAEL	8,000	3.00
5.	JAPAN	142,000	105.00
6.	KOREA – NORTH	46,500	14.00
7.	KOREA – SOUTH	38,000	32.00
8.	MALAYSIA	128,000	10.50
9.	SINGAPORE	225	3.00
10.	TAIWAN (Formosa)	14,000	15.00
11.	INDIA	1,175,000	560.00

Each one of the above listed countries is commented upon individually in some depth in the subsequent chapters.

Material Resources

5

Before considering the present state of the nation, a quick look is necessary at the basic advantages the country possesses. In the earlier chapter, the benefits of having a well developed infrastructure adequate for the needs at that time have been indicated. The advantages, arising out of the topographical lay out as well as the mineral wealth is briefly indicated in the subsequent paragraphs.

Geographically India is a vast country of almost 1.2 million square miles – an enormous area by any standard. The topography extends from the ice cold northern regions in the Himalayas to the burning deserts of Rajasthan. There are the lush green forests of the North East. The vast Indo-Gangetic plains fed by Ganges and a number of other rivers, the Southern region has its thick forests, a number of rivers and mountain ranges with heights not exceeding 2000 meters, resulting in a mild climate throughout the year. In short, India has every type of climate which can be found on the earth, making it extremely lucky in the variety of fauna, flora and biodiversity. The long coastline extending over almost 8000 miles has made of golden beaches. The ocean can provide abundant quantity and variety of fish, not only for feeding the millions of Indians but also for export. Undersea resources have not yet been explored, but vast quantities of metals like nickel, etc. are reported to be awaiting systematic exploitation by Indians. With along the coastline, extending over thousands of kms, there is ample scope for developing and harnessing tidal power.

There is an almost unlimited variety and quantity of underground resources like coal, iron, manganese, bauxite, etc. to name a few common minerals. But what is more important is the existence of vast quantities of titanium, beryllium, rare earths commodities in great demand for making special alloys, etc. needed in the advanced technological age. In addition to these, there are almost unlimited quantities of monazite-sands, uranium, etc. The demand for all these items will increase rapidly with the enormous strides being made by scientific research and new application being found for these materials in the 21st century for some products still in the conceptual stage.

As regards energy sources, apart from coal, petroleum, natural gas, uranium, there are numerous rivers, some of them snow fed, others arising in the hills of Central or Southern India getting adequate rain during the monsoon, and are a source of hydroelectric power and irrigation There is abundant sunshine throughout the year over most of India; a number of regions are suitable for tapping wind power – both these sources can provide non-conventional, non-polluting, renewable and practically inexhaustible source of power.

Nature has bestowed almost unlimited variety and quantity of natural resources on India. But no matter the extent of natural resources available, the conferment of the benefits on the citizens of a nation from nature's unusual bounty depends ultimately on the human factor. The subsequent chapters are devoted to considering the extent to which India has over the last 50 years since 1950, utilized the abundant natural resources.

As stated earlier, this is not an empirical or statistical study. It is meant to analyze in practical terms the general perception of India's progress or lack of it in the last half a century after attaining freedom. An ordinary citizen is not concerned with the GDP or the annual per capita wheat or rice crop, or any of the parameters used by economist to measure the progress of a nation. His most vital concern is to ensure having two square meals for himself and for his dependents, a shelter to protect him from the elements, reasonable and affordable healthcare, and most importantly a safer, healthier and much better quality of life for his children.

In 1950 India became a Sovereign Independent Democratic Republic. Prior to 1947, the people of India dreamt of becoming independent and taking over the reins of power so as to make India a vibrant prosperous democracy, responsive to the needs and aspirations of even the poorest people residing in the remotest villages and forest. After the lapse of more than half a century of attaining independence and taking over the reins of power with the consequent freedom to plan and implement the schemes for the nation's welfare, it is high time to look at the nation's achievements or the lack of it.

Aspects of India's Development

6

The progress of a nation over the last fifty years can be gauged by various parameters. But as stated earlier it is the general perception of the citizens as to the extent to which their aspirations of a better quality of life have been met by the Government ever since attaining independence 50 year ago is a true indicator of progress. Statistics is a useful tool no doubt, but reference to statistics brings to mind the story of a 6 feet tall non-swimmer who drowned while trying to cross a river reported to have an average depth of only 4 feet. For a non-swimmer, it is not the average depth which is important, but whether any spot in the river exceeded 6 feet. Hence the statistic whether they pertain to per capita income/availability of food/water, etc. far below the average, or the extensive and almost unlimited areas of conspicuous consumption available and enjoined by small percentage of the total population, enjoying an income far above the average.

Besides statistics relies on figures; it does not bring out the qualitative aspects of different sectors of nations activities. In the subsequent chapters, the various sectors, though interconnected, have been considered separately, purely for the sake of convenience under the following heads:

(i) Water

(ii) Agriculture

(iii) Health-medical services/Hygiene/Sports, etc.

(iv) Education-systems/Archeology/History/Heritage, etc.

(v) Transport and Communication-Air/Rail/Road/ Riverine/ Sea/Power/Village Linkage, etc.

(vi) Development-Industry/Ecology/Environment

(vii) Defense/Security-External/internal/coastal marine resources/ economic zone (maritime)/economic warfare/ fake currency, stamps/financial scams, etc. relations with neighbors/ strength of economy, etc.

(viii) Banking/FIIs

(ix) Democracy-(a) legislature corrupt particularly Lok Sabha-bedrock of democracy, criminals becoming ministers, providing police protection-from whom and why (b) Judiciary-collapsed (?), decades for judgment (not justice) why vacancies not foreseen or suits politicians? more and more resort by people to criminals for settling disputes (c) Executive ICS Steel Frame, IAS frame- why prior Government permission to prosecute IAS? Security of well paid with official/unofficial perks-need for IAS? permanent cadre, standard of administration down

(x) Summing-up

By their very nature all aspects are interconnected to some extent. Hence some overlapping in the contents is unavoidable. The above classification is made for the sake of convenience to focus on the state of affairs existing in each of the sectors considered vital. It is neither feasible nor possible to go into details, but an attempt is made to provide adequate summarized data, where considered necessary, to enable readers to form an informed opinion.

There is a common tendency to consider highly of one's own achievements, however little or insignificant they may be. An individual running 100 meters in 5 minutes or managing a high jump of 3 feet may consider it a big achievement. But a realistic appraisal requires a comparison given more or less similar parameters. When comparing the process of a nation with that of other nations, the realistic parameters would be the achievements in various areas over the same period of time.

The progress of a few mainly Asian countries, showing remarkable progress since 1950, has been briefly described in the subsequent chapters. But as the book deals with India, the various aspects of national activities have been dealt with in greater details.

7

A Few Instances of Major Easily Avoidable Inefficiencies

To achieve success in any field, even an individual has to meticulously plan his future course of action and monitor the progress on an ongoing basis. The moment any unwanted deviation is noticed, it is essential to ascertain the causes and rectify the shortcomings so as to achieve the aims or at times, even modify or alter the aims or methods, depending on the circumstances. Even the smallest deviation or shortcomings may at times conceal a major fundamental defect. It is like constructing a tower involving thousands of nuts and bolts or having a chain having thousands of links, but the strength of the tower or chain depends upon the weakest nut or bolt or the weakest link. Similarly a grandiose plan can succeed only if due attention is given to the smallest component, however insignificant it may seem. Inadequate attention or lack of timely attention to such components on the mistaken plea of it being trivial or too small a component can lead to failure.

So let us start by looking at items which are not considered important enough to merit attention, but any shortcoming in such items denotes a basic lack of competency in handling even small matters. This naturally leads one to question the capacity of the planners and implementers to handle big long-term projects when even small items exhibit important shortcomings which remain unrectified for decades or worse still, are not even noticed by the concerned authorities as grave shortcomings.

An example is given below of the incapacity to handle competently even a simple matter but one affecting every one of the million of average citizens of India on a continuing and daily basis. The cropping up of this problem is all the more surprising as bureaucrats generally prefer to follow precedents and tread the worn path and are wary of deviating from the routine. A tried and proven system in existence for centuries and convenient to all concerned, where size, shape, color and design distinguished without the slightest difficulty for even a blind person, the denominations of coins and currency notes, was suddenly changed about four decades ago, without in any way conferring the slightest benefit to any citizen. On the contrary, it is a source of annoyance and possible loss to individual average citizen. Hence it is elaborated in the subsequent paragraphs.

India is a poor country with majority of the population living in rural/semi-urban areas or in the tribal areas. The rate of illiteracy is also high in these areas particularly the most important item handled by the poor and average citizen is currency in the form of mainly coins and to a lesser extent, currency notes. The general poverty makes possession of whatever few coins and notes a citizen handles a very important aspect of life. For a poor person, even one false coin or currency note of incorrect lower denomination has an extremely adverse effect on the person.

For almost a century before independence, British India had a coinage system consisting mainly of pie, paisa, half-anna, anna, eight-anna and rupee. Each coin had a distinctive size, shape and color and it was impossible to confuse between the coins. Even a blind person could know immediately the denomination of the coin. For instance, the two anna coin was square shaped, while the paisa at one time was shaped like a washer with a hole in the center.

In the 1950s, India changed over to the metric system and the rupee consisted of 100 paise. Today the coins in circulation are of mainly 25 p, 50 p, Re. 1 and Rs. 2, and a recent addition the Rs. 5 coin to replace the Rs. 5 currency note. All these coins are circular and made of nickel alloy, having a shiny nickel color. There is practically no difference in the size of the coins of various denominations. The diameters of the 50 p, Re. 1, Rs. 2 and Rs. 5 coins are 20 mm, 22 mm, 24 mm and 20 mm respectively. The thickness of all the coins except Rs.5 is 1mm and 2mm that of Rs. 5 coin. Only Rs. 5 coin has milled edges. One cannot help reiterating that in a poor country with a large illiterate population, where most of the daily transactions of the vast majority of the people involve the use of coins, even in daytime it is difficult to distinguish between the various denominations of the coins. In poor light and especially with the poor electricity supply even in the metropolitan areas, and the lack of supply mainly in the tribal and rural areas, and the task of differentiating the various denominations becomes highly impossible, resulting in losses to many an ordinary citizen.

While distinguishing between the coins of various denominations there is no doubt a serious problem but with a simple solution, the more serious problem is the frequent shortage of coins experienced periodically all over the country. Over the years, since independence it was obvious that the population was increasing rapidly and has already touched 1 billion. Along with the increasing population, the extreme poverty of the masses making unavoidable, reliance on coins in the day to day transactions, it was obvious that the supply of coins would need to be augmented on a regular basis for decades to come. But the periodic shortage of coins indicates the lack of due attention to the problem of increasing demand for coins. Security mints were set-up in India more than a century ago. They were adequate to meet the internal demands of the variety of coins then in existence. But it is reported that during the last 25 years, India had to get the major part of its coins minted abroad due to inadequate facilities in the country. What is more remarkable is the fact that, as per reports, India's recent requirement of millions of coins is met by a country which did not have the slightest industry about 50 years ago, but is today one of the leading Asian Tiger economies. It is more remarkable as it had been an agricultural country for centuries, faced a civil war between North and South. The industrialization started only in the 1950s and it is this country, which can meet the demand for millions of coins at a time for a country, viz. India which had mints catering to the needs of the numerous rulers extending over a period of thousands of years.

A similar scenario exists more or less as far as currency notes are concerned. Prior to independence, currency notes were issued in denominations of Re. 1, Rs. 5, Rs. 10, Rs. 100,

Rs.1000 and Rs. 5000. Each denomination was of a distinctive shape, size and color. The paper used in the high denomination note was of extremely high quality, had a distinctive feel and crinkle. As a matter of fact, Indian currency was freely circulated in the Gulf region till recently. These were the coins and notes issued by the British Indian Government. However, the Indian rulers had their own coinage and currency as a rule. But there was never any confusion between the coins of British India and those of the Indian States.

The Rs. 1000 and Rs. 5000 were demonetized decades ago leaving only Re. 1, Rs. 2, Rs. 5 and Rs. 100 denomination notes. But each denomination was distinctive in color, design and size and could be differentiated at a glance. Subsequently printing of Re. 1, Rs. 2, and Rs. 5 has been discontinued. Today the notes in circulation are of Rs. 10, Rs. 50, Rs. 100 and Rs. 500 denomination. But the Rs. 100 and Rs. 500 notes are of almost the same size, design and color. It is difficult to distinguish between the two and the only way to be absolutely certain of the denomination is to carefully check the denomination printed numerically.

But again the same mind-set which has been designing the coins has apparently been dealing with the designing of currency notes. Any illiterate village child could suggest changing the shape of the coins and change in color, design and size of the currency notes with a view to removing the slightest difficulty in differentiating the various denominations. But like awareness of ones ignorance being the first step towards seeking knowledge, recognizing the existence of the problem is the prime necessity to initiate action in solving the problem. But as nobody in authority seems to have recognized this as a problem or even a short coming in the system, one cannot resist suggesting the authorities to look at the currency notes of some countries which display flora and fauna in attractive designs with various colors and sizes as to ensure distinguishing between different denominations without the slightest difficulty.

Considering the vast population and the enormous volume of cash transactions in the country as also the widespread poverty resulting in the major part of the dependence on the coins and currency notes to meet the daily commercial transactions and the normal inflationary pressures, it would have been only prudent to plan for the increased and still increasing demand for coins and currency notes.

Many examples displaying lack of prompt and appropriate action in regards to vital areas can be cited. For instance, despite numerous technical reports over the decades, suggesting immediate measures of safety on the Indian railways, having been prepared, no action has been taken inspite of continuing loss of thousands of lives and destruction of railway property running into thousands of crores of rupees. At the other extreme is the example of one bolt not having been replaced in time, resulting in the lock-gate collapsing in the Mumbai docks and entire movement of steamers including fully loaded steamers ready to depart, coming to a standstill for 5 days. This happened in July 2001.

On the one hand, India claims to have a well developed judicial system, based on English jurisprudence, set up about 150 years ago. But there are lakhs of cases pending for disposal since decades at various judicial forms all over India. The enormous backlog did not develop overnight, but was built up over the last 5 decades. Merely looking at the enormous time-lag involved in deciding cases and without going into the quality of judgments, it is obvious that the judicial system has almost collapsed resulting in people resorting to rough and ready systems of settling disputes, quite often entailing assistance of criminals. Even with the best of intentions it is difficult to imagine any drastic reduction in the judicial process and enabling the ordinary citizen to obtain justice within a reasonable time and at a reasonable cost.

While delays in the judicial process may result in justice delayed being justice denied, yet instances of people charged with committing a number of heinous crimes and not even being caught and tried in a court of law, are increasing. The classic example is that of one Veerapan reported to be a sandalwood smuggler, active for decades in illegal activities, including killing of police personnel, in the states of Karnataka and Tamil Nadu.

For decades the joint police teams of both the states had not been able to curb his activities. With such instances occurring, it is hard to describe India as a nation where the law of the land prevails. Justice must not only be done, but also must be seen to be done.

Since the last 20 years or so, land grabbing has assumed alarming proportions, even in metros. Land by the side of railway track belonging to railways is encroached upon and pukka structures built with hundreds of thousands of people occupying such lands illegally. The illegal pucca structures in Mumbai, abut on the rail track. Men, women and children carry on their normal activities like cooking, bathing, playing on/near the rail track with suburban, mainline trains and goods traffic going on. Consequently, the speed of the local trains has to be curtailed thereby reducing the number of trips for every rake. This naturally greatly diminishes the total number of passengers carried by the local trains. Despite the blatant illegality and the loss to the nation and increasing the tension for the motormen driving the trains, the process of removing them is a time consuming and slow process with the courts insisting on railways to provide alternate accommodation for such encroachers. Now encroachments have taken place even on airports. Thousands of pukka slum colonies have come up on airport land, some of them almost touching the runways, particularly in Mumbai. This is despite the authorities being aware of the strategic and commercial importance of Mumbai airport.

Thousands of instances indicating the lackadaisical and at times complete lack of concern for the nation's safety and well being can be cited. But one can't resist citing two more examples showing the utter lack of concern for the lives and welfare of the thousands of servicemen carrying on selflessly their duty of defending the nation.

Indian troops are posted on the Siachin glacier, the coldest place in the world, where even normal breathing is difficult. All the supplies have to be carried on their backs from the base camps. So it is necessary to provide snowmobiles for transport. Now snowmobiles are in common use all over the world in cold countries and can be easily purchased. But for years the babus at the Ministry of Defense, New Delhi, kept on delaying on some pretext or the other, no matter if hundreds of servicemen suffered from intense cold and frostbite and also resulting in delays and shortages of materials. Ultimately it is only because of a new and firm Minister of Defense who arranged for immediate supply of adequate number of snowmobiles.

One more tragic case of the callousness is exhibited not only by the babus of the Ministry of Defense but also by all the politicians who have been MPs over the last almost 40 years.

India acquired supersonic MIG 23 jet fighters over 3 decades ago. But proper training is a prerequisite for flying any aircraft, and particularly a supersonic jet fighter. During all these decades, the Government has not met the demand by the IAF for Advance Jet Trainers (AJT) aircraft before entrusting the young pilots with the supersonic MIG fighters. Every country in the world acquires AJTs to train their pilots before entrusting them with supersonic fighters.

But for almost 4 decades, the babus in the Ministry of Defense and more important the politicians have failed to acquire AJTs, despite more than 300 MIGs having crashed since 1971 with more then 160 gallant young pilots having lost their lives in these crashes. In addition about 50 civilians have been killed on the ground. But even recently acquired Jaguars which are also supersonic jet fighters have also crashed with more young pilots losing their lives due to the callousness of the politicians and the babus. Even during the last 3 years since 2001, the IAF has lost over 100 supersonic fighters and more then 50 young pilots.

These pilots are in their early 20's and the fittest people in the age group. They joined the IAF to fight for their country and prepared to die in the line of duty. But neither the politicians nor the babus have ever felt the slightest twinge of conscience for the needlessly tragic waste of such young lives.

Nowhere in the world will such staggering losses of men and material be accepted without any protest by the citizens of the country. About 4 decades ago, West Germany had acquired some fighter planes from USA. But about a dozen fighters crashed resulting in the death of the pilots. These planes were dubbed as Coffin Makers in the West Germany. The resultant hue and cry in the country forced the Government to take immediate remedial action.

But needles to say, India has not succeeded during the last 30 years in manufacturing AJT or likely to do in the near future. Without AJT, the training today to these brave young pilots flying old supersonic fighters can only be described as 'substandard'. Even pilots flying commercial planes are expected to be experienced in flying the types of planes for which they are licensed. But the Indian Air Force pilots are required by the authorities and the politicians to fly airplanes without proper training. Most of the crashes have been described by the IAF 'human error' which can be the result of substandard training or even poor maintenance standards or even out dated machines.

It is reported that a contract has been signed in March 2004 to acquire Hawk AJT, but deliveries of a few AJTs are not expected before 2008, till then more gallant young lives may continue to be lost needlessly.

The citizens of India as a rule do not appreciate the sacrifices made by the servicemen. Long before Independence, the British had set up in 1917, a technical institute at Khadki, Pune for providing disabled servicemen a means to learn a skill and earn a living. It was meant for thousands of men in uniform, maimed in war or peacetime as also their dependents to pick up some skills like welding, repairs to vehicles, etc. tailoring, weaving, machinery repair and now even computing.

The initial corpus of Rs. 10 lacs was provided in 1917 by Lady Willingdon, wife of the then Governor of Bombay and others. The Maharashtra Government gives Rs. 3.6 lac p.a. for payment of salaries to instructors. But the buildings are crumbling, the need is to expand and introduce new courses and new staff, etc. but the Central Government has not replied for years to their new proposals for creation of new corpus of Rs. 10 crores to supplement their existing Rs. 1.5 crores corpus. But neither the babus nor the Central Government nor the politicians have shown the slightest interest.

There have been numerous fires in recent years in specially constructed ammunition dumps resulting in financial loss of crores of rupees. In some instances, ammunition shells have landed in nearby villages causing damage and consternation. But all over the world such fires and explosions in ammunition dumps are extremely rare. In India, frequent explosions even in specially prepared ammunition depots do not cause any worry among the politicians and the babus.

Even procurement of weaponry and ammunition is a long drawn out process, extending over years, no matter how urgent the need, involving not only the politicians but also the babus of the various Central ministries. Consequently in emergencies the Armed Services find themselves desperately short of much needed supplies, whether they are warm clothing for fighting in the Himalayan ranges or ammunition for the weapons. It is reported that during the Kargil war, in 1997, the army had to import ammunition on an emergency basis.

These examples are merely indicators of a serious malaise affecting the entire nation creating serious misgivings regarding the ability of the nation to become a healthy prosperous and well governed nation in the 21st century.

Bangladesh

8

Capital	: Dhaka
Area	: 55,000 sq miles
Pop	: 62.00 mil

At the time of partition of the Indian subcontinent in 1947, Pakistan consisted of two wings, the Western wing consisted mainly of Sind and Punjab, and the Eastern wing consisting of East Bengal with India in between. In 1971 after violent struggle, the Eastern wing separated from Pakistan and formed a new nation called Bangladesh consisting mainly of Bengali Muslims.

The country has few natural resources. The region has for long been known for its jute crops. The major part of the raw jute crop continues to be exported. With a large population of more than 62 million and lack of natural resources, it is making every effort to raise the standard of living particularly, health. What is remarkable, is the approach to improve the standard of the masses by starting from the grass roots level instead of stressing and concentrating on mega industrial projects. While industries are no doubt necessary for any country, the improvement in overall health, literacy, housing are the basics for the development of a nation according to some of the nation's public servants who are making a significant contribution toward this goal. The actions of two of the nation's distinguished citizens are briefly given in the succeeding paragraphs.

Finance is a necessary ingredient for ameliorating the economic status of the masses. But the experience of Prof. Mohamed Yunus is worth studying in his attempt to improve the lot of the deprived section of the nation. He has made a remarkable success of the Grameen Bank which provides financial assistance to poor village women through almost

30,000 branches of the Grameen Bank spread over Bangladesh. His views on poverty and its banishment are worth quoting;

"Poverty is not created by the poor, but by financial apartheid by insisting on collateral.... Women are generally sincere and honest. The money they get is more likely to stay with the family and put to use. They will not use for gambling or alcohol like men with almost 30,000 branches of the Grameen Bank in the villages, the personality of women has changed ... level of school going children including girls has increased, housing and health has improved, women have adopted to family planning. Housewife, even an illiterate one knows how to balance her family budget if she is allowed .... Village women now operate cellular phones and man mobile phone booths." This, according to him, has proved that people need opportunity not charity and free market economy required for success.

While Prof. Mohamed Yunus has done commendable work in improving the economic condition of the poor and particularly women, through the network of about 30,000 branches of the Grameen Bank in the villages, Dr. Zafrullan Chaudhary has made an extremely noteworthy contribution towards improving the health of the citizens through his bold drug policy. His national drug policy of 1982 has ended the monopoly cartel of multinational pharmaceutical companies and forced them to put health before profit. His policy is based on:

(i) 250 drugs, mostly generic, as specified by WHO are adequate to treat all the world's ailments.

(ii) These 250 drugs only to be manufactured in Bangladesh.

(iii) Introduce tight control on 8 MNCs operating in Bangladesh—a key element of his strategy, and insisted that what cannot be produced locally, cannot be produced by MNCs.

(iv) No drug other than the listed 250 drugs can be produced or imported.

(v) MNCs barred from producing high priced drugs like antacids, vitamins and syrups to enable local companies to enter this market.

This stopped MNCs from cost cutting such as using local small scale factories to manufacture drugs. Dr. Chaudhari secured the full backing of the then Government in implementing his policy despite enormous pressure from MNCs, some of whom threatened to leave. But no one has left. On the contrary, two more companies have since come in. According to him, most countries are afraid to criticize MNCs under the impression that MNCs bring in valuable foreign exchange. He has given some telling examples to prove the contrary. In 1989, total investments of MNCs in Bangladesh was 382 million takas and profits takas 973. Pfizer invested T.11.4 million and took away T.200 as profit.

His policy has resulted in transferring production to local companies whose volume of production has increased and also resulted in improving the quality of medicines. Even the cost of medicines remained steady since implementation of his policy despite rise in the level of other price and taka being depreciated in terms of US $ and imposition of taxes on drugs. There has been remarkable improvement in the quality of drugs with the improvement in the quality control on drugs. Most of the drugs are single ingredient or generic products, which enables faster testing. As against about 35% of the drugs being found substandard before introduction of his policy, at present about 7% are below standard.

But in addition to implementing a practical drug policy, he believes in demystification of health and medical procedures. Gonoshastreya Kendra, charitable trust set by him, covers over 10 divisions of Bangladesh, makes it a point to educate and more importantly involve women whose role is crucial in Muslim and agriculture societies. Women have been taught to take blood pressure, give injections and even perform tubectomy. These measures have resulted in dramatic improvement in these areas as can be seen from the fact that infant mortality is 65/1000 (Bangladesh average (120/1000) and maternal mortality 1.2/1000 (Bangladesh average 6.9/1000). The trust has also concentrated on consumer education as according to him, drug is like any other commodity-consumer decides when buying other commodities but doctor decides the purchase of drugs for patient. In most cases the doctor has no first hand knowledge of the drug, but relies on the sales talk given by the medical sales representative.

Bangladesh is a poor country with a population of more than 65 million, crowded in an area of 55,000 square miles. It has very few industries. The manner of tackling the problem of population control, health improvement and general economic upliftment, particularly of the poor, through imaginative and voluntary measures with the co-operation of the people is noteworthy. The decision to restrict manufacture of drugs to only 250 drugs as recommended by WHO along with involvement and education of women whose role in Muslim and agricultural society with extremely low level of literacy, is of crucial importance to the success of the nation, indicates the ability to formulate a plan which attacks the core problem and the means to achieve successful implementation of the same. Both, Dr. Zafrullah Chaudhari and Prof. Mohd Yunus have successfully formulated and implemented plans for the welfare and upliftment of the masses without any grandiose looking schemes, involving massive sums of money and creating an army of bureaucrats. It would seem to be a highly desirable way to improve the standard of living in villages, without large financial outlays.

Perhaps the most noteworthy feature of Dr. Chaudhary's drug policy is the fact that it is entirely based on the recommendations of the Hathi committee set up by the Government of India in 1974. Dr. Chaudhari had to overcome fierce opposition from the drug lobby, particularly the MNCs. But the successful results of the drug policy are evident. Unfortunately Government of India did not implement Hathi Committee Report and today there are more than 60,000 drug formulations in India, with the rapid and widespread decline in the health of the people.

China

9

Capital	: Beijing
Area	: 3,692,000 Sq. miles
Pop	: 740.0 mil (App.)

Broadly speaking, China is bound on the North by the great steppes of Mongolia, on the West by the Gobi desert, to the South West lies Tibet beyond the Kunlun ranges, to the South are the smaller mountains and thick jungles, to the East lies the Yellow Sea and South China Sea – and in the centre lies China, the Middle Kingdom.

Mountain ranges and great rivers divide China into several regions. The people in each of these regions have evolved their own customs and dialects of the Chinese language. Geographical factors have had perhaps the most important influence on the history of China's minority people like the Uighurs on the West and the nomadic Mongols of the North, and on the relations of these people with the Han Chinese. About 90% of the population lives in the Eastern Third, almost 94% of the population are Han and the balance made up of more than 50 minority groups.

China is a vast country with an area of more than 3.6 million square miles and a population of more than 740 million. Apart from the vastness of the country and the teeming population, what is noteworthy is the fact that it is the only country with a recorded history of more than 4000 years. China has passed through very turbulent periods in its long history but the overall trend has always been to experiment and find solutions to their problems without depending on outsiders. As a matter of fact, China always had and continues to have a policy of discouraging outsiders from entering their country. But despite such a policy, it has been successful in absorbing the latest technology in diverse fields like steel manufacturing, microelectronics, nuclear physics, etc.

Chinese culture and technology was flourishing as early as about 1100 BC. Iron began to be used extensively. Large-scale irrigation projects and canals for transportation were in existence. Metal coins and glass were in common use. Confucianism, Taoism philosophical debates and literature flourished during this period. Rapid increase in trade saw the growth of a prosperous merchant class who were seen as threat by the old landed gentry, whose power was based on ownership of land and literary achievements. So the landed gentry created four classes:

(i) Scholars were given the highest status as they performed the function of recording, preserving and transmitting the ancient heritage.

(ii) Farmers were next as they fed and clothed the nation.

(iii) Artisans functions were not considered as important as that of farmers.

(iv) Merchants were at the bottom of the social scale as they were considered exploiters.

This ranking system lasted till about the fall of the Imperial Empire in 1911.

Till about 220 BC, the feudal states were normally warring with each other without any powerful central authority. But around 220 BC, one of the lords managed to gain control over all the territories which was henceforth called Ch'in and called himself Emperor of China. Since then, despite occasional setbacks, the empire continued to expand southwards.

Inspite of periodical invasions by Mongols and other tribes from the North, and frequent internal warring by feudal lords, technological discoveries and inventions continued to take place. Literature and art also flourished.

For centuries the Westerners had admired the splendors of Imperial China and conducted a restricted traded. But the nineteenth century saw the Chinese empire growing weaker and simultaneously under increasing aggression by the Westerners.

The first and most significant western influence in the early 19th century on the people was the import and sale of opium to Chinese by British traders in open defiance of Chinese law.

Till about the 19th century, Chinese self-sufficiency resulted in the balance of trade with Britain being always in favor of China. So the British traders had to settle the adverse balance of trade by paying China in silver. By ensuring addiction by the Chinese to opium despite the fact that smoking, cultivation and import of opium was banned by China, the increasing opium imports by China led to change in the balance of trade in favor of Western countries and had to be settled by payment of silver by China. China's attempt to prevent import of opium led to the opium wars of 1842 and 1860. China lost these wars and had to suffer humiliating defeats.

Some of the important consequences were:

(i) Six cities were opened to British trade and foreigners were governed by their own laws and Chinese laws did not apply to them.

(ii) Maximum duty which could be imposed by China on imports was fixed at 5% thus opening the country for flood of cheap manufactured articles from West and resulting in closing down of a large number of local industries.

(iii) Large cash indemnities had to be paid by China.

(iv) Control of foreign trade passed over to the Westerners.

Finally, as a result of the incapacity of the stagnant Imperial system to meet the Western challenge, the end of almost 3000 years of Imperial rule came in 1911, when a new republic came into existence under the leadership of Dr. Sun Yat Sen.

Some of the reasons for the easy victories of the Westerners in the 19th century over the Chinese can be attributed to:

(i) China had become weak, corrupt and lacking central authority.

(ii) Military power had been allowed to decline as the threat of war on the Northern border had been removed during the earlier periods.

(iii) The Manchu forces had medieval equipment and had no idea of modern war techniques, hence large number of Chinese troops were no match for a few well trained and well armed Western troops.

The humiliating defeats led to a search for new ways to deal with increasing foreign threat. Li Hing Chang presented a detailed and well considered plan in 1872 to the Emperor stressing the need for strengthening China economically and militarily against Western intrusion. Extracts from his plan are given below in some detail to indicate the extent to which his ideas are still valid for all countries, particularly developing countries:

"...We cannot preserve and protect our territory unless we have the right weapons.... They (Westerns) are daily producing weapons for supremacy and victory, pitting their superior techniques against our inadequacies.... The method of self strengthening lies in learning what they can do and in taking over what they rely upon .... Moreover their possession of guns, cannons and steamships began only within the last 100 years or so...their progress has been so fast that their influence has spread into China.... If we can really and thoroughly understand their methods, can we not expect that after a century or so we can reject the barbarians and stand on our own two feet?.... Japan is just a small nation, recently begun to trade with Europe; she has instituted iron factories and built many steamships...she has changed to Western Weapons.... She is merely planning for self protection...but never the less oppressing and looking down on our China...all expenditure of our nation can be economized, but expenses on defense measures and building warships should never be economized...if we try to save funds, we shall neglect all these defense measures, the nation will never have anything to stand upon and we shall never be strong...we will strengthen the aggressive ambitions of the foreigners...building of ships, cannon and machinery will be impossible without iron and coal.... England is powerful because of possession of both coal and iron...our arsenals in Foochow and Shanghai daily need huge amounts of imported coal and iron because Chinese product is most unsuitable...even foreign ships coming to our ports have to carry foreign coal...if all our ports are closed by foreign boycott, then not only our iron factories will close down, but our steamships will not be able to move an inch without coal...but more threatening is the frequent request of Westerners for permission to open coal and iron mines in the interior on the plea that China cannot develop its national resources on its own... Japan is adopting Western methods for opening coal and iron mines and thus helping her shipbuilding and machinery industry.... If our people can be persuaded to borrow and use foreign machines and foreign *methods only* but not allow foreigners to do the whole job on our behalf, then surplus funds from articles so produced can be used to maintain our ships and train our soldiers." A variety of projects were initiated but overall plan implementation was tardy and hence resulted in failure.

The 30 years from 1860s when the West actively started occupying China, saw serious attempts by China to industrialize by commencing the building of railways, factories and opening mining operations. During this period Japan successfully laid the base for future industrial growth. But the lack of progress in this direction by China can be considered due to:

(i) Conservative bureaucrats sabotaged modernization efforts.

(ii) China, unlike Japan, was continually besieged by Western powers after the Opium wars.

(iii) Lack of firm commitment to large scale Western type performs unlike Japan during the Meiji restoration.

(iv) Floods, famine and droughts were frequent during this period.

The vast Chinese empire suffered a stunning defeat in 1895 at the hands of Japan, considered insignificant because of its size. This victory of the small Japanese nation which remained in isolation till about 30 years earlier was entirely due to industrial and military reforms based on Western models.

Tian Su Tung was one of the leading advocates of reforms in 1890s, based on the Western model. But according to him, social and institutional structures were needed to be changed along with technological innovations in industry. His views are also extensively quoted below in view of their relevance even today.

"...We have more than one arsenal but at time of need there are no guns and cannons, we have more than one shipyard but at time of need there are no ships.... Helplessly we have to purchase from foreign countries who know we have no means of testing the quality of ships and weapons...so they sell to China obsolete weapons at exorbitant price...Chinese diplomatic envoys in Europe seek a share of the profit ... consequently higher the price, the poorer the weapons...In this way China has wasted several decades...we should supply water, electricity and gas for the use of the people... when streets are well kept, sources of pestilence will be cut off, when hospitals are numerous, medical treatment will be excellent...we should have parks for public recreation and health.... Need to learn thoroughly written and spoken language of all countries so as to know what other countries are doing all around us, and train men of ability as diplomats...we should adopt all the good points and avoid their bad points...as a result there will be none of the ships and weapons which we will not be able to make and none of the machines which we will not be able to improve."

In 1911, a republic under the leadership of Dr. Sun Yat Sen was proclaimed, putting an end to 3000 years of Imperial rule. Dr. Sun Yat Sen had examined in detail over the years;

(i) Why were China's people so miserable?

(ii) Why was China so weak and humiliated by all the nations including small nations like Japan and Britain?

He concluded that China's ills were due to China being weak, uneducated and divided. As a solution he offered three principles:

(i) Principle of Nationalism – China must win back her sovereignty and unity – special privileges to foreigners must be withdrawn. China must be disciplined and acquire all the powers that any foreign nation had.

(ii) Principle of peoples' democracy – China must be a nation where the Government serves the people and is responsible to them – literacy must spread to all people and eventually all people must be enfranchised – system must be introduced whereby authority runs upward from the village and commands the highest authority.

iii) Principle of people's livelihood – foundation of modern economic system had to be strengthened and peasants' lot to be alleviated.

But this republic did not last long and there was a period of confusion as feuding warlords continued their authority with a weak Central Government.

The Chinese Communist party was formed in 1921. But subsequently there was a sharp division among the people, resulting in 2 major parties being formed, the CCP and the Kuomintang (KMT). From mid-1930s all the energies of the CCP were devoted to defeating Japan which had occupied parts of Northern China and uniting Chinese people around their leadership. Ultimately CCP was victorious and the KMT had to flee to Taiwan (Formosa).

The economy inherited by CCP was in shambles. Since the fall of the Manchu dynasty, there was almost anarchy throughout China. The only industrialized zone of Manchuria, had been looted by Russians as war reparations.

In 1949, China was a poor and backward country. More than 80% of population was engaged in agriculture. There were serious social inequalities. 10%of population owned more than 70% of land. The industrial base was small and concentrated in Manchuria and Eastern sea coast and predominantly owned by foreigners. In such a vast country of 3.7 million square miles, there were barely 10,000 miles of railway, mainly in Manchuria and the East coast. Very few roads existed. The few motor cars could not travel over most of the country in the absence of roads. The industrial base was smaller than that of Russia in 1914 and very much smaller compared to India.

The immediate objective was the rehabilitation of the economy. The program of land reforms was taken up and completed in 3 years by 1950, benefiting over 300 million peasants. Smaller independent industrialists were tolerated for their skills which were needed for developing the nation. By 1952, almost 25% of industrial production was from this sector.

The Government was *clear in its objectives*. Apart from *land distribution, literacy and health* were high on the agenda.

The plan to spread universal literacy throughout China was an extremely ambitious one considering the complexities of the Chinese language, both written and spoken.

Chinese language has no alphabet, in addition there are numerous dialects. Though the written script is common all over the country, the different dialects varying from region to region made communication very difficult. The script was extremely complex. For instance, a simple word "I" required seven brush strokes. It was estimated that it takes a child at least 2 years just to master the rudiments of reading and writing. It was estimated by an expert that the total numbers of characters in the language were between 40,000 and 50,000.

The Government immediately took up the task of simplifying the script so as to make the entire nation literate. In *1950, less than 15%* of the population was literate. But by *1965, almost everyone*, men and women, above school going age were literate enough, not only to read newspapers but carrying on a national debate through huge big character posters put up on every wall in Peking. There was a deluge of these posters containing denunciation/approval/analysis/suggestions of national events and policies. Consequently, the entire population could participate in nation building process and understand the different points of view.

By 1980, China was still a poor country but people were healthy and robust. They did not depend on advanced medical systems, but relied on spirit and organization in providing enough housing, clothes and food for all. The state *systematically attacked drug abuse, VD, etc.* and fought conditions which allowed these diseases to exist.

The establishment of an efficient health care system was given priority in 1949 – the basic points of the system were:

(i) Medicine to serve workers, peasants and soldiers.

(ii) Preventive medicine takes precedence over cure.

(iii) Traditional Chinese medicine to be integrated with Western scientific systems.

(iv) Health care system to be combined with mass movement.

By 1970, the number of hospital beds had increased to about 1 per 700 compared to India's 1 per 1000. A campaign was launched against illiteracy and superstition. Mass campaign was also launched against rats, flies, mosquitoes and bed bugs. People were helped in building sanitation facilities. Diseases like smallpox, cholera, plague and typhus were completely eradicated.

Incidentally, Russia provided massive aid in the form of loans and hundreds of technicians. But by 1960, China broke with Russia as China's greatest resource was large labor pool and hence plan needed to be labor intensive. But Russian model was capital intensive and emphasis on development of urban areas. China's plan of rapid industrial advance based on wider technical foundation of skill among Chinese people rather than reliance on foreign aid was successful. Within 4 years of the departure of Russian technicians, China exploded her first nuclear device without any foreign assistance. By 1965, Russian debt was paid off and self sufficiency in oil achieved.

The essential goal cultural revolution was to prevent Chinese leadership from becoming Soviet Style bureaucratic ruling class – in which China seems to have succeeded.

The remarkable progress of China within 30 years from 1950 to 1980 needs to be noted. From a poor country wracked by decades of civil war, it had become a super power having not only the world's largest population but also largest standing army, third largest navy and third largest air force.

A comparative study of new Shanghai and Mumbai by an Indian researcher in 2001 as part of a project approved by Indian Council of Social Science Research, makes very interesting reading and gives an indication of the work ethic and energy of the Chinese.

Shanghai, like Mumbai, was a thriving international commercial centre and had a thriving textile industry since about the last century. The textile industry declined and closed down recently in both cities – but in Shanghai employees of closed mills were provided with alternate employment, unlike Mumbai. There are no slums or pavement dwellers though Shanghai is a thriving new City and now the financial centre of China with illuminated skyscrapers, green patches, excellent roads with 3 tier flyovers and absence of pollution. Already about 100 of the top internationally acclaimed companies have offices in Shanghai. It has a better social and economic infrastructure compared to Mumbai. The land belongs to the state and given to foreign investors on contract basis.

In Mumbai, the decline of the Textile industry has led to hundreds of thousands of textile workers being rendered jobless and homeless. The attempt to develop Navi Mumbai across the creek has not decreased the pressure on Mumbai. About 60% of the area of Mumbai city is now occupied by slums. Thousands of people have made pavements their permanent homes. But hundreds of skyscrapers (over 15 to 40 stories high) are coming up rapidly, but not affordable homes on rent for the ordinary people. Besides, basic infrastructure like adequate, water conservancy services and other common services like roads, public transport, etc. have failed to cope up with the ever increasing population of Mumbai.

There is a glaring contrast between the planned development of Shanghai and civic services and conditions in Mumbai.

The Chinese, over the centuries, have always shown themselves to be pragmatic. After half a century of experience in political struggles, the great Chinese leader Mao had concluded "…. Apart from uninhabited deserts, wherever there are groups of people, they are invariably composed of Left, Middle and Right…yet in the long run, the three are not fixed for all time."

Finland

10

Capital	: Helsinki
Area	: 130,000 sq miles
Pop	: 4.90 million

A country with a democratic set-up situated above 60° North Latitude and almost a third lies in the Arctic Circle. A country with more than 150,000 lakes, 80,000 islands, with thick forests—a country always in awe of its neighbor, the big Russian bear on its Eastern border – a country almost landlocked as the only route to the rest of the world is through the narrow passage between Denmark and Sweden. Apart from the geographical disadvantages of a difficult terrain with hundreds of lakes and forests, a bitter cold climate throughout the year, a location in the remote corner in the far north, it is a sparsely populated nation with a total population of barely 5 million. Considering all these factors, it would be natural for most of the world and particularly Indians to presume Finland to be a non-descript nation incapable of even the slightest attempt at achieving anything other than basic survival.

Because of its geographical location it was adversely affected by World War II (1939-45) when one of the most devastating wars was fought in Europe and particularly Nazi campaign against Russia. But despite all these adverse factors, today Finland is the leader in communication industry and also manufactures eco-friendly paper. Even in India, the Finnish communication industry has succeeded in making its mobile phone, NOKIA capture the major part of the market, despite stiff competition from other international manufacturers.

This is the result of forward thinking by the Finnish people and their Government. For decades, the entire economy was based on the only abundant natural resource viz. wood. And became the international suppliers of quality and eco-friendly paper products. But despite the use of large quantities of wood, care was taken to preserve the ecological balance.

But the country realized that it could not depend on one type of industry for ever. And so in due course, it switched over to microelectronics, especially in communication equipment, particularly mobile phones. Today 'Nokia' has almost become synonymous with quality mobile phones all over the world.

But the country is not resting on its laurels in having achieved such remarkable international leaderships for years in the electronic communication system. It has already started looking out for new areas to explore and achieve international success once again. This is characteristic of a forward looking nation where people do not rest on their laurels, but continue to think in terms of achieving international leadership in the economic sector.

It should be remembered that Finland is located in the Arctic Circle and away from the busy international populated areas. It does not have any minerals or other natural resources. But like all other progressive and developed nations, the achievements are an indication of the national will to make the most of its valued resources viz. human resources to gain international recognition for the quality of its products.

Israel

11

Capital	: Jerusalem
Area	: 8,000 sq miles
Pop	: 3.0 mil

A tiny piece of land lying between Lat 30° N and 33° N extending about 200 miles North/ South and average of about 50 miles East/West, with the port of Eilat on the Red Sea at the Southern end and Haifa on the Mediterranean on the Northern end.

Originally a part of the Ottoman Empire and was claimed for centuries by the Jews as their original homeland from which they claimed having been banished centuries ago. Entire area was known as Palestine for centuries. After the slaughter of millions of Jews in Europe during World War II, the demand for the creation of Israel as a Jewish homeland intensified. Ultimately the state of Israel was created in 1948. The carving out of a separate Jewish state out of Palestine was strongly resented by the Arabs. Right from the inception of the state in 1948, Israel had to contend with resentful and hostile neighbors. The 6-day war of June 1967 with Israel on one side and Egypt, Syria and Jordan on the other side resulted in Israel gaining territory unto the Suez Canal in the West and the river Jordan in the East.

With the creation of Israel, Jewish refugees from Europe and Jews from countries, including India started pouring into the new Jewish state. But this resulted in periodical military action against Israel by the surrounding Arab states. Hence Israel decided to have a long term plan which envisaged security in (i) defense (ii) food for the nation, and most importantly (iii) assured water supply for the newly created desert state.

The Jews who started settling in Israel were of diverse cultures coming from different nations. They did not even have a common language. European Jews consisted of German, Polish, French, Italian Spanish, Latvian, Lithuanian, and Balkans, etc each of them having their own language. But right from the inception of the state, they were of the unanimous view of having Hebrew as their national language. Now the enormity of the task in implementing this resolve can be gauged from the fact that Hebrew was a dead language for almost 2000 years. And it was this language which was to be used by the newly born state to achieve their goals of attaining excellence in economic, technological and military power with not only complete security in food production but also assured water supply. The people brought the Hebrew language to life in a short space of time and it has been and continues to be used, very successfully in all spheres of activity – not only in daily life but more importantly in art, literature, nuclear physics, biochemistry, electronics, space and missile technology, agriculture, etc.

Israel has practically no natural resources. From the establishment of the state in 1948, they had to have a multi-pronged strategy. On the one hand they had to have high degree of military preparedness which involved training of armed forces and acquiring necessary weaponry, on the other forging rapidly ahead in agriculture related activities. This would be a daunting task for any nation similarly situate and would also be a time consuming process – more so when it is realized that the entire nation had to develop the dead Hebrew language to meet the requirements of a forward looking modern state looking to meet the emerging challenges; but also the fact that Israel did not have the manpower for a full-time defense force and simultaneously carrying nation-building activities. The solution was to provide compulsory military training to every able-bodied person for at least 2 years and then keep them as reserves to be called up for duty at a moments notice.

Today, the nation has developed nuclear missile technology which naturally implies an extremely high level of proficiency in basic technology like alloy making, etc. but also in advanced technologies like aircraft designing and manufacturing, microelectronics, etc. without having to depend on any country for latest design or technology. On the agricultural front, it not only feeds itself, but also exports fruits, flowers, vegetables, milk products, etc. in a big way particularly to Europe. This itself is a big achievement as the area was a barren desert about 50 years ago. An example of the high level of production in absolute terms can be had from the fact that the annual yield of milk per head of cattle is more than 9000 kg as against India's production of about 500 kg.

As far military preparedness is concerned, it has shown the world over the years its will and strength to keep all hostile forces at bay and build up a reputation for its military prowess notwithstanding its small size and being surrounded by hostile nations.

Considering all these factors, the achievements are all the more remarkable in every sphere of activity—a result of long-term vision and national determination at all levels to achieve the goal.

Japan

12

Capital	: Tokyo
Area	: Apx 142,700 sq. miles
Pop	: 105 million

Japan consists of a group of islands lying between 35° & 45° N Latitude; a land of great natural beauty but also subject to severe storms and earthquakes.

It has a democratic set-up with a duly elected parliament. But the Emperor is a highly revered person, without any powers. Till 1850s, it chose to be completely isolated from the rest of the world. It existed under a feudal system with various lords holding sway over various parts of the country. These lords would often fight against one another resulting in lack of unity among the Japanese. Ultimately the people decided to unite as a nation under the Emperor. This process, known as the Meiji restoration took place about 1865-70. Henceforth, the nation was united under the Emperor.

Having come into contact with the European world in the 1850s, they had seen the products manufactured by European industries. They were quick to grasp the significance and importance of rapid industrialization of the nation from the military as well as the commercial point of view.

In order to learn and master Western technology, they hired Western technicians and also sent high level delegation to the industrialized Europe and USA. The delegation took about 2 years to study and learn the methods adopted by the West to industrialize. The main idea was to rapidly industrialize the nation and develop design and manufacturing capacity without depending on foreign technicians or know how.

The main factors which profoundly influenced them were the need for national unity and universal education. With this in view, they immediately introduced universal education for both boys and girls – but an education appropriate and flexible for emerging industrial, scientific and commercial needs and simultaneously preserving their cultural identity with stress on national unity along with instilling commonsense virtues like discipline, industriousness, punctuality and loyalty to the nation with the Emperor as the head. Now these were extremely radical reforms for a society which so far was not only divided among itself but also a traditional agricultural society with no contact with the Western World.

They also realized that time frame for industrialization was important and its aims could only be achieved with careful selection of the industries to be started. But keeping in mind the historical background of dissensions among the lords, the slow pace of agricultural life for centuries, the vital need for national unity and sustained approach at all levels with extremely high levels of enthusiasm for achieving their targets in the shortest time was kept in mind by all. They adopted a pragmatic and practical approach to achieve their aim. The introduction of universal education for boys and girls was a radical departure from the past. Even the traditional dress for men and women was discarded in favor of the western dress which they found more appropriate and convenient for an industrialized society. Every Japanese citizen – from a child to the oldest person takes pride in being Japanese.

After about 30 years of the Meiji restoration and the commencement of the initial process of planning the economic structure based on the need for complete change of the national outlook from an agricultural society, it had by 1900 already laid down a firm foundation. By 1930, it had acquired a reputation of manufacturing and exporting cheap imitations of western goods like toys, etc. But on the other hand, developed the ability to design and manufacture arms, warplanes, vehicles, naval ships, etc. of very high quality. The general impression of Japan being a manufacture of cheap goods was widespread and continued till about the 1960s, despite having designed and mass produced first rate fighter planes and warships during World War II.

Japan was completely devastated during World War II by conventional bombing. As though this was not enough, two atom bombs were dropped on Hiroshima and Nagasaki. These bombs not only physically destroyed the cities, but were likely to harm generations unborn. Despite the devastations in physical terms as also the enormous loss of human life in the war, and also having onerous terms thrust on them as losers in the war, Japan has attained a remarkable position as one of the 7 most powerful economic nations within about 40 years of the end of the war.

Though lacking natural resources and dependent almost entirely on imported raw materials required by one of the most industrialized states in the world, it has emerged as a leader in the manufacture of a wide variety of products ranging from micro electronic items to technologically advanced items like TVs, washing machines, music systems, cameras, videos, range of automobiles from small passenger cars to luxury cars and heavy duty trucks. Japan is also a leader in designing and production of ship building including very large Crude Carriers (VLCC) of 200,000 MT capacities and above, locomotives, and rolling stock include the fastest train in the world, heavy duty cranes, motorcycles, generators-portable as well as giant ones, textiles, etc.

This wide range of products has a tremendous demand all over the world due to reputation for quality and economic pricing. The most important point to note is the fact that the entire range of products from taps, toys to ship building including warships for their navy is wholly based on indigenous design and manufacturing capability. Initially technology was imported in a big way. But as a matter of national strategy and pride, the Government and industry decided to absorb and modify the imported technology to suit their requirements. It was not merely a question of copying the imported technology but to adapt and acquire design and manufacturing capability for which purpose industry and government jointly decided to invest in technology and human resources development. But this investment in developing core competency in new technologies was not confined to senior technologists and senior bureaucrats but care was taken to involve all the people involved in the manufacture, particularly the junior most shop floor worker as they clearly understood the importance of 100% involvement of all participants including the junior most unskilled worker. Besides, the bureaucrats, businessmen, industrialists, traders and most importantly the workers have realized that rate of change in various technologies is increasing day by day and rapid obsolescence in technology and products is a fact of the life which cannot be wished away. Hence even the junior most workers are aware of the need to be prepared mentally to accept the rapidly changing technologies involving the acquiring rapidly new skills to handle such technology – a quality exhibited by all rapidly developing countries, particularly the Asian Tigers.

Needless to say, the people enjoy a high standard of living. To maximize food production to feed their large population, not an inch of land is wasted. Even the hills are terraced to maximize production of rice, their staple food. Despite industrialization on such a diversified scale, there are no displaced persons from rural areas, nor any shanty towns. Inspite of the high state of industrialization, the people are very conscious of art, culture and natural beauty.

Japan has the second largest merchant fleet in the world including VLCCs of 300,000 MT capacity and the entire Japanese fleet is indigenously designed and built.

The Korean war of 1950s helped Japan revive from World War II in a big way. Industry made windfall profits. They studied US techniques of mass production of ships using techniques perfected by USA in World War II. USA had perfected mass production techniques of building ships. Parts of a ship were built inland and railed to the launching sites. The Japanese improved upon these techniques and could build a ship in 7 months against normal 2 years. So orders poured in. By the end of 1950, i.e. within 5 years of the end of World War II, Japan took over the lead from Germany as the biggest ship builder in the world. Besides their ships were cheaper and more reliable.

The high standards of education helped make diligent and adoptable workers, and hence the workers could be adapted for new emerging technologies like TV, radios, washing machines, refrigerators, air conditioners, electronic goods, etc. The ties between the workers and the higher ups in the organization were strengthened in every company by all participating every morning in singing the company song 'We shall send our products all over the world'. But research in every sphere continued unabated. The fastest train service in the world was introduced in 1964 between Tokyo and Osaka. Japan also staged the Olympics in 1964.

Just one example of the ability to plan and construct even the most modernistic, versatile and utilitarian yet aesthetically beautiful structure can be seen from the construction of the Sappero Dome in 2002 primarily for the World Cup football tournament.

Japan and South Korea were to co-host World Cup football matches in 2002. They remade or built 20 new giant stadiums – each of them a showpiece. Japan is said to have spent on an average $ 240 million and S. Korea about $ 160 million on each of these venues.

In 1998, after years of lobbying and having been elected as co-hosts for the World Cup, the city of Sapporo held a design competition for a new stadium. Saporo is Japan's extreme north. It's known for its winter sports and the annual snow festival. Unlike other stadiums in remote areas of Japan, the Sapporo Dome was planned with many future uses.

The design had to meet the following main requirements of FIFA: (a) provide a natural grassfield, (b) seating for at least 40,000 spectators and (c) also satisfy Sapporo's need for a warm facility for baseball and winter events.

Renowned Japanese architect, Hiroshi Hara, designed the Sapporo dome, which some consider the 8th wonder of the world.

He felt everything should be changeable and adaptable to nature. He devised an innovative method to combine an indoor stadium with natural grass pitch with multiple uses. Even the shining roof is designed to move with the weight.

The $ 430 million magnificent aesthetically aerodynamic, moveable Sapporo Dome has the following unique features:

(i) An innovative method to combine an indoor stadium with a natural grass pitch.

(ii) Through the use of moveable lower sections of seating and more than 100 custom designed rollers, the same central area can be transformed from a rectangular soccer pitch into a diamond shaped baseball field and when needed into a wide berthed concert stage.

(iii) It has a single slope seating stand – does not have second tiers or upper decks; so every seat has an unobstructed view of the playing field and the sweeping roof.

(iv) The foul line seating for baseball swivel to turn into viewing areas virtually centimeters from the football action.

(v) To make for more concentrated viewing, mechanized curtains drop down all round to darken the stadium's edges and make for concentrated viewing.

(vi) Acoustical panels make the cheering sound amazingly crisp and hardly any echo.

(vii) Background is vast, bow shaped gang plank backed by see through glass, where cafe patrons can still get a view of the match.

Natural fields wilt after 4 hours inside a stadium. It takes about half a day for the 8,000 ton planter box holding the pitch outside the stadium to be eased on 34 wheels into the stadium through sliding glass walls at the rate of 4 meters per minute, guided by about a 100 magnetic sensors developed by NASA. The raised concrete planter box is reduced to 1/10 of its weight by raising it on a bed of pressurized air. After this, the pitch is rotated 90° to fit snugly against the moveable grandstands. The natural lawn has an underground heating system to take away the severe winter chill of Sapporo, the most Northern Japanese city.

Eighty workers need 5 hours to change from football to baseball and cost Yen 2.6 million, yet in the first year itself it made a profit of 36 million yen.

This is a democratic country which has emerged as an international leader in a highly competitive international market manufacturing a vast range of goods, from tiny microprocessors to cameras, cars, calculators, heavy duty cranes, VLCC, etc. with the resultant prosperity shared by all. But despite their leadership in so many spheres, research continues in all spheres.

The character of the nation and the determination of its citizens can be seen from their achievements within 20 years of the end of World War II, and that too by a war ravaged country, which also has the unique distinction of two of its largest cities, viz. Hiroshima and Nagasaki being destroyed by atomic bombs.

13

North Korea

Capital	: Pyongyang
Area	: 46,500 sq. miles
Pop	: 13.5 mil

Not much is known about the technical and social economic developments within the country. The economic policies adopted have not been consumer oriented but more defense oriented. It is observed that the country has developed nuclear technology and also developed nuclear missiles along with systems to deliver the missiles over a range of more than 1000 km. This clearly indicates an extremely high level of not only design capability but also capability of manufacturing and fabricating special alloys and micro electronic gadgetry with zero error accuracy.

Korea was an agricultural country without any industry whatsoever. It was only in mid-1950s that UN enforced a peace treaty among the warring North & South Korea. So the real progress can be said to have commenced in the early 1960s. Again like the other Asian Tigers, it has no natural resources and relies on its most important resource, viz. human resources.

South Korea

14

Capital	: Seoul
Area	: 38,000 sq. miles
Pop	: 32.0 mil (apx)

Korean peninsula juts out from the China border and lies between 35° & 45° N Latitude.

Undivided Korea was a poor agricultural country without any claim to the slightest importance and was ignored by the world for centuries. It was occupied by Japan in the 1930s till about 1945. With the cessation of hostilities in 1945 and withdrawal by Japan, civil war broke out between North and South Korea. The South was supported by USA and the North by China. Ultimately peace was restored by the UN in 1953 and the Korean peninsula was divided along the 37th parallel north. The upper half with its northernmost frontier touching China adopted the communist system of governance while the southern is a democracy with an elected parliament and adopted the socio-economic structure based on the USA model.

The Yellow Sea lies on the western side of the peninsula and the Sea of Japan on the eastern side.

The development and growth can be said to commence only after 1960. Today the stage of socio-economic development by South Korea in about 35-40 years can be considered to be a miracle. A country which was purely an agricultural country for centuries, a country without any industrial background what so ever, a country whose people suffered during the war years till 1945, a country which suffered a civil war and ultimately a partition – is today within the time span of about three decades, one of the leading industrial countries with a very high standard of life shared by all.

The country has a democratic set-up with an elected parliament. With the partition of the country into North and South Korea, and restoration of peace in 1953, the country decided on a development strategy which concentrated, not on agriculture, but on attaining an extremely high level of technical competency in the newly emerging technologies. The sectors decided upon by the nation for developments were electronics, steel-making, shipbuilding, refrigerators, TVs, calculators, automobiles, etc. The choice of sectors seems all the more surprising as it did not have any industrial background, not even small scale industry. It did not have any trading back ground or any international exposure, consequently the people had no contact with the rest of the world or even a trace of industrial culture. On the contrary the country was an agricultural country for generations having a population accustomed to the traditional agricultural way of life. For such a nation to get not only used to industrial culture, but also to acquire excellence in absorbing and handling the latest technology within such a short span of time and keeping abreast of latest technological progress by developing their own designing and manufacturing competency, denotes a universal will of the people to make every effort to ensure the rapid and sustained growth in all spheres of national activities including sports and cultural areas.

South Korea, like Malaysia, Japan, Israel, China, etc. as a national policy invested and keeps on investing enormous amount in research and development and has developed and achieved design and manufacturing capability and are not dependent on any country for designing or manufacturing of any item. In less than 4 decades, it has achieved an extremely high degree of excellence in the manufacture of electronic goods, automobiles, steel production, ship building, etc. Their goods have flooded not only the Indian markets, but also markets all over the world, including distant countries like Europe and South America. It may also be noted that India had provided technical expertise to a limited extent in 1960s for setting up a steel plant. Today Korean Steel is exported all over the world, including India and is competing with the domestic steel in India.

Now it is considering of investing about US $ 8 billion in setting up a modern steel plant in India considering the availability of high grade iron ore, which at present Korea imports from India, which India prefers to export such high class ore rather than utilize it to produce steel.

What is more noteworthy is the fact that all the items produced in Korea or services provided, incorporate the latest technology and effectively compete in the international market. All their products have earned a reputation for quality as well as economic pricing all over the world.

Malaysia

15

Capital	: Kuala Lumpur
Area	: 128,000 sq.miles
Pop	: 10.5 mil

Malaysia consists of two separate parts:

(i) West Malaysia – a thin peninsula with Singapore at the Southern end just above the Equator and the Northern region touching the border with Thailand about 10° N Latitude. On the Western side are the straits of Malacca and on the Eastern side lies the South China seas. This is the main part of Malaysia.

(ii) East Malaysia – lies about 500 miles to the East and separated by the South China seas.

Originally consisted of more than a dozen independent states, each with a local ruler, but under the overall control of the British, was occupied by the Japanese in World War II. After the defeat of Japan in 1945, there was an attempt at taking over power by the local Communists. Ultimately the Communists were vanquished, though sporadic violence continued till the early 1970s, particularly in the Northern regions.

Britain relinquished power in 1963 and a federation consisting of a dozen or so states under the local rulers, along with Singapore, Sabah (N Borneo) and Sarawak formed with Kuala Lumpur as capital. Subsequently, Singapore separated from the federation in 1965 and now exists as an independent republic since then.

Though the communist insurgency was put down by the British in 1960s, sporadic trouble continued to erupt till the early 1970s, but since then put down completely. It is a democratic republic with a mixture of ethnic Malay, Chinese and Indian population, with the ethnic Malay naturally being in the overwhelming majority. There were ethnic clashes in 1969, but since then there have been no ethnic clashes and race relations continue to be harmonious.

Till the early 1970s, Malaysian economy could be described as a plantation economy as it depended entirely on rubber, palm oil and tin. There was no industry as such. Within about 25 years, it has transformed itself into one of the most important industrialized economies in the world. The government is clear in its focus on the development of the nation. It aims at all round development. Not only does it focus on consumer goods, computers, advanced microelectronics but also on heavy industry like manufacture of steel as also petroleum, chemical industries, automobiles, etc. It encourages direct foreign investment but the aim is to absorb the latest technology for manufacture of all types of products with indigenous expertise after achieving complete design capability.

The Malaysian government has been and continues to be extremely forward looking in its all round development strategies. It is planning to develop latest information and energy technologies, microelectronics, biotechnologies. In order to realize its vision, it is increasing substantially the percentage of GDP devoted to research in the respective areas.

The very fact of having converted itself from a plantation economy to one of the most important industrialized economies of the world within a period of less than 25 years leads one to the conclusion that a determined nation can always achieve its target with proper guidance, planning and leadership. An important factor to be noted in the remarkable change from plantation economy to a highly developed nation is the fact that this progress has been achieved without harming the ecology – more than 50% of the land continues to be forest. Progress has been planned and implemented keeping in mind the importance of maintaining the ecological balance. Despite the rapid development and industrialization of the country, there are no uprooted rural people thronging the cities and living in shanty towns.

The rapid transformation and growth of the Malaysian economy within the short space of 25 years has demonstrated that given a clear plan of projected development, as also the backing of the people, and more importantly an enthusiastic and efficient bureaucracy it is possible to achieve the desired level of achievement in a democracy.

The sectoral development was clearly plotted as early as the early 1970s. For instance, the government planned to exploit the natural advantages like the beautiful beaches of Penang, described as the 'Pearl of the Orient'. Hundreds of European / American hippies had descended on the beautiful beaches and alleged to have indulged in drug taking and other undesirable activities. The poor villagers in the nearby villages were dragged into such activities with the lure of money. The presence of such people and undesirable activities led to the well to do tourists avoiding such natural beauty spots. The Government found a simple solution. One night in 1974, the police picked up all such foreign undesirable characters, took them by trucks to the international airport at Kuala Lumpur (about 250 miles away) and put them on the first available plane out of the country. After this, the well-to-do high spending tourists started coming in large numbers and naturally such high spending tourists continue to be an important source of foreign exchange, incidentally, possession of banned narcotics and drugs carry the death penalty.

The pragmatic course of action adopted by the Government and the people of Malaysia continues as can be seen from the stiff measures adopted by the Government during the East Asian financial crisis of 1997 reportedly precipitated by Mr. Soros, allegedly an international rogue currency speculator, whose actions are believed to have sent the currencies of Thailand, Indonesia, South Korea, Philippines and Malaysia in a free fall, heavily damaging the economies of these countries. While financial experts, economists, IMF and World Bank rushed to help solve the severe economic crisis of these countries, only Malaysia refused to go begging to IMF for financial bail out package and stood firm against the advice tendered by those experts and chose to battle alone and save the country's economy.

Some of the measures taken are briefly stated below just to indicate the tough stand taken:

(i) Repatriation of profits not allowed to foreign investors for one year.

(ii) Strict short term capital control measures.

(iii) Malaysian Ringitt was made non-convertible and holding abroad was banned.

(iv) Tough credit restrictions imposed.

(v) Domestic tourism boosted.

(vi) Government employees banned from foreign travel.

(vii) Malaysian employees returning home from foreign assignments were banned from bringing home cars.

(viii) Agencies for corporate debt restructuring, for asset management and for refinance set up; these three agencies together helped industry to recover.

(ix) 1999 was declared tax free with no corporate income tax for one year, resulting in increased spending and consumption. In less than three years, i.e. by June 2000, Malaysia had recovered from the East Asian financial crisis, without begging for financial aid from IMF or World Bank, and getting bogged down with the burden of foreign currency loans, or for that matter resorting to advice from foreign economists. The successful action in recovery was managed without availing the services of foreign economists or advisors.

It may also be noted that Malaysian peninsula is about 500 miles long from North to South, with Thailand on the Northern border and Singapore at the Southern tip. There is a single meter gauge rail line from North to South, but an excellent road network which carries not only the heavy freight traffic for the industrialized nation, but also heavy passenger traffic. Incidentally with the heavy tree cover over most of the nation, it rains frequently and in some areas even three—four times a week. But despite the heavy traffic and frequent rains, the roads retain their smooth surface without any potholes.

Telecommunication set up has always been up to international standards. Proper planning has ensured adequate supply of quality electric supply.

Malaysia lacks natural resources like coal, iron, manganese, etc. but has the most important resource, viz. human resource ready to learn, accept and employ the latest technology in every sphere and a leadership which is clear in its vision about the future of the nation and a bureaucracy responding to the changing needs of the nation.

Since 1970, the policy of gradually reducing the role of expatriates in all organizations was implemented with the aim of ensuring the local Bhumiputras (sons of the soil) taking over the task of running the country at all levels within about a decade. Stress was also laid on providing education in the local language viz, Bhasa Malaysia but care was taken to ensure that not only was the standard of education maintained at a very high level, but also learning of English and obtaining higher education abroad was encouraged. Today, the nation can proudly claim success of their policy, looking at the remarkable progress made since 1970.

Singapore

16

Capital	: Singapore
Area	: 224 sq. miles
Pop	: 3.0 million

An island city-state, at the Southern tip of the Malay Peninsula, with an area of only 224 sq. miles. Its population consists mainly of ethnic Chinese, Indians and Malay. It was part of the Malaysian federation formed in 1963 but seceded in 1965. Since then it is an independent republic.

Its location at the tip of the Malaysian peninsula facing the Indonesian archipelago across the narrow Malacca Straits being at the crossroads of the heavy shipping lanes connecting the Indian Ocean to the South China Seas and thence to Thailand, Vietnam, Philippines, Hong Kong, Taiwan, Korea, Japan as also Southwards to Australia and New Zealand is an extremely important advantage for trade and Singapore has taken full advantage of this location and reaped the benefits.

It has no natural resources. When Mr. Lee Kuan Yew took over as Prime Minister in 1965, it was an old colonial trading centre with elementary infrastructure. Even the drainage system consisted of open drains. There were bungalows for those who could afford and cramped quarters for the rest. But it was an important transit and trade centre being located at the cross-roads of the most heavily traveled shipping lanes. The very fact of being a tiny island of barely 225 sq. miles, without any natural resources would normally have disheartened the citizens of a similar country. But the Singaporeans, under the dynamic leadership of Mr. Lee Kuan Yew, the Prime Minister, were bent upon building up a prosperous democratic republic where poverty would be abolished, and where every citizen, even a street vendor or a daily wage earner would get the benefit of proper housing, health care and opportunity to improve his status in life.

With this in view, the state decided on a multi pronged plan. The town planning scheme was drawn up to ensure proper zooming with plenty of greenery Housing Schemes and implemented so as to benefit all classes of citizens aimed at providing decent housing at affordable rates.

The location at the crossroads of the Indian Ocean and the South China Sea, an educated and eager to learn and hardworking population, living in harmony, a mild tropical climate, seemed to be the ideal requisites for building up Singapore as a major international financial centre. The infrastructure including communication facilities were set up at the highest international standards. By 1970 Singapore had become the leading financial centre along with Hong Kong. Hundreds of international banks, financial institutions, shipping and commercial ventures set up offices here. The housing schemes also developed very well and by 1970 even daily wage earners were provided with adequate and affordable housing accommodation. Well laid out roads, shopping malls, amusement centers along with efficient bureaucracy resulted in Singapore being not only a very important financial centre but also one of the most popular tourist centers. An efficient law enforcement agency as also judicial system has been a major factor in the development.

The benefits of the resultant prosperous economy are shared by all sections of society. But even with the prosperous economy and influx of millions of tourists every year from all over the world, the state has maintained its high standard of public health and safety. The material prosperity has not resulted in roads being clogged with bumper to bumper traffic with resultant pollution as the Government has imposed heavy taxes on ownership of vehicles. The charges for taking a vehicle into the city business centre are also very high. But public transport is efficient, clean and cheap.

Singapore has its own airline – Singapore International Airlines (SIA) which is acknowledged to be one of the best airlines in the world.

But all this progress of a tiny island state can be ascribed to having a clear vision of the future and determination of the Government and more importantly its people, to succeed in implementing its plans for the benefit of all its citizens.

Taiwan (Formosa)

17

Capital	: TAIPEI
Area	: 13,900 sq. miles
Pop	: 15.0 mil

An island of less than 14,000 sq. miles area, lying about 200-250 miles East of the Chinese mainland and divided almost in half by the Tropic of Cancer. During the 1940s, civil war raged in China. On the one hand were the communist forces led by Maotse Tung and on the other hand were the forces led by Gen Chiang Kai Shek who had to retreat to the island of Formosa (now Taiwan) whose original inhabitants led a simple pastoral life.

The Chinese who fled from mainland China and settled here by 1950 had to start from scratch – even the country was a new one without any elementary infrastructure. By mid-1950s, the process of developing the new homeland had started in earnest. By 1970, Taiwan had built up an industrial structure capable of manufacturing textiles, electronics, consumer goods, etc. Agriculture and fishing industry was also being developed. Despite the fact that the nation had to literally start from scratch in a new homeland, today it is not only militarily geared up to defend itself, but also one of the leading nations engaged in the manufacture of textiles, electronics, etc. While mainland China followed the communist way of life, Taiwan follows the US pattern of free enterprise.

Today the people enjoy a very high standard of living. Their industrial products have succeeded in winning markets all over the world. Even as early as 1970, Taiwanese textiles and electronic toys were available at very reasonable prices all over the world. Their fishing fleet exploits not only the seas nearby but also the Western Coast on India.

So it can be seen that despite a late start and settling in a new homeland, Taiwan has made enormous progress and built up a society with practically no unemployment and enjoying a high standard of living. Like all other Asian Tigers, it has no natural resources, but is rich in the quality of human resources who are always trying to develop and absorb the latest technology.

United States Of America

18

Capital	: Washington DC
Area	: 3,615,000 sq. miles
Pop	: 204 mil

Strictly speaking, USA cannot be compared with the countries described in the earlier chapters. USA today is considered as an extremely rich and prosperous country. But millions of people believe that USA was always prosperous and never experienced the pangs of hunger and unemployment on a national scale. But there was a fall from extreme riches to extreme poverty and it was not a gradual one but a precipitate one which caught the nation completely unprepared. Almost overnight millions of Americans found themselves without jobs and without any income, without shelter and most importantly without understanding the reason for the precipitate fall from prosperity to poverty.

This did not happen during 1940 or 1950, but much earlier. The World War I had ended in 1918. The subsequent decade saw a period of unparalleled growth in the economy. The period from end of 1929 till about 1939 came to be known as the Great Depression. The entire world suffered from the Depression.

The US Government was naturally fully aware of the need for action to restore the national economy. President Hoover in December 1931 assured the American public that all steps would be taken to set up an Emergency Reconstruction Corporation to strengthen the weak spots and thus liberate the full strength of the nation's resources. With this in view, the Reconstruction Finance Corporation Act was passed in Jan 1932. The aims were to "stop deflation in agriculture and industry" and thus to "increase employment by the restoration of men to their normal Jobs". President Hoover also paid tribute to the patriotism of both houses of the Congress who gave proof of their devotion to the welfare of the country irrespective of political affiliation.

Amidst today's prosperity, even Americans have almost forgotten the severe economic crisis which gripped the nation in the early 1930s. Almost 15 million Americans had lost their livelihood and were without any source of income. Others, who still retained their livelihood at reduced levels, had daily nightmares of being sacked or losing their livelihood at any moment.

The extent of depression can be gauged from the fact that market for durable goods had ceased to exist, the demand for consumer goods was restricted to the bare minimum necessary for survival. Agricultural prices had plummeted to a level at which the sale proceeds did not cover the major part of cost of production.

New methods to assist various sectors of the economy were set up. For instance, Commodity Credit Corporation to assist agriculture, RFC mortgage corporation to assist market for real estate mortgages, etc.

The president as well as the Congress realized that giving out doles was not the solution. What was needed, was putting the nation back on its feet by devising and implementing schemes where the nation could get back its pride in gainful economic activity. At the same time, financial outlay had to be considered not only from the employment point of view, but also by creating and improving infrastructure. But all this by self- liquidating schemes.

Congress authorized RFC to provide loans on self-liquidating basis, to states, municipalities, local bodies, etc. The results of this vital legislation passed by the congress urging the Great Depression, to put the country back on its feet are many and varied. The variety of projects financed, included water works, sewer systems, modern low cost housing, aqueducts, bridges, expressways, electric power plants and transmission lines, etc. Some of the noteworthy projects are; San Francisco Oakland Bay bridge, 250 miles aqueducts carrying water from the

Colorado river to Los Angeles, San Diego and more than 20 smaller communities in California, tunnel carrying traffic beneath Hudson river and similar tunnel under New York Bay from lower tip of Manhattan to Brooklyn.

But financing such grandiose schemes was not the only task of RFC. The loans varied in size from only $ 500 to put up a small canning factory upto $ 200 million for Colorado Viaduct. There were hundreds of small town improvements arranged on a pay for itself basis requiring only a few thousand dollars.

Such schemes provided directly thousands of jobs all over the country on these projects. But many hundreds of thousands of jobs were created in supplying, transporting and other ancillary activities. The multiplier effect helped put the nation on its feet again and put disposable incomes in the hands of hundreds of thousands of people who were jobless and without any income.

It financed the Rural Electrification Authority in its early years to enable people in thinly populated rural areas to enjoy the boon of electricity. This enabled hundreds of thousands of people to buy all sorts of electrical appliances like refrigerators, pumps, vacuum cleaners, dairy equipment, etc. on easy payments which private finance companies had been unable to do. The availability of electrical appliances on easy financial terms led to a surge in the demand for electrical goods, which in turn boosted the manufacturing/distribution sectors, and more importantly gave thousands of people a means of livelihood and put the nation back to work.

The RFC assisted rural electrification in a big way. The idea of spreading the benefits of electrification to rural sector and particularly, scattered rural communities was mooted by a senator from a rural state. The idea was for groups of farmers to organize themselves into societies/co-operatives. The RFC lent money on the security of the notes issued by such societies. Later on Congress passed the Rural Electrification Act. Through the early years till about 1955, REA had lent more than $ one billion to co-operatives/societies/municipalities/other local bodies to finance the construction and operation of facilities to provide electricity in rural areas. The power from such schemes served more than 2 million consumers all over USA including Alaska. Thanks to electricity provided under these schemes, rural sector started using labor saving devices, etc. enjoyed by the urban areas.

More than 95% of the loans were disbursed to cooperations and default/delays were less than 1%.

Apart from the REA which helped rural electrification, the Electric Home and Farm Authority's operation made loans to hundreds of thousands tenants/house owners of moderate means to facilitate installation of modern heating/cooling/labor saving devices in these homes. The average individual loan amount was $ 150.

The main problem with small loans is the proportionately heavy administrative costs involved in processing and collecting these small loans. The EH and FA overcame this problem by arranging with utility companies supplying gas/electricity to do the collecting. The utility companies were compensated by EH and FA paying a percentage of the monthly bill charged to the consumer.

With wartime (World War II) restrictions on manufacture of a number of consumer appliances and ban on installment buying, the EH and FA was liquidated under Government orders in 1942. By having the dealers doing all the selling of equipment/appliances, and collection of loan installments being done by the utility companies, the administrative expenses were kept extremely low.

Despite borrowing as much as $ 15 million at a time in the money markets, the EH and FA repaid the government its capital investment of $ 850,000—and also a profit of $ 175,000 – the losses amounted to less than one-fourth of 1%.

RFC started with a capital of $ 500 million and authority to borrow $ 1500 million from the treasury. Though this appeared to be a lot of money in the depression years, but ultimately the flow totaled more than $ 50 billion to fight first the depression and then World War II.

In the struggle against depression, the RFC used more than $10 billion without loss to the tax payer. The money was all returned to the treasury with $ 500 million profit after payment of all expenses including interest on moneys borrowed to finance operations.

For the World War II efforts, RFC authorized expenditure of more than $ 34 billion of which about $ 9 billion was unrecoverable but was foreseen and specifically authorized by Congress as a small part of the price of victory.

The job of pulling the country out of the worst depression had been substantially accomplished by 1939. The national income had reached $ 78 billion almost double that of 1932 and previous all time peak of $ 80 billion.

The RFC did a remarkable job in pulling the country out of its worst depression and that too, within a period of about 8 years. There was not a single instance of fraud in those years despite the vast sums involved. At the peak period the staff did not exceed 12,000. The Directors drew a salary of only $ 10,000. But it was not merely money that enabled RFC to assist the nation in overcoming the Great Depression. Most of the time, the entire staff had to put in extra long hours–seven days a week. They also had to find solutions to new problems which cropped up every now and then.

Not only the staff of RFC, but also representatives of business and industry were ever willing to assist RFC in its activities – often at considerable financial and personal sacrifices.

In brief, the success of RFC in pulling within less than 8 years, the USA out of the Great Depression can be attributed to the intelligent planning, diligence, probity and a constant willingness by each and every individual, from the President to the member of Congress to put the country above self.

Water

19

It is impossible for life to exist without water. Plants, animals, birds and human beings – all require water for survival. In a way nature has been generous in providing abundant water, particularly, rivers, glaciers, ponds, lakes and subsoil water. Four-fifths of the earth's surface is covered with water. Nature has also been generous in replenishing the store of fresh water through rains and snowfalls. But man's greed and wasteful use of water combined with the complete disregard for maintaining the fragile ecological balance has led to a situation where large parts of the world have started feeling the terrible effects of the growing shortage of water. The stage is fast approaching of possible wars between nations merely for access to supplies of water. Already, in India, states like Tamil Nadu and Karnataka, or Punjab and Haryana are engaged in battle of words and also legally for share of river waters.

One very important aspect that distinguishes lack of water from lack of food, is the fact that food or substitutes can somehow be arranged for but, so far, no substitute has been found for water. And without water, life whether it is plant, animal, birds or human beings, cannot survive.

After 50 years of independence, what is the position in India regarding availability of water? Has the position improved or worsened over the last 5 decades? Of course any improvement would be a source of great comfort to the millions of Indians. But the slightest worsening in the situation would be cause of great concern.

Unfortunately, the situation has considerably worsened over the years and has now reached alarming levels. It must be realized that shortage of water affects every aspect of existence.

Apart from drinking purposes, water is a necessity for numerous purposes, some of which are briefly touched upon below:

(i) Needed for cooking, washing, sewerage, etc.

(ii) Agriculture cannot survive without adequate water nor can animals and birds.

(iii) Existence of modern domestic/industrial/agricultural activity not possible without adequate electrical power mainly hydel even Nuclear generators need huge quantities of water.

A cursory glance at the map of India lead to the conclusion that India should not suffer from shortage of water. A number of rivers have their source in the snowfed glaciers in the Himalayas. The North Eastern region should have no shortage of water for its river as it is forested region. Besides the mighty Brahmaputra, arising in the Himalayas and flowing through parts of Tibet, again enters India and flows through the N E region. The Central and Southern region has a number of rivers arising in the forest hills and mountain ranges. There are thousands of lakes and ponds scattered all over India, including the desert regions of Rajasthan, a number of them created artificially over a period of centuries. In addition to the rivers, lakes and ponds, there is plenty of subsoil potable water even a few yards from the sea coast in a number of areas. For instance, in Mumbai city, which originally consisted of 7 islands, there used to be dozens sweet water wells even a few decades ago, some only a few yards away from the sea coast – most of them have been filled up now.

But despite having dozens of snow fed and rain-fed rivers, in addition to thousands of lakes and ponds scattered all over the country, plus plenty of subsoil water, India has arrived at a critical stage where acute shortage of water is being experienced almost everywhere. Even with an almost normal rainfall over the country in the recent past, the situation is fast deteriorating.

Over the years, the increase in population has naturally resulted in increased demand for water from not only the domestic sector but also from agriculture, industrial and hydel generating sectors. But increased demand was foreseen even 50 years ago. Dozens of mega projects for harnessing river water by building mega dams all over the country with a view to meet domestic, irrigation, industrial and hydel demands were drawn up.

So despite having foreseen the potential increase in demand and having drawn up numerous schemes to build mega projects to meet the anticipated requirements, why has a situation of acute water scarcity arisen? Did the plans for mega projects underestimate the potential requirements? Or did the actual demand outstrip the projections? Or was the faulty implementation of projects result in serious under achieving of the targets? Or was it the sole dependence on mega projects to the exclusion of other methods of water conservation/ distribution? Or is the supply of water from snow fed/ rain fed rivers decreasing? Or is it the result of combination of all these factors compounded by recklessly overusing the underground water by digging wells and ignoring the time tested water conservation/recharging methods in use for centuries?

There are numerous projects where no benefit or negligible benefits have been obtained despite massive investments of thousands of crores of rupees over decades.

A glance at some of the mega dam projects shows an incredible gap between targets and achievement in these projects. Only a few glaring examples are given below: over 470 projects have spilled over into the Ninth Five Year Plan from earlier Five Year Plans, resulting in huge cost and time over-runs. Maharashtra has spent during the last 50 years over Rs. 25,000 crores on various irrigation projects, canals, and dams but only 15% of land gets irrigated, 85% still depends on seasonal rains. Maharashtra has an average annual rainfall of 600 mm and suffers from water shortage but USA with an average annual rainfall of 210 mm per annum does not. Of course the capacity of the soil to retain the rainwater is an important factor.

	Project	Date started	Original estimate	Revised amount	Projected potential	Actual irrigation achieved (1000 hectares)
1	Waghur – Maharashtra	1975	12.0	110.0	24.0	0.0
2	Gosikhurd	1980	460.0	2100.0	251.0	0.0
3	Chaskman	1977	23	347.0	38.0	0.0
4	Lakhwar Vyasi U.P	1975	140.0	576.0	40.0	0.0
5	Khunga – Manipur	1980	16.0	150.0	15.0	0.0
6	Zankari – Gujarat	1980	19.0	90.0	24.0	0.0
7	Kallada – Kerala	1961	13.0	492.0	-	0.0
8	Bhima – Maharashtra	1965	42.0	920.0	226.0	176.0
9	Kukadi – Maharashtra	1969	18.0	919.0	-	75.0
10	Thoubal – Manipur	1980	47.0	391.0	33.0	4.0
11	Rajghat II – MP	1957	309.0	525.0	117.0	10.0
12	Idamalayar – Kerala	1980	18.0	107.0	43.0	5.0
13	North Koel – Bihar	1975	439.0	815.0	105.0	35.0
14	Champamati – Assm	1982	15.0	80.0	25.0	0.32
15	Jamrani – UP	1975	61.0	280.0	66.0	21.0
16	Muvattapuzi Valley Irrigation proj – Kerala	1975	21.0	425.0	Original target 17.4 reduced to 8.5	0.0

Note: No.16 Experts state: "Project area not geographically sited for canal construction, needing construction of bridges and aqua ducts, some aqua ducts to pass over railway lines but security risk. Even land survey was done in haphazard manner without observing norms according to locals".

A glance at the above chart indicates the gross inefficiency and colossal waste of time and taxpayers' money involved in these projects. But one cannot resist drawing specific attention to items no. 1 to 7 above where the actual irrigation achieved is nil after continuing to spend thousands of crores of taxpayers' money over a period of more than 20 years.

Finally item no. 16 deserves special attention as it clearly brings out the utter lack of considering even the basic facts relating to a project before spending hundreds of crores of rupees on a project, where the impossibility of the project was obvious from inception. This only highlights the fact of utter lack of planning in focusing on the genuine needs of the people by proper planning and, without wasting thousand of crores of taxpayer's money.

Politicians and bureaucrats continue to put forward many excuses for the cost over runs extending to thousands of crores of taxpayers' money and time over runs extending to decades in practically every project without resulting in any benefit to the affected people. On the one hand massive investment has swallowed up thousand of crores of rupees since independence without any commensurate benefit; on the other hand, periodic draughts are aggravating problems for the nation.

The first sector to be affected by draught is the rural sector-crops wither away due to lack of water. This is not the only adverse effect on the farmers. Lack of water means failure of crops and generally also loss of cattle – which in turn results in the inability to repay loans. In India, the farmer as a class, is honest and believes in repaying his debts. A number of suicides by farmers are being reported all over India every year due to their inability to repay their debts. At the cost of being accused of digressing, one cannot help contrasting the attitude of the poor farmers who cannot face the ignominy of failure to meet his commitments involving a few thousand rupees and that too normally on account of factors like rain or market prices, outside his control with that of big industrialist/businessmen whose luxurious life style remain unchanged even if enterprises become bankrupt and all their liabilities amounting to hundreds of crores of rupees including dues to workers, remain unpaid.

Anyway, coming back to the topic of shortage of water, the agriculturists' existence and well being is linked with that of his cattle. Shortage of water results in lack of water for cattle also apart from the resultant shortage of animal feed. A time comes when the farmer is compelled to dispose of his few cattle in a forced sale, rather than see them die for want of animal feed and water. Besides, the lack of water also forces the farmer, together with his family, to migrate to urban centers in search of means of livelihood. Of course there is acute shortage of water, even for drinking and domestic use but over the years, the poor rural populace as a rule, is reconciled to fend for itself and somehow try to exist on what meager supplies of water they can manage.

But existing reservoirs, lakes, ponds do not get filled up in times of insufficient rains. The storage capacity of reservoirs and lakes is also diminishing due to siltage and lack of desilting operations over the years. Severe deforestation along the banks of reservoirs and dumping of industrial and domestic waste in such storage areas are a major cause of reduction of storage capacity and also contamination.

Now reservoirs are also the main source of water to urban areas apart from providing irrigation facility to rural areas and also generation of Hydel power. A substantial fall in the reservoir level due to inadequate inflow of water would have the following adverse effects:

(i) Inadequate supply for irrigation and consequently shortfall/ failure of crops.

(ii) Inadequate supply to towns/cities.

(iii) Inadequate generation of electricity.

So it becomes all the more necessary to ensure proper storage and distribution of water.

To overcome the difficulties posed by inadequate supply of water, authorities, over the years resorted to digging more and deeper wells to meet the ever increasing shortage of water. The water problem has been aggravated by the falling water tables due to over exploitation of ground water. The indiscriminate digging of wells, even in areas near the sea, has resulted in ingress of sea water, resulting in the entire subsoil water in that area, becoming brackish and unsuitable for drinking and even for agriculture.

A number of areas self sufficient in water about 40 years ago, now face acute water scarcity. It is not the rural poor who are the only sufferers from water scarcity. Even the urban population is facing this problem. Mumbai, the financial capital of India, and a modern, progressive, clean city at one time, now faces water shortage. Even areas considered exclusive and occupied by the very rich, have to depend to a large extent on water supplied by tankers daily, due to inadequate supply from the municipal corporation. But despite acute water shortage, hundreds of high rise skyscrapers (20 to 60 stories high) continue to mushroom in the city and also in the distant suburbs. On the one hand the municipal corporation permits construction of such skyscrapers, while on the other it admits a daily shortfall of a 1000 million gallons of water. But the municipality has publicly stated its inability to supply water to these new buildings before 2008. It also admits that no new water augmentation schemes were taken up since 1995.

But the continued national neglect and mismanagement of water resources as also the excessive dependence on mega dams and mega projects, is leading to an explosive situation which is being further aggravated by the melting of glaciers due to global warming. After all, none can deny the indisputable fact of water being an absolute necessity for survival. Shortage of food can be met by imports but shortage of water cannot be met by imports. A nation has to rely on its own ingenuity and resources to ensure adequate and equitable distribution of water.

The experience of the last 50 years since independence indicates the failure of massive investments in mega projects and mega dams in providing adequate water and power. On the contrary, the locking up of thousands of crores of taxpayers' money in such projects without any commensurate benefit to the nation compels one to consider possible alternatives. Besides a realistic measure of the social cost of uprooting hundreds of thousands of children, women and men from their ancestral lands and submergence of thousands of acres of land with a high percentage of fertile lands and rare medicinal flora as also taking a toll of varied fauna all over India, has to be measured against the benefits supposed to accrue from such projects. As a rule, the uprooted people are the losers most of whom receive meager compensation after delays extending over years, and are unable to start a new life in different surroundings or environment. It is a universal fact that the bonds of an agriculturist with his land are extremely strong and efforts to uproot from their ancestral lands and traditional way of life are always strongly resented.

So, would it not be better if projects for ensuring availability of adequate water are devised keeping in mind the human face of progress? This could be achieved by:

(i) Participation of people likely to be adversely affected, is ensured right from the beginning at the planning stage itself.

(ii) Means other than building of large dams are sought and implemented expeditiously.

(iii) Tried and tested traditional methods, simple in operation, are utilized to the maximum extent possible.

(iv) The cost of such schemes are affordable by the locals.

(v) Due consideration is given to preserving the ecology.

Building of mega dams and projects on a large scale all over India is a new concept being implemented on such a large scale only after independence in 1947. Though the country as a whole receives a large amount of rain annually, it is not spread evenly throughout the year. At times there are droughts. So over the last hundreds of years, Indians have perfected the art of water harvesting. There are many ways to harvest and these techniques have been successfully used by the people. The success of the traditional water harvesting system lies in the fact that the system has evolved over the centuries by the people who used it.

Many individuals and NGOs have over the last few decades started involving themselves in studying, implementing and improving the traditional water harvesting systems. Considering the fact that thousands of crores of rupees are locked up in projects which are yet to be completed even after 25 to 40 years of commencement and resulting in incredibly high time and cost overruns, it would appear to be high time to consider the extent to which reliance can be put exclusively on the schemes for building mega projects involving mega dams to solve the extremely critical and to a large extent avoidable shortage of water all over the country in rural areas and in urban areas, in hilly areas and in plains in the interior and the sea coast.

A large number of NGOs periodically come out with well documented reports stressing the need for implementing traditional water harvesting systems rather than go in for mega projects, each costing hundreds of crores of rupees and taking decade's for completion without any certainty regarding the accrual of benefits to the people. The essential point to be noted is the fact that the traditional water harvesting methods are time tested over centuries by the people themselves. But there is a tendency among a large number of Indians to decry the achievements of their forebears over the centuries, but it is time to give the ancient knowledge its due.

Water harvesting, storage and distribution techniques have been practiced in India for centuries. The importance of water harvesting, storage and distribution particularly in a hot tropical country with seasonal and uncertain rainfall, has been understood by the people of India over the last thousands of years. The need for adequate supply of water throughout the year for agriculture as also the general population at large scattered in farms, villages, hamlets and towns was catered for by using simple well designed techniques. But apart from the need of the population at large, a very important application of knowledge and techniques can be seen in the thousands of forts, most of them on hills and mountain tops and some of them even jutting into the sea.

All the forts were self sufficient in water. Thousands of people, combatants and others, lived in these forts. In addition to the large human population, hundreds of animals, including horses and elephants, had to be taken care of even at times of siege which could last for months. Even palaces and towns built in the desert were assured of adequate supply of water to all—be it a fort on a hill top or a town in the desert.

But the stress on mega projects after achieving independence more than 50 years ago, resulted in the neglect of century's old tested techniques and systems. Even techniques like drip irrigation considered by many to be a recent development, were in vogue centuries ago. Farmers in Meghalaya have been using for centuries, bamboo pipes for tapping river waters, which is transported through these pipes over hundreds of meters and finally released in drips where needed. This not only indicates the practical application of water conservation by drip irrigation, but also the ability to use bamboo which is available in plenty locally.

But gradually, despite bureaucratic, political and public apathy, and at times, strong opposition, the time tested water harvesting, storage and distribution techniques are coming back into their own, albeit slowly. It needs to be noted that water harvesting and conservation techniques are also being successfully tried out in urban centers by utilizing monsoon waters which used to run waste from concrete roof tops.

The Indian Institute of Planning and Administration has stated that there are numerous examples of areas being hit by draught where traditional water harvesting methods have been phased out. Piped water supply has resulted in failure to maintain the culture of water conservation. The recharging process through water harvesting and conservation has been completely ignored since independence. The absence of recharging coupled with excessive overdrawing has resulted in continuous falling of groundwater levels.

According to the protagonists of water harvesting and conservation, the reasons for floods and draught are the same, viz. ignoring catchment areas and not involving the communities directly affected by the projects. In a sample study, it was found that people in more than 20 river basins were facing acute water shortage. The cause for this tragedy affecting thousands of lives was the untrammeled and unscientific 'Progress' by conducting large scale mining, which has completely destroyed an elaborate water harvesting system created centuries ago after carefully mapping the terrain.

A number of individuals and organization have been taking keen interest in the ancient water harvesting, storing, transporting and distribution systems. Numerous examples of such ancient systems can be found all over India but only a few are briefly described below.

1. Burhanpur (Madhya Pradesh)

There is a 24 km long underground canal constructed about 400 years ago during the Moghul period by a private citizen, supplying water to Burhanpur town. It is a technological marvel. The entire canal runs 20 feet underground with channels more than 20 ft high and 6 to 8 feet wide. Water is collected, not from the rivers, but by collection of water seepage through special holes. It has aeration towers at short intervals. The water flows to the town due to a suitable gradient. The canal is a rare example of Moghul water supply technology and one of the few examples of underground water transport systems round the world and based on unique principles.

Though this is a classic and unique example of water supply scheme without resort to dams or pumping station, it has been completely ignored and neglected by the Government authorities despite attention having been repeatedly drawn by locals and other experts. Even though it is in state of disrepair, it still supplies about 100,000 gallons of water a day. The continued neglect, heavy deforestation and building of roads near by is affecting the canal badly. It is sad to see such a technological marvel created more 400 years ago facing continued neglect and official apathy during 50 years of independence. This marvel should not only be protected but strenuous effort be made to learn and replicate the ancient techniques.

2. Jodhpur (Rajasthan)

Somewhat similar is the case of the centuries old water supply system to Jodhpur town. Again it is the individuals and private societies which are trying to preserve and re-energize the centuries old canal water supply system. This canal system, if repaired and maintained properly, can provide the major requirement of water to Jodhpur town. But the Government and even most of the citizens continue to be indifferent to this historical, scientific and economic water supply system.

3. Udaipur (Rajasthan)

Udaipur was known for its large number of natural and man made lakes in the desert. The rulers of Mewar had built palaces, some of them in the lakes, and took great care of these lakes as they were the source of water for the people throughout the year. Today, after more than 50 years of independence and abolishing of the Princely Indian States, the lakes are drying up. In some cases like the Mutasagar Lake, and other lakes, the situation is so bad, that people and cattle walk across what was once the middle of the Lakes.

Decades ago, much before India became independent and the merging of the princely states with India, the rulers permitted the locals to dig up the silt in summer. This had a two fold effect, the farmers got free silt which was good manure and the populace in general benefited by this annual dredging which helped in preventing of silting up of the lake and thereby preserving the water storage capacity. Today, government rules and regulations, formal or otherwise, have resulted in stoppage of this ancient and beneficial practice. Naturally the lakes are silting up.

The farmers do not get free manure and the populace at large suffers water shortage. At this rate, the lakes in this desert region, which had adequately met the needs of this region for centuries, will dry up resulting in untold suffering to the people. Lakes are crucial for the economy of this region as they form the catchment area of neighboring Barmer, Chittorgarh, and Udaipur districts. The state has not shown any urgency in finalizing or implementing various scheme even in a state which is mainly desert, and the need for water all the year round, is all the more critical.

4. Hyderabad (Andhra Pradesh)

Hyderabad was also known till about the 1950s as a city with almost dozen lakes. These lakes were interconnected, so the rain water was harvested and distributed throughout the city. Consequently there was no shortage of water. Today the citizens face water shortages, particularly severe during summer, as the interconnecting system has fallen into disrepair, due to neglect. As is the general practice in India today, garbage, sewage, etc. is dumped in the lakes. Legal and illegal structures continue to sprout all over the lake side. In summer there is acute shortage of water, in the monsoon there is heavy flooding in the city due to blocking of natural water channels.

5. Raipur (Chhattisgarh)

Raipur had more than 130 ponds built and maintained properly during the centuries of rule by the previous rulers.

Today barely 25 remain. Even the 600 year old Buddha Talao is not maintained. It is now the dumping place for garbage. Documented records show that due care was taken previously to keep water clean and prevent misuse. All the ponds were interconnected to allow circulation of water, not a drop was allowed to be wasted. The ponds used to keep the water table high and the city cool. But today the ponds are utterly neglected. Now even the Buddha Talao stinks. As per the State Pollution Control Board, its water in the pond is not fit to be touched, but people have their bath in these dirty waters. Government now intends erecting a statue of Swami Vivekananda near Buddha Talao, instead of trying to clean up the talao.

6. Thane (Maharashtra)

Thane is almost a suburb of Mumbai. It had dozens of lakes, but nobody had taken any interest in maintaining these till recently. A newly appointed commissioner decided to clean up not only the city and its roads, but also to clean up the dozens of lakes. So far, he has succeeded in not only cleaning up the city and broadened its streets, but also cleaned up a number of lakes. For that matter even Mumbai had a number of ponds/lakes/talaos but over the years they have been filled up.

So far the neglect of ancient lakes has been described. While in the past, not only the rulers but also the tribals realized the importance of water resources management, it is seen that during the last 50 years the ancient water management systems have by and large been allowed to fall into disuse. But there are instances of lakes created during last 50 years, also being allowed to fall into disuse. The facts about the lake in Chandigarh make disturbing reading. The facts are briefly stated below about the lake in Chandigarh.

Chandigarh was meticulously planned and constructed immediately after independence with the latest concepts of urban planning with plenty of open spaces and parks. It has been seen earlier that lakes created centuries ago, continued to serve the purpose for which they were created. But this no longer holds true.

This is the story of Lake Sukna, planned and created in 1958 at Chandigarh, the capital of two prosperous states viz. Punjab and Haryana and declared as a National Wetland in 1988. A comparison of some of the parameters is given below to indicate the apathy display by the authorities:

	1958	1980
Average water level	17ft	less than 6 ft
Total holding capacity	10 cu mt	4 cu mt
Surface area	560 acres	340 acres

It is only the voluntary efforts by some public spirited citizens which have prevented the lake from being completely silted up. There have been Government plans to dredge the lake with the assistance of the Dredging Corporation of India. But this has been in the planning stage for more than 2 decades with no progress in finalizing a plan. There is a limit to citizens' voluntary efforts. So with the continued apathy displayed by the authorities where even dredging plan cannot be up, let alone being implemented, there are also fears that the lake will very soon be converted into a marsh before being sold to developers for constructing buildings. And this is the fate of a lake in a modern, planned city which is the capital of two prosperous states.

The fate of this lake highlights the glaring contrast between the planning, construction and upkeep of lakes centuries ago and the present lake constructed barely 50 years ago and declared a National Wetland.

There are numerous examples of neglect of ancient water conservation and distribution schemes which have been allowed to fall into disuse and aggravate the acute water scarcity problem. The reservoirs are allowed to silt up. Every year stop gap arrangements to supply water are carried out. Digging wells is the commonest method of trying to satisfy the needs of the people. But these have been done over the last 50 years without taking into account the basic fact that there is a limit to drawing water, and the most important factor viz. the necessity for recharging of wells and subsoil water have been completely ignored. Consequently the level of subsoil water has drastically fallen. There is very little subsoil water available in large parts of the country. In the attempts to draw water, wells have even been dug near the seashore as a result, the subsoil water has been contaminated by sea water, and millions of litres of water have been rendered unfit for any use. Besides, industries discharge their effluents frequently in the rivulets, lakes, ponds, thereby contaminating the entire water supply.

Water being a prime necessity for survival of humans as also flora and fauna, a large number of individuals, groups and NGOs are involving themselves in solving their own problems rather than wait for any action by the Government. The number of such groups is increasing day by day. Some of the schemes launched by them have shown remarkable success. A few such successful schemes are indicated below. It must be stressed that only a very small sample is given below, when there are hundreds of successful schemes all over India.

1. Ralegaon Siddhi (Ahmednagar Dist., Maharashtra)

This village situate in a draught prone region of Maharashtra was a typical village with extreme poverty – no supply of water, no school or medical aid and addiction to liquor being rampant. Today it is a model village with schools for boys and girls, well constructed residential accommodation, hospital, etc. in short, everything needed for a decent healthy life for all its citizens. An important factor is the voluntary ban on liquor – as a matter of fact all villagers have taken a pledge to abstain from consuming or dealing in liquor.

The initial concept and spade work was done by an individual without any scientific education. Today Ralegaon is internationally known for the excellent development without depending on Government schemes or action. But the entire credit goes to a modest individual who wanted to improve the living conditions of his village and believed that this could be achieved only if all the villagers could unite and share a common vision of improving the lot of all the people in the village, without waiting for Government to draw up schemes. He could successfully inspire the people, not without struggle, to unite and build a model village.

Today, there are schools attended by boys and girls, provision for higher education for the deserving, medical aid, etc. The villagers are now assured of a better future for their children and women no longer have to trudge for a few pots of water everyday. Incidentally, Shri. Anna Hazare, the man with vision and burning desire to improve his village is not a highly educated person. He was a simple army truck driver and continues to be a simple person, unaffected by the national and international fame achieved by him.

2. Raj Samdhyala (Rajkot Dist., Gujarat)

A village with a population of about 1,500 adopted water harvesting techniques in 1985, by building about a dozen dykes for storing water and using it for irrigation. The locals fought with the state authorities for the implementation of their scheme and obtained Rs.2 crores spread over 15 years, which was adequate as labor, was donated by the villagers themselves. The locals also realize the importance of tree cover, which has grown in about 20 years to about 50,000 trees from about 2,000 trees in 1980, thus raising the water table adequate for almost 300 wells.

But not only has water harvesting resulted in adequacy of water throughout the year, but there has also been an overall development of the community. The children now attend the newly started village school. But what is more noteworthy is the fact that more than 600 of the 1,000 students are girls. So though the present generation of women are illiterate, the coming generation of girls will be literate and hope to participate actively not only in the development of their village, but some of them also hope to be in the nation building activity at the district and state level and may be at the national level. The villagers may be illiterate, they are fully aware of the necessity of preserving the ecological balance by enacting strict rules for preserving the flora and fauna.

3. Dedakadi village, Savarkundla area (Rajkot Dist., Gujarat)

It has been lucky to have guidance and assistance of a NGO for almost a decade for tackling the water scarcity problem of almost 100 villages in the surrounding area.

With the growing prosperity, schools have been set up for boys and girls. As a matter of fact even a hostel has been set up at Dedakadi village where girls from other villages can come and stay for their studies.

4. Jamkhandi (Bijapur Dist., Karnataka)

In 1987, the UKTR Sangh, arranged on their own with the help of concerned villagers covering irrigation of about 35,000 acres spread over 30 villages. Potable water was also implemented for providing water to 3 lac villagers by constructing 430 meter long and 8 meter high barrage. It was constructed in just 11 months at a cost of only Rs. 93 lac, as against Government estimate of over Rs. 2 crores. The food grain output also increased from 4,000 MT to 1.5 lac MT. The land value also increased from Rs. 10,000 per acre to Rs. 2 lac per acre. It is maintained by farmers association.

5. Sariska (Rajasthan)

Shri. Rajendra Singh of Tarun Bharat Sangh, a NGO, decided a decade ago to make villagers accept the right of wild animals over forests. TBS connected this concept to conservation of water. With this in view, they helped the villagers construct a number of small and big ponds. These ponds have curbed the need for villagers and cattle to enter forest for fodder and water. This has also stopped tigers from straying into populated areas, thereby reducing conflict between man and animal.

6. Kalamkarwadi (Ahmednagar Dist., Maharashtra)

A semi arid and hilly tract with annual rainfall of about 300 mm. Water had always been a problem in this drought prone area. Water had to be brought by tankers to meet the shortage. Even in the monsoon, barely 50 wells were functional. Naturally the quality of life was extremely poor. But now there is a dramatic improvement in the quality of life.

More than 70 biogas units have been set up, the most important item was the providing of more than 100 toilets in the village. Primary school has been established and the girls particularly, are taking full advantage of it. Like all other villages which aim to improve the quality of life, there is a self imposed ban on sale and consumption of liquor. This is just one example, a scheme promoted under the Indo German Watershed programmed and implemented with the assistance of NABARD, though the planning and implementation rests with the village watershed, nominated by the village Sabha. The regular supply of enriched slurry from the biogas units has ensured a safe and non-harmful fertilizer, resulting in improved productivity and dependence on wood as fuel drastically reduced.

7. Pati Bloc (Badwani Dist., MP)

Tribals of Badwani district had been demanding drought water conservation works be taken up as part of relief operations. Despite furnishing all details and meeting officials at all levels, including Chief Minister nothing happened for 3 years. Ultimately a team of 30 villagers went to Alwar, Rajasthan to study the scheme being implemented by Tarun Bharat Sangh (TBS) an NGO.

On return, the villagers could convince the Gram Sabhas of 18 villages to go ahead without begging for Government aid and used even their ordinary tools. Within 4 months, the tribals had put up 20 water conservation structures in 18 villages. Water conservation experts from Samaj Pragati Sahayog, an NGO, testified to the efficacy of these works and confirmed that they would have cost the Government not less than Rs. 80 lac. But the Government was churlish in not praising the work of these tribals, who look upon these achievements as an honor for the villages and proved that tribals know as much about building small dams as engineers.

But the villagers feel that if they could achieve so much, then with proper Government help, they could do much more. But a number of dharnas and meetings with officials have resulted in more delays by the Government.

8. Gavdewadi (Pune Dist., Maharashtra)

Till 1978, water scarcity and supply of water by tankers with consequent migration to urban centers for earning a living was a normal phenomenon in this village.

Fed up with urban living and wanting to ago back to their village, a group of more than 100 villagers visited Ralegaon

Siddhi and came back convinced that they could change their village using home grown techniques developed in Ralegaon.

Gradually bunds were built along nullas saving rain water from going waste. Today the drought affected village has been completely transformed, all by the initiative and hard work, of the local villagers. Now the reverse migration back to their village is going on. They have also built schools and the local girls are also grabbing the opportunity to get an education.

9. Lav Ka Bas (Rajasthan)

After 3 continuous years of drought, more than 500 villagers of Lav ka Bas, decided to ensure retaining whatever rain fell in that area. So they decided to build check dams on the river Ruparel after managing to collect about Rs. 3 lac under the guidance of Tarun Bharat Sangh (TBS) an NGO based at Alwar.

Within 4 months the villagers designed and built a dam 80 m long and 12 m high. No sooner was the dam built, than the irrigation department officials came to demolish it. The reason cited by the Government was that the building of such check dams (small as it was) was in violation of water sharing arrangements signed in 1910, between the erstwhile Princely states of Alwar and Bharatpur. Minister for irrigation went further and asserted that even a drop of rain falling in Rajasthan belongs to the Government and no individual had the right to collect even one drop of rain.

This is a classical example of typical bureaucratic obstruction in the villager's efforts to improve their lot by local talent and effort in the most economical manner. Of course the Minister's claim to every drop of rain water is just the wide belief of a number of politicians in something over and above the ancient (but long Defunct) Divine Right of Kings.

But this is not the end of the saga. The villagers were in no mood to surrender meekly and continue to suffer from shortage of water. They guarded the dam 24 hours a day to prevent the Government from demolishing it. This high handedness of the state Government was brought to the notice of the Central Government who sent a team consisting of Shri. M. S. Swaminathan and other eminent people, who after examination of dam, certified it to be safe and a boon to the villagers. This team then enlightened the state Government the need to encourage water harvesting techniques being implemented by the villagers.

10. Iyasara (Mehasana Dist., Gujarat)

Mehsana is one of the districts in Gujarat facing severe scarcity of water, and to make it worse the abnormally high percentage of fluoride in the water has made the soil infertile. It also spreads fluorosis and other diseases. The river Rupen runs for the major part of the year except in the monsoon, when more than 90% of the rain water goes waste and nothing conserved. The land is thickly forested with thorny shrubs. There are numerous pits and gullies, some of them 30 feet deep and making the land unfit for farming, but used by bootleggers for brewing illicit liquor in a big way. But in 1997, an engineer purchased about 20 acres with plan for developing it as a farmland. He cleared the land by hiring the very people who used to brew illicit liquor in the pit. He used the excess mud from the gullies to level the land and converted the pits into checkdams. With only 5 check dams he has converted the entire area into a successful farm. The water used is the rain water collected by the checkdams and hence pure and contains no fluoride. The water table in the area is being recharged. Now he grows healthy corps, fruits, flowers, etc.

His enthusiasm has converted a barren land where nothing could be grown into a flourishing farmland. Besides he has put a stop to the illicit brewing in the area. He strongly feels that the Government and people cry over the lack of water in Gujarat but they are ignorant of such successful experiments.

Cases of Government agencies actively encouraging such initiative and community involvement by villagers in self help are rare in India.

So, it becomes all the more necessary to highlight the rare instances where the bureaucrat, working within the framework of rules and regulations makes a significant contribution towards improving the lot of the impoverished masses who had been exploited for decades. Fortunately, in India the number of such bureaucrats, who are assisting the traditionally neglected people to improve their lot, is gradually increasing. Tragically, such selfless service is, as a rule, not appreciated by the powers that be. It is this indomitable spirit and the burning desire to make India a better nation, without the slightest regard for self glorification that keeps such rare individuals continuing their perceived duty.

A number of such examples are now coming to light. But only one such example is cited below.

Orissa had been very badly affected by the severe cyclone of 1999. But even otherwise, most of the districts like Bolangir, Kalahandi, and Naupada, etc. have not seen any development since independence over 50 years ago. The large scale destruction of forests, the huge mining operations without conferring any benefit to the locals, mainly tribals, has impoverished the people without any means of earning a livelihood. To add to their misery, one of the worst droughts in decades resulted in drying up of lakes and ponds.

This is the story of one district viz. Naupada in Orissa. Thousands of villagers had to flee to neighboring states in the hope of earning a living for survival. In June 2000, Shri. B. Sethi took over as Collector of Naupada district where the officials/politicians/business men had a complete grip on the entire range of activities. As a result, the Public Distribution System (PDS) was reduced to a farce and the poor never got any of the foodgrains. Government projects existed only on paper and funds were siphoned off. But the new Collector changed all that.

The village Panchayat was entrusted with running the PDS. Up-to-date stock position was displayed now at every Panchayat office. Besides, the villagers are not compelled to buy their entire entitlement in one lot, but can do so when circumstances permit.

Depriving the poor and mostly illiterate villagers of their full labor charges was normal. Today a villager is paid Rs. 50 for a day's labor, whereas earlier the contractor would pay a maximum of Rs. 20 a day and that too not promptly. Now huge tanks for storage of rain water are being constructed. Formerly all such construction activities were carried on by contractors. But it is now entrusted to village Panchayat, where the laborers from the village elect a leader. A full detail of each project showing not only the total cost, but also the entitlement for each type of labor is published in booklet form. Besides, for emergency measures, sanction was obtained for feeding almost 15,000 villagers in emergency centers. But the attitude of the politicians can be gauged from the fact that neither the local MP nor the local MLA has contributed anything from their local area development fund despite repeated requests as the utilization and disbursement of cash is controlled by the villagers themselves without any middleman.

There are thousands of examples all over India, of local citizens, particularly in the rural and tribal areas joining together under the guidance of individuals and/or NGOs, successfully implementing water conservation and distribution schemes at a very nominal cost. It may be noted that recently, Government officers like Collectors have also started taking keen interest in such schemes and rendering all assistance to villagers in successful implementation of such schemes. But it must be stressed that such successful schemes involve all the locals from the planning stage, right through the construction stage and continuing through the monitoring and maintenance of the scheme. Such schemes envisage not only adequate water throughout the year, but also consequential improvement in the quality of life. Schemes of this sort have resulted in sustainable uplift of the people with a reasonable disposable surplus income as against the subsistence standard of living and normally being in debt to the local money lender.

This has resulted in improvement of health and even educational facilities are coming up in the villages. What is more important, is that benefits of education are being shared by both boys and girls. The migration to urban centers for earning a living has practically stopped in those successful villages. In due course agro industries are also expected to grow in such rural areas.

Apart from resulting in the improvement in the quality of life for the present as well as the coming generations, what needs to be stressed is the fact that there is no uprooting of children, women and men from the their ancestral roots and driving such self respecting people to destitution, as is the normal result in mega projects. On the contrary, their roots in their ancestral land are strengthened along with improvement in the quality of life for the present as well as the future generations.

The conception, planning, implementation and maintenance of such schemes do not necessarily depend on highly educated people. The basic concept has to come from the local community which is largely uneducated in the conventional sense but wise in ancient and practical knowledge. Once the community identifies its problems and reaches a consensus on the broad outline of a plan to improve its lot, they can now depend upon a number of selfless educated and dedicated workers, individuals as also NGOs who render all assistance to the villages in dealing with the technical aspects as also the bureaucracy.

There are innumerable success stories all over India and more are coming up every year. But only a few have been cited here briefly, just to indicate the enormous benefits reaped with minimum financial costs accruing to the local communities without depending upon mega projects or other extremely expensive schemes drawn up by Government planners.

It can be seen that the common characteristics of such successful schemes are:

(i) The entire community is involved in the planning, implementation, maintenance and running of the scheme.

(ii) Barren lands are converted into flourishing agriculture communities with the least financial investment.

(iii) The role of the Government is kept to the minimum.

(iv) With assured water supply due to storage and recharging of subsoil water, the quality of life shows tremendous improvement.

(v) Women no longer have to trudge a couple of kms everyday, just to get a few buckets of water.

(vi) Children, both boys and girls, get an opportunity to get an education, and that too in their own village.

(vii) Villagers take a solemn pledge to abstain from liquor.

(viii) Gradually economic activities like agro industries start developing in such areas.

(ix) There is a marked improvement in the health of the villagers.

(x) The villagers take pride in the uplift and improvement in their village brought about by their participation at all stages.

(xi) Such schemes are economical and yield enormous cost benefit returns within a short period, sometimes within 2 years.

But the general and widespread indifference exhibited by politicians, bureaucrats, and the citizens at large, in ignoring and running down time tested, cost effective water management systems and environment degradation, particularly indiscriminate destruction of forest cover on an unimaginable scale even in the catchment areas of dams throughout the country, along with polluting of rivers by dumping millions of tons of garbage and sewerage in the rivers and lakes everyday, is the real tragedy of independent India.

The extent of apathy exhibited towards water resources management over the last 50 years can be seen from the following.

Almost 500 projects from earlier 5 year plans have spilled into the 9th 5 year plan with huge time and cost overruns. Total cost of major, medium and small projects is Rs. 1,26,000 crores and the spillover itself is Rs.80,000 crores. Even foreign aided projects lag far behind schedule. The ministry of Water Resources itself is compelled to admit the progress as slow and 'not satisfactory'. A few such examples in a couple of states are given below.

Orissa

Utilized only 46% of aid under the US$ 300 million water resources conservation target, even after 64% of project period had lapsed. Grant of EU 11 million by European Economic Community for minor irrigation projects also allowed to lapse.

EEC had approved work plan in 1998 but Government failed to issue necessary executive instructions for implementation of schemes. EEC has now stopped investment.

Madhya Pradesh

Rajghat Canal irrigation project was planned to irrigate 1.2 lac hectares in 6 districts through canal system. Japanese agency has pledged Rs. 420 crores. Only 11% utilized though 60% of project period lapsed.

Maharashtra

Agreement signed in 1999 with KFW, Germany Donor agency, for minor irrigation projects covering 17 districts. But formalities incomplete for project where thrust would be on farmers' participation in management and operation.

Krishna Valley Irrigation Development Corporation (KVIDC) is a mega irrigation project involving more than Rs. 7,000 crores initiated in 1996. Though the long canal is aid to be almost complete, there are reports about workmanship of the canal being extremely poor. It is reported that even a 100 HP engine cannot sustain supply of water beyond a stretch of 10 meters.

Due to bureaucratic and political delays, out of total irrigation potential of 140 million hectares, only 90 million hectares have been brought under irrigation since independence.

The frightening reality of rapidly diminishing supply of water all over the country, in rural as well as urban areas, has made a number of communities realize the futility of waiting indefinitely for benefit from such schemes launched by Government decades ago.

Apart from the incredible cost and time overruns, a cursory look at the cost-benefit ration analysis of the crores of rupees spent on mega schemes and the benefits to the community as a whole, indicates a completely skewed picture where massive expenditure involved in these schemes, benefits a very small per centage of the agriculturists. Just a few examples from one of the most economically advanced states are given below.

Maharashtra Government has spent till now about

Rs. 40,000 crores on irrigation projects including construction of dams. But so far, only about 1 crore acres of land out of about 4.5 crores of cultivable land get the benefit of irrigation and 50% of this benefit goes to sugar cane growers. Now cane and bananas are major water guzzlers. Cane growers' consume about 96% of drinking water, though their total production was a mere 4% of the state's total production.

But despite massive investment in building dams and irrigation schemes, it can be clearly seen that massive investment of taxpayers' money has resulted in conferring benefits on an extremely small percentage of citizens. Inspite of the growing water shortage all over Maharashtra, the Government has licensed more than a dozen co-operative sugar mills which will push up the demand for water guzzling cane corp.

But it is not only the state Government which appear to be averse to reviewing the role of dams and taking urgent steps to meet that growing water famine and which will seriously affect not only suppliers of water to the common citizen (rural and urban) and also agricultural sector, but more importantly seriously hamper hydel generation which will have a cascading effect on the entire national economy.

In May 2001, a 2-day world conference on dams was held in India. A report entitled "Dams and Development – a new framework for decision making" was released over 2 years after intensive debate among various interest groups all over the world. Now this report represented a deep and intensive study carried on over a period of 2 years by independent forum of 68 members with none of them representing any Government organization. Participation in the deliberations of the conference would have provided an opportunity for Indian officials to interact with an independent forum presenting a detailed and exhaustive unbiased report on the type of dams which has been of great significance and continues to fascinate Indian planners.

The topic was of great relevance to the Union Ministry of Water Resources. But despite the 2 day conference being held in New Delhi, the officials of the Ministry did not attend the conference. No decisions were expected to be taken at this conference. Participation by the Ministry would have proved beneficial to all the participants and perhaps brought some new thinking to bear on the policy of mega dams and irrigation projects in the background of massive cost and time overruns, with meager returns.

An extract from the report released recently by the World Wide Fund for Nature from Switzerland is quite informative. This report, is based on case studies on role of dams in flooding in Honduras, Nigeria, and Mekong Basin, West Bengal and Southern Africa.

Dams built with intention of reducing flooding can often exacerbate the problem with catastrophic consequence. Referring to West Bengal where the original concept of damming the river Damodar was by building a series of dams on the Damodar river, an idea based on the Tenessee Valley Authority (TVA) scheme, USA. The TVA scheme built in the 1930s was a comprehensive scheme involving irrigation, hydel generation and also tourism. This proved extremely successful. But the DVC scheme has not been successful in any of the areas unlike TVA, the report goes on to state "Some of the worst flooding in Murshidabad district (West Bengal) where Mayurakshi flowed, swollen by dam release – also Burdwan in the lower reaches of Damodar, below 2 reservoirs managed by DVC". Faced with the risk of overtopping and structural damage at the height of the floods, DVC engineers decided to release 70,000 cusecs a second from Maithon and 30,000 from Panchet. Water hurtled down the Damodar and over the Durgapur Barrage, flooding towns as it headed towards Calcutta. At the height of the floods, roughly 40% of 230,000 cusecs of water passing over Durgapur barrage was the result of releasing water from the 2 dams.

"These floods are manmade and unnatural", dams carve up landscape like a jig saw puzzle in the name of providing benefits to people but the pieces often never fit again and fragmented nature can result in greater losses for generations to come as per the WWF Freshwater Programme. WWF has called on Government to "expend efforts on technology that provide water and energy to people without destroying their natural environment".

While the NGOs and individuals have assisted communities in a big way in water harvesting and distribution techniques, the urban sector is also now experimenting with such techniques successfully. The schemes launched in a few urban centers for harvesting rain water from the roof tops of buildings, have shown encouraging results and are being gradually implemented in a number of cities.

Ultimately it is the community involvement and not merely investing thousands of crores of rupees in schemes involving mega dams and canals that is the solution for lasting and assured water supply for centuries to come, without uprooting thousands of villagers and upsetting the ecological balance.

It is a universal truism that adequacy of unpolluted water is a sine qua non not only for survival but also for progress and improvement in the quality of life. Hence the need for involving all sections of society in preserving the sources of water and also making every effort to ensure the continued availability of adequate water to each and every citizen not only for today but for generations to come.

20

Agriculture

Ensuring adequate food to all its citizens is one of the prime duties of any Government. But more than 50 years after independence, millions of Indians – children, women and men suffer from constant pangs of hunger and many parents watch helplessly their children wasting away from hunger in slow painful stages. That millions of citizens all over the country, particularly in tribal areas and numerous villages and hamlets in a number of pockets, suffer from pangs of hunger for months and years on end, often subsisting on roots and shrubs, is a sad commentary on the political system and functioning of democracy over the last five decades.

Why has the nation come to such a stage where it cannot provide even a daily bowl of food to each and every citizen? Is the production of food grains inadequate to meet the rapidly increasing population? If the production is adequate, then is the system of collecting from production centers, and the transport and distribution system seriously flawed? Even if adequate food grains reach the affected areas, then why do millions suffer the continual pangs of hunger? Are the existing systems inadequate to cope with the need for discharging the prime duties of the state in ensuring at least the minimum quantity of food to each and every citizen particularly the extremely poor? Are there any other reasons for millions of poor citizens having to suffer the pangs of hunger for years on end? Why do hundreds of thousands of infants and children die of malnutrition and hunger every year even in 'rich' states like Maharashtra?

Before proceeding to analyze the probable reasons for the millions of poor having to suffer from acute shortage of food, it is necessary to glance briefly at the situation over the last 50 years.

The partition of India in 1947 resulted in the fertile Punjab region being truncated and India losing the major part to Pakistan. Subsequently due to various reasons, there was also a shortage of food-grains in India. To meet the problem, on the one hand it was decided to continue the system of food rationing introduced during World War II (1939-45) and on the other to import adequate food grains from USA. Under PL 480, the import continued till about late 1950s.

Production

The Centre decided to take all steps to increase food-grain production with the aim of achieving self-sufficiency. The agricultural scientists played an important role in increasing the production of food grains dramatically. With the increase in production, India became self sufficient in food grain by 1960s. Since then, production of food grains has been more than adequate to meet the nation's demand and the Government has been building up buffer- stock over the years to meet unforeseen contingencies. Today after the hue and cry over the reported deaths of the thousands of people due to starvation in various parts of India, the Government admits that millions of tons of food-grains stockpiled over the years are rotting in the godowns. India has the unique shameful distinction of having millions of citizens unable to get even a bowl of food for months and years on end and trying to survive on wild roots and shrubs while millions of tones of food grains rot in the godowns.

So, the production of food grains is more than adequate to feed each and every citizen of India. But a situation has been allowed to develop over the last few decades where millions of tons of food grains involving expenditure of thousands of crores of rupees have been permitted to rot, rather than ensure at least a daily bowl of food to the very poor.

Collection and Storage

As production is not a factor leading to starvation, let us examine the next factor, viz. collection and storage. Over the years, many schemes have been introduced by the Central and the State Governments. To ensure economic returns to the producer, a number of agriculture produce societies have also been set up all over India.

The methods of disposal by growers differ from area to area. For instance, in Punjab, the growers bring the produce to the mandis but in Gujarat, the buyers normally deal directly with growers. The Government agencies buy the produce at prices fixed by them. Such produce is packed in gunny bags and stored in godowns, scattered all over the country. But conventional storage methods by stacking gunny bags in godowns, rather than in silos, have serious drawbacks. The first and foremost drawbacks were the presence of rats, insects, pests in these godowns. Rats reportedly destroy not less than 10% of such stocks. In India the Government has recognized the existence of these factors and permitted 2% rat droppings in these food grains. The very fact that Government permits rat droppings to the extent of 2% and other impurities in food-grains, is an indication of the indifference of the Government to the quality of food-grains consumed by its citizens.

The stocks acquired and stored during the year are not disposed of in the same year. Every year there are left over stocks. Consequently the bags at the top are disposed of first, and the old stocks remain at the bottom. As a result of this policy of last in, first out, the old stocks accumulate at the bottom of the stack. Thousands of bags are reported to have burst and contents lost or destroyed all over India, resulting not only in loss of millions of tons of food-grains, but also financial loss of crores of rupees spent in acquiring, transporting and storing such stocks.

But what is stored has to be protected. Adequate measures have to be taken to protect such stocks against various risks such as rain, seepage, rats, insects, thefts, etc. Naturally a large administrative organization has to be maintained to oversee and control all the activities, including periodical receipts and deliveries at all storage centers scattered all over India. With millions of tonnes involved, adequate steps have also to be taken to cut down losses due to theft, pilferage, etc. All this involves naturally recurring financial outlay running into hundreds of crores annually. But the present system of collecting and storage has failed to prevent millions of tons of food-grains from rotting in the godowns. The lack of any action over the decades to ensure proper storage has resulted in the tragically absurd situation where godowns are packed to capacity with million of tons of mainly rotting food-grains, and new stock acquired every year have frequently to be stored in the open due to lack of covered storage godowns.

Transportation

One would normally expect the Government to facilitate transport from surplus areas to needy areas within the country. But over the years, policies have been framed in such a manner that interstate, and in some cases even inter district within the same state, are not permitted. Transport of food-grains are beset with numerous bureaucratic hurdles. The present rules hamper every attempt to transport food-grains from surplus to deficit states in times of scarcity. For instance, under the present rules, Kerala can import food grains from abroad without difficulty but to get the same from surplus Punjab would involve about 3 bureaucratic hurdles in getting the licenses with the resultant delay.

Distribution

The agencies of the Central Government, acquire stock from the growers and then transport and store them in godowns scattered all over India. But actual distribution to the consumers is done through the PDS by the respective states. The State Government purchases the stocks from the Central Government and arranges to transport to various outlets (normally Fair Price Shops) all over the state. Such stocks are sold by the shop to ration card holders. The idea of the PDS was to ensure availability of at least minimum quantity of essential food-grains at reasonable prices against ration card.

While the intention of the scheme is laudable, a number of shortcomings have been noticed, resulting in the poor being deprived of even the minimum food-grains at a reasonable price.

(i) This system depended upon the existence of fair price

shops, not only in urban areas, but particularly in remote villages and tribal areas.

(ii) Possession of a valid ration card was a prerequisite.

(iii) Buyers had to purchase the periodical (monthly/weekly) quota at one time.

Obtaining a ration card was a costly and time consuming process, particularly for illiterate and poor villagers living in hamlets and village far from any state administrative offices. Generally those few who were lucky enough to get some sort of occasional work, had to forego their earning for completing the formalities and getting a ration card. Even today millions do not possess ration cards though entitled.

After getting a ration card, there was no assurance of getting ration quota. Even in urban centers, the consumers generally could not get all their entitlements against the ration card at one go due to reported unavailability of one item or another. They have to approach the shop a number of times to get their periodical entitlement. But the situation in villages is much worse. There are numerous cases where cardholders have not received food-grains for over 2 years against valid ration cards.

Now mismanagement is a completely manmade problem in the post independence period. A basic analysis of the problem indicates the following facts:

(i) Inspite of periodic and localized failure of monsoon and other natural causes over the last 50 years, the aggregate production of food-grains has been such as to enable stockpiling of more than 60 million tones of food-grains: adequate to feed 100 million people for 2 years – a large part of the stocks are rotting.

(ii) An elaborate Government mechanism (FCI) costing hundreds of crores of rupees annually has been built up over the years to collect and store and distribute the food-grains.

(iii) While collection from producing centers and storage at hundreds of godowns all over the country is the responsibility of the Central Government agencies, the delivery to the ultimate consumer through Fair Price Shops against ration cards is the responsibility of the State Government.

(iv) Lack of purchasing power with the millions of poor all over the country.

(v) Failure to devise and implement practical income generating socially helpful schemes with the village as the focal point drawn up with the wholehearted involvement of the affected villagers, hamlets and tribals.

(vi) Rampant corruption in collection/storage/distribution of food-grains.

(vii) Excessive bureaucratic/political hassles in ensuring minimum entitlement to every citizen.

But does the existence of the problems listed above make it impossible to see that each and every citizen gets at least a daily bowl of food? Is it not possible to rectify this tragic situation? It must also be realized that suffering the pangs of continuous hunger is not an occasional phenomenon confined to a few pockets in remote areas in some economically backward states like Orissa or Bihar but such victims are found in lacs even in 'prosperous' states like Maharashtra, Andhra Pradesh, etc. in other words, it is an all India problem with pockets of plenty alongside pockets of starvation.

Hence the immediate aim should be to:

(i) Ensure availability of food grains all over India, even in the remotest hamlet, all through the year.

(ii) Ensure adequacy of income to every citizen of India to purchase at least the bare minimum quantity required for survival.

For attaining these aims, the following steps are suggested:

The rationale behind numerous restriction on transport of food-grains within or outside district, state or country need to be examined with a view to ensure availability in every village and remote hamlet. Even more than a century ago, one of the measures taken at times of famines was to publish food-grain prices at various centers all over India, and free movement was permitted within the country. This helped in making available food-grains in scarcity affected areas.

It is for the politicians and bureaucrats to set aside their preconceived notions and carefully work out a complete and drastic change in the present system of collection, transport, storage and distribution also all over India, with the aim of providing minimum quantity of food on a continuing basis at reasonable prices to the needy citizens of India.

Incidentally, apart from food-grains, there are problems with transport, storage and sale of almost all agriculture produce periodically. There are occasional reports of farmers throwing their bumper crops of potatoes, onions, etc. due to unhelpful Government policies. It is indeed a failure of the politicians and bureaucrats for permitting such a situation to arise where farmers suffer due to plenty, and advantage of bumper crops cannot be taken to distribute such crops to the needy and ensure a reasonable return to the producer.

But apart from the immediate need for ensuring minimum quantity of food-grains in every village and hamlet all over India by a complete change in the present system, the most vital factor leading undernourishment and starvation is the lack of purchasing power among the tribals and the poor. The absence of any practical schemes for ensuring adequate income on a continuing basis, even in areas identified officially as inhabited by the extremely poor and suffering often from natural calamities has resulted in the continued existence of millions on a bare survival level.

In a number of cases, the 'development' process has left villagers, in a penurious state, as their natural habitat and source of food supply has been destroyed by various causes like discharge of harmful chemical effluents by industries or other commercial activities, mining operations, acquisition by Government for mega projects, etc.

Numerous schemes have been introduced over the years by the Government, to ensure availability of adequate food to the poorest of the poor. There have been attempts to introduce food for work schemes for the poor. But introduction of such schemes have not resulted in banishing pangs of hunger and ensuring at least the bare minimum of food necessary for survival to millions of Indians even 50 years after independence.

The main reasons for the failure of the schemes have been:

(i) Non-involvement of locals in planning and implementation of such schemes.

(ii) Complete lack of commitment in linking such schemes to income generating and socially useful schemes, like improving village sanitation (and consequently health), building good roads linking to nearest highway or town (benefiting movement of people and produce), community schools, etc.

(iii) Confining such schemes merely to breaking of stones for future road building by women (including pregnant women in scorching heat and children and men; also dumping mud for road building but in almost all cases the mud is blown away by the winds or washed away by rains).

(iv) No attempt at cost benefit analysis by independent body of any of the hundreds of thousands of such schemes involving thousands of crores of rupees in the aggregate, undertaken all over India since independence.

(v) The practice for decades all over India of measuring relief measures undertaken, in financial terms – equating achievement with money shown as spent on such schemes, in other words, greater the amount shown as spent, the greater is the credit taken by Government for ameliorating the lot of the affected villagers.

(vi) The rampant corruption in the execution of almost all such schemes.

There are pockets where no food-grain have been supplied for 2 years, resulting in ration card holders being deprived of food after undergoing the travails of managing to get a ration card. But despite well documented reports of rampant corruption in a large number of areas in regard to implementation of schemes to alleviate the pangs of hunger of millions of starving people, no effective action has been taken to punish the guilty profiteering in human misery resulting in slow lingering, painful existence of millions of children, women and men.

But it is not only in states considered economically backward or poor that poor including tribals, suffer from lack of food, or rampant corruption. Even in states considered as prosperous like Punjab or Maharashtra, the poor continue to suffer due to rampant corruption or indifference of the authorities. In Punjab over 70% of food-grains distributed through PDS vanish without reaching the poor. Maharashtra considered to be a prosperous state, also contributes to the sufferings of the poor. Just 2 instances out of the many of widespread starvation and suffering are given here. In Nandurbar district, where more than 60% of the population consists of tribals, more than 300 children have died due to starvation in just a few months in the year 2000. In Thane district, barely 50 km from Mumbai, the financial capital of India, the poor including tribals did not receive any food-grains under PDS for more than 7 months in the year 2000 – a fact admitted by the local development project officer. Most of the children there can be seen to be obviously malnourished. A number of them are in extremely bad shape and cannot hope to survive. But the district collector stated that deaths are due to various diseases like pneumonia, etc. but not starvation – a normal Government reply all over India. This is more fully described in the chapter under 'Health'.

Now Anganwadis were created for the benefit of the children and Government appoints women to look after the Anaganwadis. They are also required to maintain records of the children under their care. But incomplete records are maintained at a number of Anagawadis. The reason for the incomplete records is that almost all anganwadi workers are illiterate, though Government rules stipulate minimum Std. VIII pass as they are required to maintain records. But the appointment of Anaganwadi workers depends upon the local MLA and Zilla Parishad workers, who appoint staff in complete disregard of Government rules, and thereby ensure the utter neglect of the poor, particularly the tribals who not only do not get minimum food but also health care.

The Government makes loud protestations making available adequate wheat for the nation and in 1996 the Government decided to import wheat so as to depress the domestic market. The aim being to make the farmer sell their crops to FCI. 30 lac tons of wheat were imported at an average price of Rs. 680 per quintal which was Rs. 205 above the domestic procurement price; plus Rs. 125 as freight and handling charges, thus was making this imported wheat Rs. 330 per quintal more expensive than the local procurement price. Ten lacs of wheat imported from Argentina were so bad that the Government knew there would be no buyers and hence no point in sending it to the shops. The Government noticed the conditions of the wheat only when it reached JNPT docks at Mumbai – so nothing could be recovered from the shippers and it was a total loss of Rs. 805 per quintal, i.e. Rs. 805 crores.

The PL 480 imported some 40 years back had brought the infamous 'Congress grass weeds' which is still proliferating and cost the farmers heavily. Now about 15 lac tons of wheat arrived from Australia but without complying with the mandatory norms laid down. Neither pre-shipment inspection nor adherence to prevention of Food Adulteration was carried out. It is mandatory to obtain a phytosanitary certificate prescribed by the UN as per norms laid down by the Destructive Insects and Pests Act.

But the FCI merely ordered that the wheat should not be moved to wheat producing areas in the North West. Further if the wheat is milled, all the debris and the spillage should be burned to avoid the spread of toxins.

Any Government having the interest of its citizens at heart would have refused to accept the substandard shipment. A small country like Sri Lanka turned back ships bringing ship load of sugar damaged by rain water. They did not accept such damaged sugar for their citizens.

It may be also noted that when importing wheat in 1992-93 about 50 officials had been posted at the source of wheat loading from the agriculture ministry.

But in India a peculiar situation exists where farmers suffer badly even when they harvest bumper crops. A few examples are given here to indicate the tragic consequences of bumper crop.

In Orissa there was bumper rabi and kharif crop in 2001-2002, of over 80 lac mt. – a record in over a decade. With a population of about 4 crores it can consume only 50 lac mt. including 9 mt. as seed, wastage, etc. leaving a huge surplus of over 30 lac mt. In addition the Centre provided about 1 lac mt. under various schemes. But Orissa farmers have always been victims of distress sales, mainly because of poor market network and little help from the Government. FCI is the only agency, but it procures from the millers and not directly from the farmers, FCI procured only 4 lac mt. much below the target of 15 lac mt. citing lack of storage facility as Orissa is reported to have only storage facility for 6 lac mt.

In response to a petition, HC had asked the state and FCI to purchase paddy directly from the farmers of Bolangir on experimental basis and appraise it of advantages and problems. It is reported that the FCI had made all arrangements to purchase directly from farmers in the district but instead of taking up the work, the state cabinet decided to challenge HC in the SC.

Bumper crops of wheat surpassing targets has ruined farmers and increased their debts in MP, Punjab, Haryana, AP, etc. Some have even committed suicide. In MP, Government suddenly stopped procurement on support prices without any official declaration. Government normally declares support prices every year and food-grains bought by it at these prices. Consequently, prices crashed. Market is totally controlled by traders. Crop insurance schemes have proved to be failures. The need is for proper infrastructure, plus a distribution network, proper counseling so that farmer is able to participate as an equal member of the new economy.

But the Government appears to have ignored the farmers in tackling technical and financial issues involved in establishing and managing storage areas particularly cold storages. In Dec.2004, over 300 delegates discussed for 2 days the institutional technical and financial issues of cold storage management and rural management at Mumbai. The stress was on establishing such storages closer to the producing areas – the conference was keen on educating farmer on merits of preservation and storage of farm produce. There are approximately 4500 cold storages in the country with a total capacity of about 18 million tons mainly used for storing potatoes. But concept of multipurpose cold storage was now gaining popularity.

This conference dealt with problems involving farmers – but it was held in Mumbai, not a single farmer was invited and the proceedings were carried on in English. So one cannot help wondering at the sincerity of the Government, in trying to assist the farmers. With such conferences, taking into account the avowed purpose of the conference, being to educate the farmers on the merits of storage and preservation of their produce.

India has an arable land area of 184 million hectares. It produces 90 million tons of milk (highest in the world), 150 m tons of fruits and vegetables (second highest in the world), 210 million mt of food-grains (third in the world) and the highest number of livestock at 480 million. But processing levels are extremely low: fruits & vegetables – 2%; poultry – 2% milk. 14% poor shelf life and absence of market connectivity result in wastage of food. Processing activity in some countries: Philippines – 45%; China 23% and India 7%.

Faulty regulatory systems prevent farmers from directly marketing their produce except through designated agricultural markets. Currently food laws span 9 ministries. Besides states have their own control orders. Organizations responsible for enforcing these regulations are poorly staffed or trained and represent the vestiges of post independence license permit raj.

All over the world norms lay down that total pesticide residues in a typical diet for average person should fall within the acceptable daily intake. The pesticide residue consumed is calculated, based on Minimum Residue Levels *fixed for every pesticide* before it is registered. In India MRLs are registered for less than half of all pesticides.

An unprecedented nationwide study of pesticide levels in our food conducted by top Government agencies came up with figures so shocking that it was withdrawn soon after it was released in 1993. Its findings of toxic levels and its drastic change in policy have been buried. After the Coca Cola findings, the JPC asked for the 80 page report "surveillance of food contaminants in India" but not produced the report. The report had been prepared by the Indian council of Medical Research and team of country's top pesticide experts. The report has exposed the magnitude to problem. It is the first official report to acknowledge no one was measuring the food safety levels despite presence of 2 safety indices the world over, viz., (i) Acceptable Dietary Intake (ADI) and (ii) Minimum Residue Level (MRL) for all pesticides.

Numerous official reports have since been prepared: (i) 1996 – ICMR found 51% of food contaminated with pesticides, out of which 20% had limits exceeding their MRLs (ii) 1999 – study conducted by All India Research Project (Union Agriculture Ministry) showed 60% food commodities contaminated with pesticides, out of which 14% were above MRL limits (iii) 1999 – AIRCRP showed vegetables and fruit samples from 16 states to be 100% contaminated (iv) 2000 – study conducted by CERC Ahmedabad found that most of wheat flour brands were contaminated with pesticides, some of which were banned in India.

Other reports continue to show increased contamination of food, fruits, and vegetables with pesticide far above safety levels.

The essential point is that India is prey to uncontrolled, unmonitored and unseen pesticides. No other civilized country has poison in every element of our food chain. But tragically we do not have even the most elementary regulation to monitor that or the political will to bring in even elementary regulation to safeguard the populace. Our farmers, almost all illiterate, are encouraged by traders and manufacturers of internationally banned DDT, Lindane, Chloropyriphos, and Sevin, etc. Various Government ministries have refused to take any action against flagrant use of such banned and dangerous chemicals in our food chain.

Recently 470 products containing suspected carcinogens have been recalled in 15 nations at a cost of £ 15 million. While the Government is anxious to ensure purity in food products, the business community is refusing to take remedial measures, as it would cost too much. The Government's proposed law will help pinpoint the various stages at which contaminants are introduced in food items. But the food processing industry including spices and beverages are not willing to list ingredient and contaminants such as pesticides on their labels as they feel such labeling will have a negative impact on sales. The food and beverage industry, including the spices trade have clearly indicated their concern is with their bottom line, i.e. profits and not with the health of the consumer.

Government's plan is in keeping with international laws like EU 2002 which makes it mandatory for food products to be able to trace from production to processing to packaging. India's lack of concern for the consumer and guided only by the profit motive have often resulted in food products like meat exports having been rejected over the past few years. It will be necessary to implement the new laws strictly keeping in view the businessmen's profit motive supreme no matter what happens to the consumer. But as no country will touch Indian food and beverage products, ultimately, business compulsions will force the business community to abide by international quality standards, despite their aversion to take any steps for the protection of the Indian consumer particularly. In due course, the businessmen will learn that what is good for the consumer is good for the business.

Earlier we had stated that the PDS and other poverty alleviation schemes are riddled with corruption. The Planning Commission evaluation division has found that in 2003-04, more than 50% of food-grains meant for people below the poverty line, did not reach them. In financial terms, more than Rs. 4,100 crores of subsidy for PDS did not reach the targeted people. The subsidy was wasted. Planning Commission survey found that: (i) 20% of people above poverty line eat up benefits meant for the poor in AP, Himachal, TN, Kerala; (ii) maximum leakages in Bihar, Punjab, UP, Haryana where 500 mt of grains just get lost.

Food Corporation of India (FCI) was set up in 1964 in the era of food scarcity with the following main functions:

(i) Ensure remunerative prices to farmers for their produce.

(ii) Assist in stabilizing food prices throughout the country.

(iii) Feed the Public Distribution System (PDS) also set up simultaneously.

It was also supposed to be the buyer of last resort to save farmers from exploitation by traders by offering minimum support price.

Over the years, the role and function of FCI has changed under political pressures. It is forced to buy at prices much higher than the market rate and in bigger quantities than required as buffer stocks. The market prices of wheat and rice often fall below PDS prices, with the country becoming surplus one instead of being in deficit. So off- take from PDS often fell. Besides lack of purchasing power is also one reason for the poor off take. Thus sales through PDS fell and unsold stocks with FCI increased.

The quality of stocks acquired is also often substandard. But the small farmer does not benefit. For instance in 2003-04, Punjab farmers sold paddy for Rs. 250 per quintal. But commission agents who buy from the farmers at low prices, made huge profits by selling to FCI @ Rs. 500 per quintal. But so rampant is the corruption that a former Chairman of FCI termed it as Food Corruption of India.

It has a huge organization spread all over India engaged in procurement, storage and distribution of food-grain with a well paid staff of over 200,000 including 11 IAS officers at the top and an annual age bill of over Rs. 900 crores and average salary of about Rs. 20,000 p.m.

In 2003, its godowns were overflowing with 46 million mt. of food-grains. This is 3 times the buffer stock supposed to be maintained by Government and about 35% of total wheat and rice produced in the previous year.

At least 1 million mt. was rotten and 200,000 mt. classified as damaged and naturally unfit for consumption. The cost of holding such excess stock, including that unfit for consumption is estimated at Rs. 16,000 crores. Food-grains costing about Rs. 500 crores is said to be lost in transit every year.

But FCI has no control on the price, quantity and quality of its purchases. Now FCI's relevance is in question. Perhaps the responsibility of holding their own stocks could be passed on to the respective states.

Today the FCI continues the buying and storing system as followed for the last 100 years. Government had agreed that mechanized handling should be introduced without delay. It can also study modern storage technology from Israel where food-grains can be stored up to 100 years without any deterioration in quality.

A few of the shortcomings in the making available food-grains to the poor and also the poor quality of food-grains have been indicated above. So far the official stress has been on thinking in terms of providing food through the PDS forever. This betrays an utter lack of innovative thinking and commitment to providing adequate affordable food to every citizen. Attention needs to be given urgently to providing adequate purchasing power in the hands of the poorest of the poor.

Besides food does not mean only rice, wheat/coarse grains, etc. – it also includes a variety of dairy products, fruits, fish, poultry products, etc. Naturally converting such plans into reality involves every aspect of national endeavor like providing quality seeds, proper farming techniques, adequate power (hydel, tidal/solar/thermal, etc.) not only for cold storages but also for domestic use, communication and transport systems, healthcare for humans and animals, and reforms, etc. In other words, every aspect which will materially improve the quality of life of every citizen of India will have to be taken into account.

But all this involve a radical change in the mindset of policy makers, planners/implementers in other words, all politicians from the lowest village level to the highest parliamentary level at Delhi as also the bureaucrats at the lowest village level to the highest level at the Central Government at Delhi, will have to have a vision of hunger free India and the determination to make it a reality.

So far the negative aspects have been brought out briefly but changes are already taking place. Luckily winds of change can never die down completely in a country like India. The energy, intellect and burning desire to improve the lot of the common citizen has started showing signs of arousal all over the country at various levels. Individuals and NGOs have been contributing their mite to improvement of the agricultural sector at the grass root level. A few such examples are cited here. This is only a small sample of the large number of such successful experiments all over India.

Scientists of Gujarat Agricultural University conducted soil and other surveys to gain knowledge of the type of crops to be grown and then advised the local farmers in 12 villages in Bhuj district, Gujarat. The farmers were reluctant as only thorny Acacia flourished there but the local Swaminarayan Sect assured financial support even if crops failed. The farmers are now successfully growing groundnut, millet, jowar, pomegranates, amala, and coconut and variety of vegetables.

Wardha District, Maharashtra

Over 500 farmers' families from 200 villages associated in project involving mixture of traditional wisdom and scientific intercropping with the help of Chetna Vikas an NGO, it developed counter bunding and helped in saving crops from dryness. Now this system has ensured harvesting of food items needed by farmer's family of members on 2.5 acres throughout the year. Thirty-five different crops including 80% of food required by a family of 5 can be grown under the most trying weather conditions. Vast variety of crops ensures mutual control of each other by insects. This is an example of application of scientific knowledge. Besides, farmers are convinced on seeing results in other fields, only farmyard manure is used and not chemicals.

Bastar District, Chhattisgarh

Bastar is a tribal area and one of the most backward ones in

India, and also for the grinding poverty. But for the first time can now hope for a better future thanks to Sri Chaubey who left a job as Geologist with PSU and started lemon grass cultivation in Bastar. The forest department has turned over vast stretches of barren, degraded land in and around Jagdalpur to lemon grass cultivation after suitable treatment. The ownership of the land remains with the forest department but the farmer owns the crop and all the profits. The landless tribals now earn about Rs. 20,000 per acre of lemon grass within 3 months of cultivation. Now Chaubey has also set up an oil extraction plant for which he buys all the lemon grass grown by the tribals. About 2 mt. of oil is sold every month for exporting to Germany for use in toiletries, perfumes, etc.

Yavatmal District, Maharashtra

Shri Utterwar of Yavatmal district grows mainly oranges but suffers often from lack of water with poor rainfall. But now reaping rich harvest of oranges, etc. by following the revolutionary 'do nothing' method of agriculture advocated by Mr. M. Fukuoka of Japan. He is of the firm belief that nature takes care of its offspring. His favourite question is 'How does vegetation grow so well in forests? Instead of removing grass and weeds, he only mulches them and no chemical is sprayed. Now Shri Utterwar also grows wheat, jowar, soyabean, cotton, etc. He is one of the 150 fellows of the Ashoka Innovators for Public, and a Washington based NGO. He was also invited at a seminar on control of food systems in Austria in 2001.

A weed named as 'Congress Grass' was brought into India along with wheat imported in 1950s. It spread all over India and efforts to destroy were not successful. Cattle do not eat it and causes allergies reaction in humans. After decades a solution to eradicate it is in sight. Scientists have found that the grass is the exclusive food of the Mexican beetle which devours the grass and fly to other areas. The beetles are being used as biological control agents and being bred in labs and cultures being sent to agricultural universities also.

A new trend has been introduced in Kerala by farmers forming their own companies under the Companies Act by treating landholding as equity. This has been done earlier in Sri Lanka. NGO based in Madura mobilized in 2000, a self help group of tribal women to form Gram Mooligai company – tribals cultivating and gathering medicinal herbs and operate in tribal districts of Tamil Nadu, Kerala, Karnataka and Maharashtra. Infarm Agro Movement, a charitable company set up in Kottayam, has with about 1600 rubber growers as shareholders to solve their problems. Inform procures and markets through hundreds of outlets in Kerala. More farmer companies are coming up in Kerala after the success of Infarm. This only shows that agro based enterprises formed by the farmers of the farmers for the farmers can be successful.

A number of success stories have been cited above, but regretfully even the reverse process of reducing crop out put is also on. Just one example of how the famous Saffron crops are being destroyed in the name of development of industry. Kashmir is famous in India for its Saffron, which grows mainly in that area only. But Government has permitted a cement manufacturing plant to be set up in Pulwama district, Kashmir. Now about 800 hectares in all of saffron fields are being choked by the dust from the cement plant. And output has fallen to about 1 kg/hct to maximum of 2.5 kg/hct. Already India's output is low by International standards. Spain, Iran and Greece are the major producers of Saffron with an out put of about 6 kg/hct.

But the people of India will always rise to the occasion. As seen a number of farmers have converted barren waste lands into fruitful farms, more will follow their example.

Even in the matter of land records tremendous improvements can be seen. This is a matter which gives rise to litigation and waste of time as document of ownership is a must for obtaining any aid from any organization. So far, all over India this has always been an area of dissatisfaction leading to delays.

Now in Amravati, Maharashtra, a bureaucrat has shown that matters can be simplified within the framework of the Law. Ms. Manisha Verma, district collector has evolved a system whereby the all important document, viz. 7/12 (a comprehensive document which irrevocably proves land ownership, area, crop pattern, plantation and also the wells and hand pumps) is delivered to the rightful owner free of cost in public meeting. Any dispute regarding the records are immediately attended to after consultation and consent of other villagers. However, if mutations are debated and are serious in nature, special hearing is organized in the next 15 days where the officer gives his verdict, a completely transparent, cost free process and involving the people concerned.

Despite setbacks over the years and the bureaucratic and political hurdles, one can see a bright future for new developments in agriculture. The following is the story of initial set back in as much as the Government itself just ignored the enthusiastic report of a team sent by it in 1995. The team consisted of 2 ministers, scientists from the Himachal Pradesh Council for Science, Technology and Environment and also some progressive farmers. They had been sent by the Central Government to China to study the way it had used sea-buck thorn to usher in an economic revolution. The team recommended the formulation of an ambitious project for cultivation of sea-buck thorn as also the establishment of pharmaceutical and food processing industry to replicate the Chinese experiment.

The tribals of Spiti, Himachal Pradesh cold desert area, call it the wonder plant. For generations they have used it for a variety of purposes like prevention of soil erosion, fuel, fodder and also medicines.

It also has an immense curative effect for a variety of ailments like common cold, lung and blood pressure problems, allergies, viral infections, cardio-vascular diseases, etc.

Though no action was taken on the report submitted by the special team sent by the Government about 7 years ago, now work is going on for 3 separate projects for the Defense Research and Development Organization and the Indian Council of Agricultural Research. Sea-buck thorn grows in abundance in Spiti Kinnaur, Pangi, and Tabo Keylong, areas bordering Tibet, Kargil and Leh. It has also been found helpful for soldiers posted in the Kargil and Siachin areas who suffer on account of radiation, low oxygen availability and extremely low temperatures. It already has a wide range of application in cosmetics, medicines, wines, etc. Having realized the importance of this plant, a number of countries like Germany, Finland, Britain, Central Asia, etc. have also started commercial cultivation, development and processing of the plant. China already has 12 lac hectares under cultivation.

But innovation does not come from highly educated persons only as we have already seen. One more example of innovative farming is of Suresh Desai of village Bedikhal, Belgaum district. He has studied only upto matriculation. Right from 1991 he has been following the farming philosophy of S. Dhabholkar of Kolhapur who believes in more sunlight, less water for sugarcane, this is contrary to the normal practice as sugarcane is a water guzzling crop. His 12 acre farm yielded 40 mt to the acre.

He is a firm follower of organic farming movement and is a recipient of the organic farming award from the Maharashtra Government in 2004. His technique is being followed by about 300 farmers in Belgaum. He recommends seasonal intercropping in between rows of sugarcane. Entire cost of sugarcane is recovered through seasonal crops like gram, soyabean coriander, etc. The intercrop biomass negates the need for chemical fertilizers. This method, known as Desai method has been recognized by the National Agriculture Research Centre, Nagpur, who is trying to popularize his style of sugarcane farming. There are critics, powerful ones like Vasantdada Sugar Institute, Manjri, and Pune. But as one award winning farmer has said, the real road blocks for popularizing Desai method on a larger scale, are the seed traders, the fertilizer industry, the sugar co-operations viz. all those who control pre and post cultivation operations.

It is heartening to see a wide spectrum of people taking keen interest in agriculture. Even the Chief Minister of Punjab, while attending Agriculture Summit 2003 held under the auspices of the CII in Mumbai, made it very clear that his interest in the conference and visit to Mumbai was confined to a matter connected with agriculture in his state. He was very much concerned by the suicide by over 600 farmers in his state due to the unresolved problem of plenty. But he stressed the innovative spirit of the farmers of Punjab who were ready to experiment with newer crops and diversifying into milk and food industries. He also said that though India as a whole is surplus in potatoes, yet Mac Donald's prefer to import potatoes, to make their chips instead of buying from Punjab because Punjab potatoes have more sugar and less starch content; so the Agro Research Institutes are trying to perfect the 'chipola' brand of potatoes with high starch content.

So, it can be seen that despite obstacles, the innovative spirit of an Indian cannot be put down, whether he is a simple farmer, an industrialist, scientist or an entrepreneur.

Education

21

Basic universal education is the prime necessity for the growth and prosperity of the nation. With the advent of independence in 1947, a number of institutions like IIT, IIM, and RIT for higher technical and specialized education were set up. There has been a spurt in the establishing of engineering and medical colleges, mainly in the private sector. Given a scenario with so many specialized institutions coming up providing education in specialized knowledge areas, one would expect the country to have a high percentage of literate people.

But the actual position is quite different, 30% of the total illiterate population of the world is in India. According to some estimates, barely 20% of the population is literate. Such a low percentage is bad enough, but reality is far more depressing. India is probably the only country where anyone capable of writing his name is considered officially literate. So, the official literacy rate in India is no indication of the extent of illiteracy in the country after more than 50 years of independence and is of limited help in comparing with other countries.

Literacy is the bedrock of development of a nation – more so in the rapidly expanding boundaries of knowledge and technology. While centers of highly advanced learning like IITs, IIMs, etc. were set up after independence thereby benefiting a miniscule percentage of the population, action for ensuring literacy for the vast majority of the population was not given due attention, resulting today in a nation of illiterates even 50 years after independence

Depriving the benefits of literacy to every single citizen of the nation is one of the prime causes of the lack of the desired growth in all spheres of national activity and thereby leading to socio-economic problems and resulting in dissatisfaction and tensions within the different groups all over the nation.

An in-depth study may reveal a number of causes for such abysmal performance over the last 50 years in the most vital area necessary for not only national growth, but more importantly for national unity and stability.

A few events can be said to have significant effect on the growth of literacy. These events per se cannot be considered as adverse to the growth of literacy. On the contrary, with proper handling, these could have resulted in the widespread literacy all over the country.

Till 1947, English was the medium of instruction in British India, and was the link language all over India including princely Indian states, right from the NWFP in the north to Cape Comorin in the south, Sind in the west to NEFA in the east. This facilitated spread of knowledge and commerce all over India. It also assisted international commerce and also students proceeding abroad for higher studies.

The advent of independence in 1947 led to the redrawing of the map of India, excluding areas forming West and East Pakistan. Hundreds of princely states, big and small, merged into India. Consequently, the erstwhile map of British India had to be redrawn taking into account the merger of such states within the newly formed Indian Nation. This resulted in a number of states forming the Indian union. But in the process, most of the newly formed states did not have the uniformity of language as the people of merging states had in some cases different languages. In the mid-1950s, in response to a strong demand from some quarters, the states of Indian Union were redrawn on linguistic basis. So local language was given prominence. Mere fact of giving importance to the local language is certainly not objectionable. But the infrastructure to spread quality education has to be set up and maintained. Even today the quality of contents as well as the quality of printing of the books in local language is extremely poor in almost all the states.

The other major cause of low literacy rate has been attributed by some observers to the grant of adult franchise without specifying any educational qualifications for legislators. Wisdom is not the prerogative of the highly educated but appropriate standards of education among the policy makers ensures at least stating of literacy goals and the goals for the benefit of the citizens. Proper education does not mean getting a degree which in no way assists a graduate in earning a livelihood.

There is a feeling among a large number of citizens that the present system of education is adequate, both quantitatively and qualitatively, judging from the number of graduates and post graduates being churned out every year. But the quality of education and knowledge exhibited by majority of such students is rather disappointing. Prima facie, the reasons for such inadequate performance appear to be:

(i) Lack of adequate schools and necessary infrastructure.

(ii) Poor teaching methodologies.

(iii) Poor course content quite divorced from needs of present day.

(iv) Excessive dependence on rote in passing exams.

(v) Ignoring the role of education in promoting curiosity among the students and creating awareness of their surroundings and environment.

But the process of education starts at the primary level. This is the basic stage. Most of the states have not given due importance to this fact. The course contents, the prescribed books and often the teachers do not succeed in creating any interest among the young primary students. Very little energy and time seems to have been spent by the various authorities to make the process of learning an attractive one at the primary stage, by and large the books are badly printed and often in black and white without color pictures. Such books fail to attract the children's attention, let alone encourage the young minds. It is but natural for a young child to lose all interest in studying or even looking at the prescribed books. With the loss of interest at the primary stage itself it is difficult for children to kindle interest at a later stage.

The System also discourages initiative or spirit of curiosity or enquiry, but encourages learning by rote without making any attempt at understanding . And this tendency of learning by rote is carried over by the student to the graduate and even to the post graduate level. The inappropriate course contents along with the killing of the spirit of curiosity and learning by rote leads to millions of students being unemployable in today's world where technology in all spheres is rapidly changing. Unemployment is not only a waste of national resources in providing education which has no relevance in today's rapidly changing world, but unfortunately it has tragic socio-economic consequences which may result in increased crime.

There has been some attempt at providing at least primary to middle school level education in the urban centers. But even here the poor cannot as a rule get the benefit of education. In any case poverty forces many to drop out at an early age.

The millions of poor, particularly the rural poor and the tribal are the real sufferers of the education system in force since independence. What could be the reason for millions of citizens being deprived of an opportunity to become literate? Is it the lack of funds? Is it lack of appropriate policy? Is it the apathy at the political and bureaucratic level? Is it a deliberate policy on the part of the politicians to keep the masses illiterate and uneducated and treat them as vote banks who will do their bidding? Is it because politicians find it easy to manipulate illiterate and uneducated minds given adult franchise? Is it a general aversion on the part of the students to acquire the type of education being provided now?

But when even children, the potential leaders of tomorrow, cannot be provided with increasing level of education, the question of providing means of literacy and education to elders and grown ups particularly in small towns, villages, hamlets just does not arise.

It is not possible to pin point any particular reason for the extremely high rate of illiteracy in the country. But it is also incorrect to ascribe the low rate of literacy on the lack of desire on the part of the millions to acquire the least bit of education. Given an opportunity, the strong desire for becoming literate exists in millions of citizens all over India. This desire exists even in some of the poorest tribes or villagers, who have to trudge, in fair weather or foul, for long distances or undergo inconceivable hardships to quench thirst for literacy. This is all the more admirable as generally such people have no money for education, and one child away for studies means corresponding reduction in the family labor force and naturally the family's day's income.

The political system despite its rhetoric about compulsory free education for children, has failed during the last 50 years in spreading literacy to the masses, but has made it the privilege of the few.

Accepting the high of illiteracy, is it not possible to spread literacy all over the country and make all citizens literate – young or old, male or female, rich or poor, forest dweller or city dweller? If a nation can make incredibly rapid strides, internationally and nationally, in the development of computer and information technology, does it not indicate the existence of capability to spread literacy rapidly over the entire country ?At this stage it is worth while referring to the progress made by China, by the end of the civil war in 1949, China was a poor and backward country with more than 80% population engaged in agriculture. It had just passed through a devastating civil war waged for decades. In 1950, barely 15% of the population was literate. But the Government was clear in its objectives and priorities, land distribution, literacy and health were high on their agenda.

To add to their problems of spreading literacy it may be noted that the Chinese language has no alphabet, as such. There are numerous dialects with a common script all over the country. But the different dialects made communication difficult. The script is extremely complex, just to write 'I' it required seven brush strokes, it was estimated that there were at least a total of 40,000 to 50,000 characters and it would take at least 2 years for a child just to master the rudiments of reading and writing. In comparison to India, spreading literacy in China appears to be an almost impossible task, and would take probably centuries to make a noticeable improvement in the literacy rate.

But the people had a will to improve. The Government took up the task of simplifying the script. By 1965, that is within 15 years of the end of the devastating civil war, almost everyone, men and women, had become literate. But the concept of considering peoples literate in China is different from that in India. In China the Government permitted people to express their view through huge posters put by citizens on every wall in Beijing. Huge crowds would gather and read these posters. Anyone could put up posters approving, denouncing, analyzing or suggesting events and policies. As a result of the spread of literacy in China, its citizens could understand the different points of view and contribute towards the nation.

In India, having tremendous advantages regarding the various scripts, the authorities take pride in percentage of people considered literate merely on the perceived ability to write only their names and this after 50 years of independence.

In the year 2000, World Education Forum attended by over 160 countries, held in Dakar, Senegal, pledged to achieve primary universal education, gender equality and improvement in quality of education by 2015. Latest UNESCO report states 91 countries making some progress but 35 countries including 22 sub-Saharan and India are very far from achieving the goals.

Education is considered single most factor for development of any nation. Research shows that education is the cheapest support that any Government can provide to its citizens. Kerala with half of Punjab's income has doubled the rate of literacy. Vietnam, despite going through a war has 94% literacy against 52% officially claimed in India. Providing education and knowledge may be against the interest of the corrupt politicians for whom keeping the masses ignorant serves the interest of the mafia raj. And this has permeated the entire Indian Society.

Apart from the politicians some of the bureaucrats are also assisting in sabotaging the Right to Information Act.

Unfortunately steps are not being taken to spread functional interacy, which only means the ability to read simple instructions on fertilizer or pesticide bags or machinery or markings on cartons, etc.

More than 95% of money allotted for primary education is spent on salaries and perks of teachers. Hence practically nothing is left for school maintenance and infrastructure or teaching aids. Despite increasing the salaries of primary school teachers 23 times in 24 years in West Bengal, primary education has regressed. There are many ways to improve literacy, but only if there is a strong political will. In some states the standards of literacy are abysmally low. The results of nationwide survey By Pratham presented to planning Commission showed that 61% of the age group 7 to 10 years in Bihar could not read.

But the attention given by the Municipal Corporation of Mumbai also show a pathetic picture. For instance, the municipal school at Rafiqnagar, Govandi, students far in excess of capacity and poorly maintained with broken tiles in classrooms and stinking toilets. Due to excess number of students, they are also crammed into the verandahs. But the BMC cannot claim lack of funds as can be seen from the figures below:

Year	Funds record Rs. Crores	Funds spent Rs. Crores
2001-02	20.34	1.7
2002-03	216.23	9.3
2003-04	No new allocation	17.0

There is an attempt by some to show impressive progress, at least on paper. Maha Sarva Shiksha Mohim was concentrated in showing increase in enrolment. For instance, there are five divisions in Std. I, including students in the corridor, but only two divisions in Std. V due to drop-out. Even providing mid-day meals is not much of an attraction as the poor children do not even find it palatable. Thus leading to wastage of resources and depriving poor students of mid-day meal.

BMC runs about 1200 schools of which 95 are Marathi medium and about 45 English medium. But Marathi medium is not popular as the poor want their children to be educated in English medium schools for which the poor manage to spend hundreds of rupees every month, to send children to private schools. They take a very practical view that knowledge of English is a prerequisite for any job.

But running of educational institutions including medical and engineering colleges has become money making racket in India, and highly politicized. Those controlling such institutions are now openly referred to as 'Educational Barons'. The standard of education in such colleges is generally low.

The Deemed University status is very coveted by the politicians running universities as it frees them from Government control and grants far more independence and autonomy concerning admissions of students.

Every state in India appears to have its own view point in looking at Indian history and the subject matter of history textbooks. Now guidelines for history textbooks from 2004 onwards in West Bengal have drastically reduced history of India's freedom movement to make room for modern European history replete with Communist jargon on like working class movement exploitation of workers, etc. even in Class X, but mention of patriotic Indian leaders like Bal Gangadhar Tilak, Pandit Madan Mohan Malaviya, Gopal Krishnan Gokhale, etc. is not made. The Education Minister of West Bengal, when asked about this replied, "Too much stress on Indian National history would have created a false pride and patriotism in tender minds". But even world history taught in West Bengal from class VIII ignores the Fall of Berlin Wall, unification of East and West Germany, etc. Even disintegration of USSR is given a passing reference in some books but not in others.

The process of modern education was started in Bombay in 1829 by Dr. Wilson with education being provided to boys and girls. But today the education system in Mumbai is so complex and competitive than even parents of 3-year-old kids enroll them in coaching classes. In some schools 3-year-olds are tested as to who is the Prime Minister of India, etc. Some schools quiz the parents of such tiny tots and also ask parents of 3 years old tiny tots to bring along the copy of their income tax returns, copies of parent's educational qualifications, etc. Though it is evident that this in no way helps a tiny tot to have the benefit of education. Millions of children particularly tiny tots go without any education, even basic reading and writing. No wonder India leads in the highest number of illiterates in the world.

At this stage it is worthwhile looking at a small but poor country like Cuba. In 1959, illiteracy was over 90%, but by 2003 there was 100% literacy. It is said by the common people that if there is a child in remote corner of Cuba, there will be a teacher to teach the child. Over the years, military barracks were converted into schools. The contrary situation prevails in India. Schools are taken over by security forces for weeks and months at a stretch, teachers are forced into other duties like polling duty, etc. with no alterative arrangements for teaching children. Even a large number of teachers are not qualified teachers.

It is reported that in Cuba, all teachers are trained before hand to ensure that all children receive minimum of 9 years mandatory schooling. Each child is supplied with free school uniform, supplies and meals; every child attends a school in his neighborhood.

Cuba started another education revolution in 2000 by reducing the number of students to only 20 students per class in primary schooling. If there is a shortage of classrooms and over 20 students per class then, 2 teachers are given per class, for next 3 years, 1 teacher for every 15 students. The teachers are trained to impart comprehensive education to each group of 15 students. At secondary level, complete technical support like TV and video display is available in each classroom. This has reduced requirement of more teachers for small groups of 30-40 children. Reduced class size and emphasis on providing only well trained teachers has increased demand for new teachers. A new educational training plan is being put in place. In the first year, student teachers who are in high school pass out to get institutional training in University. During the intervening 4 years, before they pass out, they work in local schools for 5 days a week. On the sixth day they attend training institutions with full teacher's salary. The student gets degree on completion of program and becomes confirmed teachers. By linking work with study, Cuba now claims 1 teacher for every 37 citizens whereas in India it is said to be about 1 per 3000.

But in India the standards of education have touched an all time low even in states like Maharashtra who had a very good record for academic standards and good governance. In 2000, the Maharashtra Government has reduced grants, delayed payment of salaries and grants. Even recruitment of teachers has been curbed. Against vacancies of almost 300 teachers in arts, commerce and science colleges, the Government has approved only 50 appointments.

Maharashtra has a history of being in the vanguard of literacy and education. It has a number of educational institutions over a century old, engaged in providing education from the school stage to the post graduate and highly specialized medical, engineering and other disciplines. It is one of the most highly industrialized states. Mumbai city has been the financial capital of India for almost a century. With such a background, it would be interesting to have a brief look at the state of education in this premier state.

In the year 2000, an official survey was conducted to evaluate the primary education system on the basis of the performance of 7.5 lac students in 6,500 schools in the districts of Amravati, Akola, Buldhana, Washim and Yavatmal, all in Maharashtra. Some of the important findings of the committee are given below:

Fourty-five per cent of the students in the 7 to 14 years age group are illiterate. Out of the 7.5 lac students recorded in school registers, more than 2 lac remained absent. The findings were based on simple and very basic tests for students from Class I to Class IV, and there were no specified content and textbooks. The aim was to check the accuracy and familiarity with words and numbers.

Most of the students of class IV found it difficult to count up to 10, and barely able to write their own names. Official statistics rank Maharashtra as a highly literate state with a literacy rate of about 75% in the 7-14 years age group. But the official survey clearly states that reality of 45% of the students in this age group being illiterate and opines that literacy levels would be just as bad in other parts of the state.

The dismal state, after 50 years of independence has been ascribed by the committee mainly to the following reasons:

(i) Teachers have mastered the art of bunking school on the flimsiest pretext.

(ii) Tendency to complete the annual course without ensuring whether students have acquired basic competency.

(iii) System of education wherein learning is a monotonous and unimaginative process.

(iv) Overall comprehensive evaluation, which has been universally accepted as an integral part of the education process, has been completely missing from the present system.

This is the state of primary education, the foundation of higher education in one of the most progressive and prosperous states with more than a century old tradition of high standards in education. But this is not an isolated example. The same disregard for primary education is replication in almost all the states in India. Only the extent of disregard varies.

Is the picture any better at a slightly higher level, viz. at the junior college level? Are steps being taken to improve the quality of education by reviewing the entire syllabus and the quality of teaching including the methodologies?

The facts given below provide self-evident answers:

The Maharashtra Government had announced in 2003 its decision regarding service conditions applicable to new teachers in Junior Colleges. It may be noted that more than 300 vacancies need to be filled up in Mumbai alone. The importance attached to education can be gauged from the Government policies regarding recruitment of new teachers for junior colleges. The terms laid down by the State Government are:

(i) Such appointments will be on contractual basis for a period of 10 months with no salary for the vacation period.

(ii) Those qualified as second class MA/MSc/Mcom or not having qualified as B.Ed will be paid Rs. 3,000 per month.

(iii) Those with minimum postgraduate degree plus B.Ed will be paid Rs. 3,500 per month.

(iv) Such teachers employed on contractual basis only stand a chance of being made permanent after 5 years, but no increment is assured.

Even in colleges, a class IV employee (Peon) starts with a minimum salary of Rs. 4,300 p.m. plus all perquisites and benefits. Such employees are not even graduates, let alone postgraduates like teachers.

Consequently, departments have to rely on guest faculty who are paid Rs. 50 (fifty) for each lecture, a meager sum by any standards. It is the educational standards which continue to plummet and the students who are deprived of the right to quality education and guidance.

But education is low on the priority of Government Payment of salaries and grants to colleges are often delayed for months together. Even payment of scholarship to students is delayed for months. Thousands of students of Std. IV and Std. VIII appear every year for scholarship exam conducted by the Maharashtra Government. All those scoring above a certain cut off point (changing every year) earn a scholarship which is largely considered prestigious. The amount is about Rs. 250-300 and normally for 3 years. For some of the students this is a big amount. But even this amount earned by young students through hard work is not paid by the Government at times for years and students and schools made to run from pillar to post.

After all, the amount to be paid is known immediately on declaration of results, but even this is delayed for years at times for lack of funds or red tape when the total amount involved is barely Rs. 3 to 4 lac. This is one more example of the utter lack of interest in education of young children and not rewarding young children promptly for the hard work put in by them. This examination is not compulsory and most of the children appear for the prestige attached to scholarship.

But the indifference towards education extends even to the college level. Most of the colleges in Maharashtra faced with severe financial difficulties as the State Government has not released even non-salary grants for over 4 years since 2000. College lecturers have not been paid salary for over 2 months. The total over dues amounts to over Rs. 31 crores.

But it is not only in Maharashtra that education is treated as a burden for the authorities. Even private medical colleges manage to get approved by the authorities without having even the basic infrastructure. Only one instance is cited to show that such institutions can flourish even when located barely a few kilometers from the offices of the Union Health Ministry.

Major shortcomings were noticed in the Santosh Medical College on the outskirts of Delhi at Gaziabad, by the inspection team of the Medical Council of India. The college was found to be training medical students when it did not have the basic requisites for teaching. But the college continued to get recognition for the previous 4 years.

But even engineering colleges are opened in a single room without any infrastructure. Maharashtra already has more than 120 engineering colleges. A large number of graduates in engineering from these colleges find it almost impossible to get suitable jobs. Under the circumstances it would only be proper for the Government to improve the standards of education imparted in such colleges. But rather than make any attempt to improve the standards, the Government encourages private, politically well connected people to open more private colleges. Master plan of Mumbai University maintains that Mumbai city does not need any more engineering institutions but colleges proliferate in Mumbai.

But the authorities merely give 2 years time to the college

promoters to acquire the requisite infrastructure, including campus, buildings, equipments qualified staff, etc. knowing fully well that cancellation after 2 years of the recognition of such colleges is impossible. As the students of such institutions will have wasted thousands of rupees and precious years, they will have nowhere to go, and leave them and their parents embittered and force them into antisocial activities.

Such ill-equipped institutions are a grave menace to the progress of education. But two other factors which need to be considered when looking at the progress and quality of education in the country are: (i) the quality of the educators and (ii) the curriculum.

Helping the disadvantaged is without doubt a noble act but classifying the disadvantaged merely on the grounds of caste, creed, community or religion is open to debate. In India, the concept and practice of caste, creed community and religion have an impact on society not seen or experienced any where in the world.

An impartial in depth, wide ranging study needs to be done expeditiously to ascertain the extent to which the present system of classifying and assisting the perceived disadvantaged helps the nation in making the best possible use of its present and future human resources. To what extent can a teacher or professor appointed or promoted solely on the basis of caste, creed or religion succeed in making the students understand the importance of imbibing knowledge and skills from the youngest age necessary to face the keen competition in every sphere, and make an earnest attempt to succeed in life?

As far as the educational field is concerned. It is vital that the best candidates be appointed at all levels, be they primary teachers or senior faculty members guiding PhD students as they are the ones who guide the minds in the proper direction.

The state of Chhatisgarh had passed a law allowing registration of more than hundred private universities, most of whom had no infrastructure, no classrooms, etc. The Supreme Court quashed the state law and cancelled the registration of more than 100 such universities in the state.

But Indian students can and do excel in every field provided they are given the opportunity and their creativity and intelligence not be stifled by politicians. In the USA, nine of the best Indian origin brains were honored in MIT technology review magazine list 2004 in the world's top 100 young innovators all below 35 years in age. Dr. Mootha, assistant professor at Harvard Medical School got an annual fellowship of US$ 500,000 popularly called in USA 'genius award' from an unknown jury, from confidential nominations without application or interviews, the only criteria being 'The Big Idea'. Dr. Mootha tracking mitochondria and tracing patients with metabolical diseases, e.g. diabetes, obesity, cholesterol and submitting his findings to medical journals. No record asked of how award spent.

In American Universities the viva voce is held within weeks of submission of PhD thesis, in most European universities within 3 months of submission, but in India it takes anything between 1 to 2 years. Besides lack of originality, copying of PhD thesis is increasing.

But no matter how illiterate a person may be in India, it would be incorrect to label such a person as a burden on society and incapable being a member of society and more importantly desirous of contributing his mite to society.

Even illiterate workers in India perform feats which are considered practically impossible by the people all over the world, particularly the Westerners. Alang, on the coast of Gujarat is the graveyard of ships, not because of shipwrecks, but discarded ships from freighters to oil tankers to aircraft carriers to VLCCs (very large container crude carriers) are brought here for being scrapped. There are no dry docks, no army of trained engineers with latest equipment only illiterate poor workers. The ships are driven onto the shore and literally beached. These huge ships are stripped systematically of all that can be salvaged. In all these years, not a single ship has keeled over due to irregular stripping and thereby affecting the balance of the ship. These workers come from all over India and earn a pittance of about Rs. 100 a day with no perks, not even living quarters, running water, medical aid, etc. Everyday a couple is badly injured and a few also die, but labor welfare measures are lacking. However, the point of this digression is the fact that after the devastating earthquake in Ahmedabad in 2001, a group of about 45 workers from Alang safely demolished in one night what demolition workers from army and fire brigade could achieve in 4 days. These men are used to working in oppressive conditions at Alang without proper safety devices like gloves and masks, and using only cutters and wrenches. This goes to show the spirit of the average Indian to tackle the task, given the spark to ignite the spirit.

A series of experiments conducted by Sugatha Mitra over 23 different locations all over India confirmed that no matter what, children don't need to be taught how to use computers. Children taught themselves how to open or close files, draw pictures, play games, surf and chat on internet, send and receive or e-mail even without knowing English, irrespective of educational background, literacy levels, social or economic background, ethnicity, intelligence or geographical location.

In the earlier part, the short comings in the present system of education have been brought leading to frustration among the children and high rate of illiteracy but the winds of change have already started blowing in India in all spheres, including literacy and education. A few such examples are given here.

At the very outset, an example is given from Bihar where the rate of illiteracy is high, and more importantly the teaching is done not in a school room, but in traveling railway bogie, packed with hawkers. Who are the students? Every morning, since 1997, an earnest teacher Vishwanath Prasad Vishwakarma, has been teaching a dozen or so hawker boys in the last bogies of the packed train. He teaches for about an hour, the time taken by the train to run from Nawada to Gaya. He teaches them reading writing and arithmetic - a necessity for hawkers. There are on an average 10 hawkers in the age group 12-30 yrs. The curriculum is need based. There are no schools for such hawkers with no fixed timings. So they take advantage of this school. They learn while they work. One of the students proudly states that he has been attending this school for a couple of years and is now preparing to appear for Matriculation exam within a year...Vishwakarma does not charge any fees.

In Rajasthan, a quiet revolution has been taking place. In Cheepivada, Jaipur, the eagerness of children to learn and the teachers to teach can be seen from the fact that in the absence of classroom children sit in the shade of a Neem tree to learn. Initially parents refused to heed teachers request to send children to school but teachers started with a handful of children. Gradually parents started sending the children to school and not only gave space in a nearby temple but also funded the building of a room.

The Institute of Development Studies, Jaipur conducted a pro-poor planning study in 1997 which among other things stated that almost all Government schools lacked even blackboards and proper furniture. The high rate of dropouts also raised question about the quality of education. Then came the Janshala project in 1999 sponsored by the UN. The community was now involved in the project to run schools. Some of the teachers worked hard on building a strong parent teacher association. The plan has been successful. Some of the parents have pulled their children out of private schools and enrolled them in Janshalas like Van Vihar.

But some shortcomings still persist. The Teacher-student ratio at present is about 1:80 though efforts are on to bring it down in 1:40.

Fourteen students of Zilla Parishad School in Maval Taluka, Pune district have made it to the merit list of class VII. What is note worthy is the fact that most of the students come from farmer families or farm laborer families and have to trek treacherous roads and hilly terrain for miles, some even bare foot. It's a hilly region and leopard menace also exists. Zilla Parishad School has about 300 students from 10 nearby villages.

In 2003, 13 students appeared in the merit list of class VII scholarship exam, in 2004, out of the 17 who appeared, 14 made it to the merit list. Shri. S. Dalvi the teacher is credited with bringing in complete turn around. Now the children are extremely enthusiastic and determined. They don't mind trekking over hilly terrain infested with snakes, insects and even leopards, they don't take even Sunday off. It only goes to show the fierce urge to learn and improve their lot in life, thanks to an unusually enthusiastic teacher.

Success has brought aid from social organizations like Rotary Club of Talegaon, donations of cupboards, plus 300 books for setting up a library, plans also for color TV, bicycles, sewing machine, etc. Zilla Parishad plans to build two more classrooms, but school has no library, no benches, no drinking water. But despite these adverse factors the children retain their fierce urge to learn with the able assistance of their teacher.

Another saga of the fierce urge to learn under extremely adverse circumstances comes from Gaya, Bihar. In a poverty stricken area in remote weavers' colony in crime ridden Gaya district. The people have shown how highly education is prized by them. Here residents of the colony who earn on an average of about Rs. 50 per day have painted slogans like "if you have seen dreams of IIT, then forget what is yours (house and family), make your resolve and rank will be yours".

Eighty per cent of weavers are below poverty line yet it boasts of scientists who work at DRDO and Indian Nuclear Centers, as well as engineers in topnotch companies like Wipro, Infosys and even in USA. It is not only past success, but students continue the tradition of doing well. In 2002, 6 boys cleared the IIT examination, 2 girls got through state level engineering exam in Kerala. Success stories in almost every year. In 1998, 3 made it to IIT, 8 in 1999, 2 in 2000 and 2 in 2001. But merely passing is not enough.

Their parents earn about Rs. 50 per day. All somehow have to manage finance. All rely on coaching classes about half an hour away. The population consists of about 1500 weavers. There is a good atmosphere here for studying. Crimes start about ½ km away but students claim not to be affected by it. Those who have succeeded and moved out, help those still studying. A trust has also been formed to help students lacking in finance to study further.

Today there is a computer driven revolution sweeping the country in various fields including literacy. More than 50 technology literacy models developed by NGOs are available in the country. But even without the computer, education is being revolutionized.

For instance more than 95 lac primary (class I to VI) school children in rural Maharashtra are being taught English as part of their curriculum. But an attempt is simultaneously being made to Indianise English and also teach them functional English words in common use. For instance age old favorite nursery rhymes have been indianised. Five year olds can be heard singing loudly "Where have you been my little Raj? I went to Agra to look at the Taj" and so on, though the children may not know a word of English. Students are casually replacing English words for Marathi words even in their normal daily conversation. The transition is surprisingly painless from Marathi to English. Incidentally, Marathi medium schools run by BMC are being replaced by English medium schools. As the poor strongly desire that their children be taught in the English medium.

In the rural experiment of teaching English, a large number of children are from the poorest daily wage earning families but even they are excited enough to teach their parents and grandparents whatever they learn in school and most of the parents reciprocate with eagerness. The children are also taught functional words like table, chair, radio, TV, engine. The process is being augmented by specially prepared audio cassettes.

Specially prepared textbooks state in their preface that it will not hamper the learning of the mother tongue. The pronunciation is not merely based on British or American pronunciation. Even the environment in which the child is placed has been taken into account to enable any primary teacher to handle English as a subject for Std. II. The teaching of English course has been deliberately spaced over 4 years as children need revision, though some teachers are confident of covering the course in six months.

Another innovation in education has been brought about by

Shrinath Kalbhag, who did a PhD in food technology from the University of Illinois and was head of the Engineering services at an MNC, in India for years. He had little faith in the conventional education system in India as it robs the children of curiosity and makes the children dependent. He quit his job and came to an arid and backward village of Pabal about 70 km from Pune. He set up the Vigyan Ashram to propagate his idea of non-formal education. His first step was to formulate a course for dropouts to equip them with basic vocational skills. The basic rural technology course teaches skills ranging from cooking to pregnancy tests, engineering design to poultry management and soil analysis, and this of course is now part of the recognized curriculum for Class VIII, IX and X in 20 schools. He strongly felt that the high dropout rate is due to the present system of education. The basic idea is to stress learning, which seems to be succeeding.

Pabal, pop 12,000 is now home to one of six world wide MIT Fab Labs that try to building 'everything from anything'. Already there is one Fab Lab in India at Bithoor and one each Boston (USA) Costarica, Ghana, Norway. It is manned by school drop-outs and underprivileged children and has a collection of hi-tech tools that can be used to fabricate instruments of any utility and configuration. The Fab lab's objective is to take technology to assist the developing world to solve local problems.

Since 1982 when it was founded by late Shri. Kalbag, it has turned out 800 dropouts into entrepreneurs. They proudly claim that even before MIT brought in funds and resources, their techniques had invented 6.5 HP mini tractor. Today the technicians, who are village dropouts, are connected to the world sharing knowledge and technology.

One more example of people with non-formal education, was not only improving the life of the nearby villagers, but also won the prestigious Aga Khan Award for architecture in 2001 by the Barefoot College of Tilonia.

The Social Welfare Research Centre at Tilonia, Ajmer District, Rajasthan was founded by Sanjit Roy in 1972 and is now known as the Barefoot College where every one is a student and a teacher at the same time. They have revised the old time tested techniques. The barefoot system is popularly called so as it means basic knowledge without a degree. Rural folk all over India survived with the knowledge gained from practical experience over the ages. Recent events have shown that village communities can develop and maintain their own store of knowledge.

Over the years a few urban educated teachers have helped local boys and girls to acquire skills as solar engineers, skilled craftsman, rain water harvesters, and house builders. Even housewives have been turned into hand pump mechanics, etc. The Aga Khan award for Architecture has been given for integrating social, ecological, cultural and educational elements in such a way as to aid rural development while promoting the architectural traditions of the region. All the buildings in the campus, including ones with geodesic domes have been constructed in vernacular style with local material by 12 Barefoot architects led by Bhanwar Jat and Mohamed Rafique. The entire place is electrified by solar power. Even in early dawn, piping hot water is instantly available as some of the pipes and boilers have been insulated. Even their computer centre with 15 computers run on solar power. The plans for the campus were drawn on the traditional courtyard format with surrounding verandahs.

Wood is scarce and expensive in that desert region and so the frames for the geodesic structure is made from readily available scrap metal from discarded agricultural implements, etc. and covered them with dense thatch. The college has provided more than 200 basic low-cost dwellings in the surrounding villages for the homeless. Women not only learned repairing handpump, but also helped in building rainwater harvesting tanks in many schools and the water lasts for about 3 months, so the girls and women can profitably utilize the time and energy formerly spent in bringing water in pots on their heads.

The people complement each others knowledge and have found out the difference between literacy and knowledge. Barefeet women can repair a handpump or solar lamp. The semi-literate women can even operate a computer and feed it with regular data. The people of Tilonia have learnt self reliance and do not depend on the Government.

Information Technology is booming all over the world, but most of developing countries cannot afford the computer system. In Brazil, where the minimum monthly wage is about $ 75 and where most of the people can't afford a telephone, a new basic computer has been developed, which can be had on monthly installments for as little as $ 15 pm. But with the general low learning power, it has been found that installing in public schools can provide internet access to more than 7 million children. This is an example of a poor country trying it's best to spread IT throughout the country at an extremely affordable price.

Thanks to the computer, an IT revolution is spreading throughout the world and India is not far behind. In Maharahstra, Tatyasaheb Kore Institute of Engineering and Technology is the main hub of Warna Wired Village project, the only one of its kind in the country and connects 70 such villages attached to the Tatyasaheb Kore Co-operative Sugar Factory of Warna Nagar, with each other and the rest of the world through the internet. IT centers have been established at 6 villages. All the 70 villages covered by project are linked to these 6 IT centers through phone and respective IT centres are in turn connected to main hub via VSAT.

It has made life easy for the farmers. Normally farmer would wait for the day, the nearby Sugar Co-operative came and collected its cane. But now all he has to do is to go to the village booth and tell computer operator that crop is ready. Its revolution takes care of the rest. Warna dairy alone has 70,000 members and the sugar co-operative has 30,000. The 6 business centers in Warna Nagar, viz. dairy, sugar co-operative bank, hospital, agricultural goods processing unit and departmental stores are linked with VSAT. A farmer can now monitor various processes sitting at his village without any need for going to the factory or dairy. The project is attempting to change the attitude and traditional thinking of the villager. The farmer is still used to the idea of turning to the Government for even simple things like forms, etc. Now the project is trying to ensure that he just has to inform village booth operator of his requirement and that will be taken care of.

Indians at all levels are finding new and diversified uses for computers and internet connectivity. A few examples are given here.

In Gujarat, a class V dropout today operates the computer and co-ordinates the village health services and also trains others like her. This is done under SEWA's Theli Phone scheme where more than 5,000 poor self employed women are given mobile phones to stay connected.

As a result of a 3 year agreement between Hewlett Packard and Andhra Pradesh Government 4 villages in the Kuppam rural community are improving literacy, creating new jobs and accessing Government services by using ICTS. It also makes it possible for them to make use of connectivity to schools, colleges, colleges and hospitals and vocational training through direct and distance learning, agricultural advice and health. The villagers can also access automated Government records for land records, birth and death registrations and on line bill payment facilities.

The Aziz Premji Foundation has set up learning centers to develop and provide curricular and non-curricular content, train teachers and promote computer assisted learning. Numerous schools are benefiting from this scheme. Some of which are mentioned below.

300 Municipal schools in Ahmedabad, more than 3,500 schools in as many villages in 27 blocks in Karnataka, 500 schools in as many villages in 10 mandals in Andhra Pradesh plus municipal schools in Vadodara and Surat. The Karnataka and APF have launched a joint campaign to obtain used computers and hardware that accelerate the proliferation of such centers. The innovative initiatives range for interactive movies to help children learn alphabets to getting the students to use handy cams and shoot small films on topics of their own choice in their own village.

Kerala is making full advantage of its strengths like a

literate population, fibre optic connectivity right up to the panchayat level and strong panchayati raj institutions. Kerala IT mission, as part of the Akshaya project, has set about 600 internet kiosks, each comprising five computers, and plans to set up 9,000 ICT centers to be used by at least one member of each of 65 lac families in the state though at present thousands of families in Mallapuram district can now learn basic computer skills and access content at the already established about 600 kiosks.

In Orissa, over 7000 artisans are working towards increasing their income by about 25% byusing the Net to reach their markets directly and by passing the middlemen. This is being done with the help of MITRA technology foundation's handicrafts e-trade centre.

While computers are generating tremendous interest all over the world, the ancient concept of 'Vedic' maths is also generating interest. A wide debate is taking place about Vedic Maths (VM) efficiency versus the Western Mathemetics.

This is an amazingly compact and powerful system of calculation used by ancient Indians, as a matter of fact the term 'Vedic' is a misnomer. The system of maths is a set of 16 algorithms and 14 sub-algorithms in Sanskrit meant for performing simple and complex computations. It was set down in the form of 'sutras' or aphorisms in an age where paper and pencil were not common and people relied on memory. It is a deceptively simple technique to shorten long calculations and appears magical to the uninitiated.

The system was rediscovered from the Vedas between 1911 and 1918 by Shri. Bharati Krishna Tirtha (1884-1960) a Shankarachaya of the Govardhan Pitha at Puri. He was a noted scholar of history, philosophy, mathematics and Sanskrit. After years of meditation he intuitively was able to reconstruct the mathematical principals enshrined in the *Atharva Veda*. He is reported to have written 16 volumes expounding the Vedic System of Maths. These books were unaccountably lost. Ultimately he wrote a single book which was published in 1965, five years after his death.

Some years later a copy reached London and well known Mathematicians like Jeremy Pickles, Andrew Nicolas, and Kenneth Williams took deep interest in the book. They extended the introductory material given in the book and gave many courses and talks in London, and a book *Introductory Lectures on Vedic Maths* was also published in 1981. Andrew Nocholson made 4 trips between 1981 and 1987 to India, to find out more about this science. Maharshi Mahesh Yogi was also instrumental in making the western countries take interest in Vedic Maths.

Dr. Das, a regular contributor to the 'Indian Journal of History of Science' states a course in Vedic Maths requires about 400 to 900 man hours compared to 2400 to 3200 man hours that is spent in the present academic curriculum for doing multiplication using Vedic Maths. Its adequate if multiplication tables are learnt up to 5×5 and simple addition and subtraction of single digit numbers is known, the rest is done by using the Sutra formula. He feels that 'Sutra constitute a formulation of maths by means of which problems in fields as diverse as co-ordinate geometry, algebras, arithmetic and calculus can be handled. He also feels that the Sutra method has to be examined as an alternate way (code language) of expressing mathematical terminology due to its simplicity and compactness as compared to the symbolic method presently in use.

The Vedic Maths is being attacked as regressive by many who do not have any idea of the potential for simplifying calculations. There are also some who are against it solely on the grounds of the word 'Vedic'. However, examples are given here to show the simplicity of using:

Multiplication: Use first sutra.

"By one more than the previous one"

For instance multiply 9,988 by 9,912

Multiply 99 by 100 (one more than the previous number)

Then multiply 88 by 12:

1st step gives 9900, 2nd step gives 1056

So the answer is 99001056

Subtraction: Second sutra

"All from nine and last from 10"

For instance, subtract 357 from 1000

Take each figure from 9;- 643

Last figure from 10;

10-7 = 3

The answer is 643

"The beauty of Vedic math approach is that for any problem, the answer can be obtained either from left to right or from right to left."

Realizing the importance of education and the high illiteracy rate, corporates have started investing heavily in setting up schools, colleges, trusts, etc. to ensure the widest possible coverage for making quality education available to the widest range of citizens. Besides a large number of NGOs have also set up facilities for providing quality education. A number of NRIs are also providing resources like men, money and materials to ensure that even the poorer and disadvantaged sections of society get the benefit of quality education right from the primary level.

Some of the richest Indians in the world have come together under one umbrella organization called the Indian Education Initiative Established in India in December 2000 with the aim of providing primary education to all children in India by 2010. The IEI members feel that the tasks of teaching about 180 million children between the ages 6 to 14 year is an achievable target even in a country like India where the illiteracy rate exceeds 35%.

IEI will base its tactics on the mode provided by Pratham. It will put children in 3 different categories: (i) Balwadi—pre-school for 3 to 5 year olds, (ii) Bridge course—for 6 years which identifies, brings together and prepares drop outs and never enrolled students for formal school and (iii) Balsakhi—for 6 to 10 years old which will offer in school remedial learning to assist potential dropouts attain basic literacy so that they can participate in class more effectively.

IEI also stressed that they would work in tandem with social service sector and the Government. Even the cost of educating has been worked out. Cost of educating for a year a child in Balwadi would be $ 7.50. The entire cost of sponsoring a Balwadi with about 20 children has been estimated at $ 150. The Bridge course would be about $ 210. Cost for a single child estimate at $ 13.50. The Balsakhi course for a single child would be about $ 5.20 and $ 210 for a unit. But education world also include teaching better hygiene and health care.

Dr. Madhav Chavan the founding member of Pratham is the inspiration behind IEI. His low-cost easily replicable community oriented model was recognized as one the three most innovative projects in the social services sector world wide for the year 2000, by the Global Development Network which is a collaboration of the World Bank and the Government of Japan. Pratham has already helped about 100,000 children since inception. It has been cited by UNESCO as being ideal model for other developing countries particularly Latin America and Africa. He strongly feels that the importance of primary education has not been realized since independence. While the well to do have been able to take care of educating their children, but the weaker and disadvantaged ones have suffered as they do not fit into the system as it exists in different states.

Education, pursuit of knowledge and scholarship were highly regarded in the past. Among the foreigners who came to India and contributed tremendously towards the spread of education was Dr. Wilson and his wife. The archives of the Maharashtra Government name Dr. Wilson as one of the founders of modern Mumbai. He came in 1829 to Bombay with his wife and mastered Marathi and Sanskrit within 6 months. In 1832 he started a school in his house in Girgaon but he made it necessary for his students to learn their mother tongue Marathi, before starting their English lessons. His wife started an English boarding school for girls, which later became St. Columba School, Bombay. He started a college section in 1836 for his school. The University of Bombay was incorporated by law in 1857, and he was named among the original Fellows in the Act of Incorporation. He served as VC in 1868. He helped decipher the Brahmi script helping scholars to read rock inscriptions at Girnar, Gujarat. He was a remarkable linguist and mastered: (i) Hindustani, (ii) Gujarati, (iii) Marathi, (iv) Greek, (v) Persian and (vi) Sanskrit and was examiner for MA for all these languages. He died in 1875.

Today's education does not lead to students taking any interest in the glorious past extending over centuries. Indians taking interest in the past and trying to kindle interest in the past are not encouraged. It is the foreigners who have tried to preserve the glorious heritage. Even preservation of flora and fauna were encouraged by the foreigners. The Archeological Society of India was founded in 1868. Similarly, the Botanical Gardens, Kaziranga Gama Sanctuary, Museums Zoos, etc. were set up almost 100 years ago. Care is not being taken to preserve atleast some of the well known, forts or architectural marvel like Forts of Shivaji, Hampi, etc. Even the Supreme Court had to be brought to issue instructions regarding preservation of Taj Mahal. Gol Gumaz, Bijapur, Karnataka is famous for its dome without support built about 400 years ago. Due to continued neglect it is in danger of collapsing. It's said to be the second largest dome of its type.

Even the Russian President Mr. Putin made it a point to visit Tipu Sultan's palace, during his visit to India in December 2004. Putin's visit was prompted by his keenness to see the rockets used by Tipu Sultan. Putin exhibited keen interest and asked many technical questions during his visit and was surprised at the technology used. But there is no publicity given to such marvels in India even in schools.

India is rich in archeological treasure extending over thousands of years. But after independence there has been a slowing down in scientific study of archeological structures. Even a city like Mumbai is rich in such history but efforts to popularize the grand history are lacking. Various historians have claimed that the distant suburb of Mumbai, now known as Nalla Sopara was none other than Ophir mentioned in King Solomon's time about 1000 BC. It is said that it was the largest trading center mentioned by Greek, Egyptian and Roman historians. Today it's neglected completely.

Hampi said to be one of the most beautiful archeological sites in India. The Portuguese traveler Domingo Paes had noted that in the reign of King Krishna Devraya's the Royal avenue running from the great Virupaksh temple complex to the majestic Nandi at the bottom of Matanga hills was of exquisite proportions. Today numerous ramshackle shacks have been erected in clear violation of all rules and regulations. It is full of beggars and touts. Many of the exquisite temples are unattended and vandalized. The Government had started building a bridge and road cutting through the ruins. Many illegal structures are coming up. The Japanese had given crores of rupees for the preservation of Hampi along with UNESCO but have since withdrawn in disgust.

But the Indians have no regard for this remarkable inheritance. There are no public toilets. The foreigners are charged Rs.450 to enter some of these monuments. Cattle roam about freely and there is dung everywhere and naturally an all pervading stink. Added to this is the crowd of beggars and touts. But neither the local people, nor the various Government authorities have the slightest interest in preserving such a masterpiece of ancient Indian architecture and city planning.

India is a vast country spread out over hundreds of thousands of kilometers. Numerous highly civilized cultures have flourished over thousands of years and left gigantic structures of surpassing beauty all over the country. Even the Taj Mahal was neglected. It was rising international concern, and the NGOs along with judicial activism assisted by the Supreme Court that at least some action is being taken to curb the deterioration of the Taj. Despite having thousands of structures which are fantastic examples of architecture, sculpture, etc. India cannot attract even a fraction of the number of tourist, which other countries can without such wonders. Paris city alone attracts 20 times more tourists than all of India. Even tiny Maldives islands attracts 4 times its population of its coral islands. Brazil is not only preserving its rain forests, but also using them to attract tourists to its eco friendly resorts. Of course they do not have the kind of wildlife (or what is left of it now) we have in India. But with all that, India attracts only a fraction of the tourists that Brazil does.

Museums are a rich source and a record of a country's heritage. The first museum was set up in 1814 at Calcutta, based on the collection of the Asiatic society of Bengal. An Asiatic Society was set up in Bombay which was a priceless collection of lakhs of books, but which is finding it difficult to maintain its priceless heritage for want of funds, making desperate efforts to maintain the collection.

The importance of museums was realized decades ago, and since independence have been placed high on the agenda of the state as the one institution capable of educating the masses in nation building and democracy. Today there are said to be more than 400 museums and the Department of Culture spends approximately one-third of its total budget on central museums. But despite all this, museums continue to be unexciting places and arousing not the slightest interest among the visitors. Is it because they are treated as warehouse where ancient artifacts are kept in showcases with no attempt to trying to arouse the curiosity of the viewer or to provide any connectivity between the objects and the viewers?

But even elementary tasks in running any organization, particularly where each and every object has an importance and an irreplaceable one, are ignored. The National Museum is situated in the capital Delhi, itself. It has more than 200,000 objects, most on them being national treasures. But after 50 years of independence it does not have a comprehensive list of all its acquisitions. It was only the pressure of a court order in response to a public interest litigation that, the National Museum has started the process to verify all its objects. The fault lies squarely on the bureaucracy as can be seen the reported remark of Director General, National Museum. "It is very difficult to have a list of so many objects. But we are in the process". The process having been commenced under courts order referred to the above.

One of the important reasons for the dismal state of museums is the fact that even today museology is not seen as a specialized discipline. Archeology and musuelogy are separate and specialized disciplines. Archeological Survey of India (ASI) manages more than 30 site museums all over India. ASI had an exclusive museum branch headed by the Director of Musuems, till mid-1990s. But since then, the exclusive museum branch no longer exists and the museums are under the control of the Circle Superintendent of ASI. But looking after museums is only one of the duties of the Circle Superintendent. He is also in charge of all monuments in that area, is also the licensing officer and the officer of state management under ASI. The Director, Conservation, ASI justifies these changes and adds that the post of archeologist and museologists are entirely interchangeable.

The Gujarat Government has made clear its indifference to the national heritage preserved in the museum. Since 1996, the post of Director of Museums is under the charge of the Gujarat Administrative Service. Gujarat state has one the best museums and picture gallery established by the former Maharaja of Baroda. But now its decay and dilapidated condition is becoming evident due to lack of proper maintenance. All this was once part of the Gaekwad's Royal Collection. The museum has a rare Egyptian mummy, which now lies unattended though it suffered serious damage about 4 years ago. The museum began preservation work on the illustrated manuscript 'Mahumalti' in about 1999, but what so far it has managed in 5 years is its fumigation. But the extent of mismanagement can be seen from the fact that a few years ago the musuem set out to buy an X-ray machine for pictures, but ended up buying X-ray for human beings. The musuem and art gallery has only one qualified guide out of staff of 80.

But basic infrastructure is poor. The National Museum of Natural History, an institution devoted to environmental education, is housed in a rented building owned by the FICCI, with whom they have to share an entrance. On occasions, for security reasons the staff including the Director are refused entry to their museum.

But there are examples of well run and well maintained museums in India. For instance, Chhatrapati Shivaji Maharaj Vastu Sangrahlay (Prince of Wales Museum), Mumbai, is an encouraging example of a well run museum, because, it is unhampered by excessive bureaucratic control, as it is an autonomous body, controlled by a close knit board of trustees. With 16 galleries it has a staff of 120, most of whom are qualified museulogists. It has been able to raise Rs. 8 crores recently for building a fully equipped conservation department and a wing for an exhibition hall.

It may be noted that a seminar on museums held in 1998 under the auspices of the Department of Culture pointed out that most of the museum have very poor conservative facilities, only a few central museums have such facilities. As stated earlier, the National Musuem of Natural History is housed in a rented premises, lacking unrestricted access, though having a committed staff, all of them have done their masters in natural science and degrees in Museulogy.

ASI was founded more than a century ago and had always distinguished archeologists at the head. But the control has passed into the hands of the bureaucrats during the last few decades. Several panels from the Sir M. Wheeler committee of 1960s to the recent BB Lal committee have suggested across the board overhaul of the ASI to encourage the ASI cadre to come up but the bureaucracy has always scuttled any such move and as seen in Gujarat, and now in the ASI, an IAS officer heads specialized body like, ASI. The ASI has a vast pool of talented scholars but mediocrity has taken root with a demoralized set up. In December 2004, the Indian Council of Historical Research in its annual congress, demanded that control of ASI be handed over to professional archeologists but looking at the developments during the last few decades, the chances of such professionalizing are remote.

India is a storehouse of countless and varied treasures. Some of them have been mentioned earlier but reference also has to be made to marvels like the famous shaking Minarets of Sidi Bashir Mosque in Ahmedabad. It was slightly damaged in the earthquake of 2001 but the Ahmedabad Municipal Corporation is digging a tank adjacent to the minaret and thereby weakening the foundation of this centrally protected monument. But neither the AMC nor the ASI are worried about the danger to this monument which may collapse as a result of the digging by AMC.

Indian subcontinent has seen the rise and fall of numerous civilizations extending over thousands of years and archeologists will take hundreds of years to unravel even a few of the buried civilizations. Harrappa and Mohenjadaro, now in Pakistan have aroused the curiosity of this highly developed civilization all over the world's archeologists for decades. Since 1997 excavations are being carried out at Rakhigarhi, Harayana by the ASI. The excavation site is located in the plains of the ancient Drishadvati river, a tributary of the now lost legendary Saraswati river. It happens to be the largest Harrappan site measuring 230 hectares and next to Mohenjadaro. There are traces of high degree of urbanization sophistication. It is characterized by writing, use of standardized weights and measures, apart from walled settlements, granaries subdivided into cubicles, variety of sanitation systems in the form of house drains. The dead were buried in long pit in north south orientation along with pots. Some of the females had shell bangles in their left hand.

Another site was accidentally found at village Mundi in western UP. This is the second site discovered in eastern up, near Madarpur village, Moradabad district. A farmer accidentally came upon a massive hoard of gold coins and jewellery among other artifacts. Accordingly to local report nearly three tones of the hoard had been taken away before the ASI came to know. The ASI have identified the hoard as belonging to the Harrappan era and had instructed the District Magistrate Muzaffarnagar to recover immediately the treasures from the locals, and even pay double the market value, for its preservation for posterity. The DG ASI described the discovery as exciting and very important from the historical point of view and added that the latest discovery proved that the region was very much a part of mature phase with which other places of Harappan civilization like Mohenjadaro in Pakistan and Lothal and Dholavira in Gujarat were associated.

The discovery of a Lothal in Gujarat in 1954 indicated its connection to the Indus valley civilization all previously excavated sites being in Pakistan after partition. Lothal is a well laid out town, 280 metres from North to South and 225 metres from West to East, a well planned and laid out town with houses being built of firebricks and paved streets intersecting at right angles. It is dated at 2200-2000 BC. The most prominent feature of the town is a trapezoidal basin. The function of which is under debate. Some consider it a dockyard others a water tank.

Indus valley civilization is considered a landmark in the civilization. In the Indian subcontinent, yet no interest is generated among the students, most of whom, even from areas near Lothal are completely ignorant of the existence of the presence of such an important site.

In May, 2001, the National Institute of Ocean Technology stumbled upon a Harappan like site deep in the waters near Gujarat. It is dated tentatively about 4000 BC or beyond. Initial under water readings suggest that the area is lined with well laid house basements, partially covered by sand waves and ripples. However, exact antiquity can be determined only upon detailed exploration of the underwater site.

Another important ancient site under detailed excavation is at Hadab, a coastal town in Bhavnagar district. Experts believe, it may be the ancient trading centre, Ashtra Kavapra mentioned in the ancient Greek works of Ptolemy. It was stated by them to be an important trade centre and a flourishing port town in the second to the sixth century AD. The ASI started excavation for Hadab at that spot as it fits the description given by Ptolemy in his works written in the second century AD. Many experts feel that the site originally known as Astrakav Kavpra (mentioned in Greek) and later changed to Hastavapra and Hatab as it is known today. The excavations seem to indicate that the area may be an elevated one, which corroborate the ancient historical description. The Greek geographer Pliny had mentioned fortified cities with moats round them in this region and Hatab might be one of such cities in the fifth or sixty century AD.

Even in Assam traces of highly developed civilizations have

been found near Guwahati. It is said that on digging a meter into the ground at any place in Guwahati pieces of pottery, broken stone images or beautifully polished stone blocks will be found. Dr. Medhi, an anthropologist of Guhati University has published in one of his research papers that a civilization similar to the Indus Valley civilization flourished in the Brahmaputra Valley. He also said that archeologists have proved the existence of the city of Pragjyotishpur which is largely said to be buried under the present day city of Guwahati. Dr. Medhi also stated that most archeologists also believed that an ancient city known as Pragjyotishpur (meaning Eastern place of astrology) is mentioned frequently in the *Mahabharata* and *Ramayana* and the *Kalki Purana* existed in Assam. The location of a temple of planet worship called Navagraha, meaning an abode of nine planets of the solar system, and its connection with an ancient research on astronomy and astrology lends weight to the theory that the city of Pragjyotishpur is buried under present day Guwahati. Dr. Medhi puts the time span of the civilization between 7th and 13th Century AD.

Even in Bihar, apart from the Stupas, recent excavation at Kesariya has discovered stupa which resembles the Buddhist temple at Brobudur, Java and is a prototype of the same.

Importance is now gradually being given in India to our ancient knowledge in diverse fields like medicine, surgery, astronomy, physics metallurgy, etc. Experts at IIT Kanpur recently claimed to have solved the mystery of the non-rusting iron pillar even after more than 1600 years. They have discovered that a thin layer of misawite, a compound of iron, oxygen and hydrogen has protected the cast iron pillar from rusting. The protective film has been growing for 1600 years and has grown only 1/20th mm. The protective film is formed catalytically by the presence of high amounts of phosphorus in the iron- as much as 1% as against less than 0.05% in today's iron.

High phosphorous content as result of unique iron making process practiced by ancient Indians who reduced iron ore into steel in one step by mixing it with charcoal yielding molten slag and pig iron that is later converted into steel.

But even ordinary citizens have made praise worthy efforts to preserve India's colorful history. The Khuda Bakhs Oriental Public Library was established in 1891 at Patna, Bihar. It is a treasure house of Muslim art and culture and has one of the richest collections of rare books, manuscripts and paintings, each an example of the best of Muslim art and literature.

It has been declared as institution of national importance after the take over by the Government of India in 1969 by an Act of Parliament. It houses over 18,000 Urdu, Persian and Arabic manuscripts, the second largest in the world, the largest being in the Istanbul Public Library, Turkey. The collection is priceless. It has over 95,000 rare and old printed books. There are manuscripts in exquisite calligraphy with enameled gold. But perhaps the rarest and most valuable manuscript in the library is the "Tarikh- I- khandan- I- Timiuriah" in Persian script. It narrates the history of Timur and his successors down to Babar, Humayun and Akbar. It is remarkable for the splendor of its miniature paintings in the delicate style practiced under Akbar's patronage. The fly leaf has an autograph note by Shahjehan stating that the work was written at the instance of Akbar. It is embellished with 112 illuminated pages bearing the works of the most notable painters of that time, with their names inscribed at the bottom of the page. Each of the paintings is enameled in gold. This manuscript alone is insured for Rs.70 crores but is priceless.

The library also contains Arabic and Persian translations of the 4 *Vedas*, the *Bhagvad Gita* and the *Ramayana*. This goes to show the composite culture of the country. It is a rich source of knowledge relating the Moghul period particularly and various research studies are undertaken at this unique library by scholars.

But another famous literary collection at Baroda lies almost forgotten. The artistically carved wooden case in the reference section of the Mandvi Central library, Baroda, houses not only photo plates of handwritten manuscripts of Lord Byron, Martin Luther, Galeleo, Francies Bacon, Benjamin, Franklin, etc. but also beautiful collection of books of interest to not only students of literature but also for students of History. But there are practically no visitors. Even the wooden case itself needs repairs.

India is a rich storehouse of knowledge and it only requires people with the desire to increase their knowledge and share it with their fellow citizens and the rest of the world. The lack of political will to ensure 100% literacy right from the primary school stage is acting as a damper to the spread of knowledge in the country.

22

Health

A healthy populace is the bedrock of a country's strength and prosperity. Unhealthy people cannot contribute to the growth, prosperity and safety of a nation. On the contrary, resources have to be diverted for the care of such people. Obviously with a healthy populace, a large part of the national resources can be better utilized for the development and betterment of the nation.

Can India be considered a country where the population is by and large healthy? Have deadly but common diseases like malaria, cholera, tuberculosis, etc. been eradicated? Are adequate and appropriate measures being taken to build up a nation of healthy people?

Today, more than 50 years after independence the populace cannot be said to be mostly free from diseases. Malaria, T.B., cholera, etc. are rampant. Health services for the populace as a whole leave much to be desired. Even measures for ensuring healthy and safe future for the infants have not resulted in any substantial improvement.

It is only proper to commence looking at the state of health of the populace by considering the health of the children who after all, are the potential wealth of the nation. In 1990, India had endorsed at a world summit along with other countries, certain goals for a healthy and safe future for the children. A review made a decade later of some of the targets and achievements are given below:

	Actual 1990	Target 2000	Actual 2000
1. Mortality rate per 1000			
(i) Infants	80	50	72
(ii) Below 5 years	109	70	105
2. Maternal Mortality per 1000	437	220	407

The economic reforms in 1990s are believed to be the cause of the sharp increase in mortality. The reforms led to neglect of social sector. The poor forced to spend 12% of income on hospitalization against 2% by rich. Hence, percentage of rural poor not seeking treatment has gone up from 10 to 21%.

In 1999, Maharashtra Government had itself set a goal of bringing down infant mortality rate from 48/1000 to 15/1000 by 2012. It was supposed to reach 25/1000 by 2005. But the figure in Jan. 2005 is still 45/100. Dr. Bang report submitted to Maharashtra Government in Dec., 2004 has stated that every year between 1.2 and 1.75 lacs children die in Maharashtra, majority in rural areas. Most of them can be saved by simple interventions that cost little but the political will and initiative is lacking.

As per the Economic Survey of 2004, infant mortality in India remains at 67/1000, whereas in Sri Lanka it is at 17/1000, China at 31/1000 and Bangladesh at 51/1000.

The actual figures may depict a much more depressing picture as health facilities, particularly outside metros and big cities leave much to be desired. The birth and death rates for the interior, particularly the tribal areas, cannot be considered to be accurate. But the fact remains that a nation which cannot or does not take adequate care of its children right from birth, cannot expect to have a healthy populace.

But a few dedicated medical staff is doing wonders in nursing back to health hundreds of malnourished children. At the Cama & Albless Hospital, Mumbai several malnourished chidden are being nursed back to health by a simple, effective and cheap method. The patients belong to the poorest strata of society and are normally about 2 years old with swollen legs and arms, protruding ribs, sunken cheeks and no appetite. The child is fed thin gruel and normally after three days, the child improves and starts eating. The mothers are extremely poor and illiterate. But this simple remedy, which does not rely on any medicine, but only on thin gruel which any one can prepare, has been found to be effective in almost all cases. Many booklets have been brought out by the hospital in Marathi and English with diagrams and simple instructions.

India is a unique country with overflowing granaries and widespread malnutrition. Comparative figures of children suffering from malnutrition in some countries are given below: India 63%, Nepal 47%, Congo 45%, Bangladesh 45%, Pakistan 38%, average for sub-Saharan Africa is 30% only. Within India, Maharashtra 76%, Bihar 64%, Orissa 54%, Madhya Pradesh 55%. Tamil Nadu is the exception as the mid-day meal program for school children is first charge on the state budget.

CAG report states that 40% of all rural households do not get 2 square meals a day.

A general attitude of callousness towards children is commonly found in a number of Government hospitals. A few examples are given here. Dr. B.C. Roy Memorial Hospital, Kolkata is the only referral pediatric hospital in West Bengal. In September 2004, 5 children aged between 3 days and 3 months died due to prolonged power cut extending over 2 hours. The hospital pleaded helplessness. But hospital did not mention any reason for not having any standby generator, particularly as it was the only pediatric referral hospital in West Bengal.

Two years ago the abysmal conditions prevailing in this hospital were highlighted when 14 children died with in 3 days due to lack of adequate supply of oxygen. The standard of care in the only pediatric referral hospital in West Bengal is indicated by the fact that apart from the above, 15 children died in 2 days in 2002 and on 12 March 2004, 7 children died in a span of 5 hrs, at night in this hospital.

West Bengal has been ruled by the Left Front Government and has the same CM for almost 25 years. It is only natural to expect the Government to provide the best possible care for the common people particularly at the only pediatric referral hospital in that state. It is interesting to recall that Cuba under the leadership of Fidel Castro claims to have the best medical system in the world for its citizens.

But the callousness of the hospital authorities towards suffering children is also exhibited even in the Central Government's Safadrjung Hospital, New Delhi. In July, 2004, 12 infants died in one day and 34 within the week at this hospital. After these tragic deaths, Supreme Court had appointed a committee of 2 doctors and 2 lawyers to examine how the situation can be improved. But no action by authorities pending report, and the same callousness towards infants and children continues. No efforts to provide minimum improvements after July 2004 tragedy. No portable X-ray, no ventilators in each ward, emergency drugs still not available. Even the shortage of potable water continues.

But the callousness of the staff at hospital continues unabated along with inefficient service. Just couple of examples are given here.

In the chilly winter in Dec. 2004, a mother (Sunita) stands at 9 pm outside emergency pediatric ward holding her 8 months old son (Sumit) with bad cough and feverish for 3days, another patient holds his one and half year old close to his chest in the bitter winter night. His son cannot open his eyes and had severe convulsion. He also had convulsions about 7 months earlier. 2 male and 1 female doctors are supposed to be on duty. But only 1 doctor is attending to patients in pediatric emergency ward. Security is very tight and no one can enter no matter however serious the patient may be. Ultimately after waiting for 2 hours outside the ward in the bitter cold winter, Sunita is called by the doctor and told to get X-ray done on lower floor. No portable X-ray though promised by Health Minister 6 months earlier.

Meanwhile the other child's (Ankush) parents advised to get his child admitted immediately and get medicine from outside as emergency medicine was not available. The one and half year old infant having convulsions has to share bed with 8 month old Shagun having pneumonia. The parents of Ankush got medicine from outside but had to give it themselves as no nurse was available.

Ankush had convulsions again but the doctor said they could not do anything and asked him to be taken away. So he was taken away by his parents in the morning to a private nursing home which is way beyond their means. They had already spent in April 2004 Rs. 18,000 in private hospitals. As regards the other patient, 8-month-old Sumit, the doctor finally saw him and the only medicine prescribed was a syrup after making the infant and his mother wait outside in the bitter December winter.

While the common citizen and the little infants and children have to suffer for lack of any medical care, the Legislators continue to be pampered. Even in Nov. 2004, additional ventilators, ECGs, portable X-ray, etc., purchased costing lakhs of rupees, and kept in special ward created for MPs in Parliament House.

Even in Maharashhtra, Association of resident doctors of Government hospitals submitted in Jan. 2005, a memo highlighting lack of facilities at J.J. Hospital Mumbai (premier Government hospital). Amongst other shortages, they highlighted lack of sonography machine, "We have only one sonographic machine for 4 hospitals J.J. group, viz. J.J. Cama, St.George and G.T."

But the callousness of the people of India towards their fellow citizens is incredible. Dr. Baba Amte, an internationally acclaimed pioneer in large scale rehabilitation of leprosy patients looks after and is responsible for well being of over 4500 leprosy patients. He runs an abode, Anandvan Ashram, at Chanda District, Maharashtra and has been internationally acclaimed for outstanding humanitarian work, and the 3rd generation of his family is also engaged in this work. But Baba Amte is 90 years old and suffers from severe back trouble but is still active. Apart from donations from well wishers from all the world, his ashram also receives grant annually from Maharashtra Government to run his ashram housing over 4500 leprosy affected inmates. But the Government had not released grant amounting to over Rs. 85 lac for 2 years since 2002. Thus not only causing distress to the inmates, but was also insulting to Baba Amte. Despite reminders, the grant was not forthcoming, forcing him to go on fast unto death. While the Government has no compunction in spending the taxpayers' money on less deserving schemes, it just ignores such deserving schemes.

The utter neglect of children can also be seen from the manner in which the children's homes in Mumbai are run. Children's Aid Society is India's oldest since over half a century and runs 6 children's homes. They are among the largest in Asia housing over 3000 disadvantaged children. In 2003, Maharashtra Government appointed Shri. Waghmode who was the Congress president of Sangola district, Maharashtra as Chairman of Children's Aids Society and was also given the rank of Minister of State. This was the first time that the tradition of always appointing a distinguished philanthropist/social worker was broken, and a politician was appointed and that too with the rank of Minister of State. The mismanagement of the homes and the public outcry forced the Lok Ayukta to appoint Justice Palker to report on the affairs of the homes. In May 2004, justice Palker submitted his report. But the babus and the Minister refused to give copy of the report on the grounds of its being confidential. They even refused to give the name of the Principal information Officer (PIC). Ultimately after a protracted and tenacious fight the report was handed over by orders of the Lok Ayukta.

The report passed severe strictures against Waghmode, the Chairman. "Remove him at once, start a detailed enquiry against him and frame corruption charges against him and strip him of his MoS Rank". He spent Rs. 17 lac in refurnishing his office when children continued to sleep on the floor just above his office, spent Rs. 1.5 lac on function for his mentor Balram Jakhar and Rs. 86,000 on private vehicles, used society's vehicles for his personal use, bought mobile phones for himself and his favourite staff, mailed Divali cards with photos of himself with S.K. Shinde and Sonia Gandhi, appointed his personal secretary as child Welfare Officer, helped himself to public money at cost of actual day to day work of children's homes.

Child welfare Committee, which adjudicates on over 50 cases at Dongri observation home repeatedly, sent letters to Women and Child welfare department stating non-existence of any stationary and adequately paid staff.

Justice Palker report also stated "grave financial irregularities committed, non-chalantly assumed powers in utter disregard of society rules, State Government turning a blind eye to blatant misuse of powers for personal gain at cost of children's welfare" Waghmode candidly admitted in writing, not knowing his powers. But the investment in each child @ Rs. 17 per day since 1994 remained unchanged even when children slept on the bare floor just above his office renovated for Rs. 17 lac.

After the report was made public, the employees of Children's Aid Society moved HC against lack of governing Council of Society (dismissed by Waghmode) consisting of and including Umerkhidi home, Chembur Children's Home and Home for Mentally Handicapped at Mankhurd (all in Mumbai) the court has observed that Waghmode not pass any further orders.

Mankhurd Children's Home meant for housing mentally challenged, hearing and speech impaired, physically disabled, normally up to 18 years of age but there is no real plan/proper treatment/training, so they stay there till they die. The oldest has been staying since 1950. In 1998 capacity raised from 280 to 350 trained but resources unchanged, monthly grant of Rs. 750 per inmate at remand homes nothing for special needs of such children. Repairs and electrical repairing not done for years, despite repeated reminders. Harsha, 16-year-old died recently of electrocution. Toilets, baths stinking, children with contagious disease can't be segregated due to lack of space. Dirt, stench flies, everywhere. Severe medical and psychological problems along with diseases like TB, AIDS, epilepsy, cancer, etc., but campus with over 1000 children has one temporary doctor and one residential full-time nurse.

Child's right to protection, survival, development and participation are all violated. The children asked for simple inexpensive things like skipping rope, football, carromboard, cricket and ball, etc. when asked by faculty of TISS. In the David Sassoon Home, clothes line not permitted in boys' stark dormitory, where they sleep on the floor above newly renovated office for Rs. 17 lac, as authorities fear children may use them for self strangulation.

Navjivan Home for rescued sex workers Dongri, Mumbai has 4 homes in Mumbai but non-functional toilets, no bathrooms, inadequate water supply, soaps/detergents in short supply, no sanitary napkins, irregular supply of vegetables and meat but now reportedly a committee appointed to study improvements.

But the conditions in some of the boys' homes outside Mumbai in Maharashtra are equally dismal. These homes were set up under the Bombay Children's Act enacted by the British more than 80 years ago, it was replaced in 1986 by the Junior Juveniles Act. These laws were enacted for the social rehabilitation of juvenile offenders. But today there is ignorance of the law by wardens of the children's homes and violation of all norms for the rights of the children.

The staffs at these homes are mostly unqualified and untrained and ignorant of the purpose of the J.J. Act. All rules are generally violated. There is not a single child welfare officer.

The boys are housed mostly in dismal shelters, sometimes unfit for human habitation. The boys Home in Latur, Maharashtra (constituency & home of the present Chief Minister), 103 boys are kept in a 'home' which was godown for storing food-grains for years. It has only one door, which is rolling steel shutter (natural for a godown). The home has had 13 superintendents from 1998 to 2001. Neither the superintendent, nor his assistant has any qualification for their post, except their proximity to important bureaucrats/politicians. The assistant proudly states that his job entails preparing monthly progress reports for every troubled inmate.

In Paithan, Maharashtra, the superintendent of the home is also a probation officer in the courts and readily admits ignorance of any norms or laws in running the home. But this official has been considered fit by the Maharashtra Government for being entrusted with monitoring NGO run homes as the Government representative on the district inspection team, Aurangabad, Maharashtra. But the number of children's homes are mushrooming rapidly in the state. With practically no control on the operations, the authorities do not appear to have the slightest interest in complying with the JJ Act or even basic amenities for children (even making them sleep on the bare floor). They appear to run as sources of income for the people in power, at the cost of physical and mental torture to children with no regard for the welfare of the children.

The main attraction for the rapidly increasing, but poorly run homes, in Maharashtra, seem to be the fact that the Centre foots 50% every states annual bill for children's' homes. Maharashtra is supposed to be a prosperous state, but it corners practically half of the Center's grants, as can be seen from the following figures:

	2001-02	2002-03	2003-04
Maharashtra	711	509	743
Madhya Pradesh	114	161	107
Tamil Nadu	190	114	107
Total Centre grant all over India	1,518	1,433	1,639

After cornering almost half the total grant from the Centre, the treatment of the children and conditions at the children's homes continues to be abysmal.

Children are frequently shackled to the beds when admitted to a hospital. The police put shackles on the ankle of every child to prevent him from running away. Even children suffering from illness are shackled. Recently 2 boys aged between 11 and 14 suffering from chicken pox were not only shackled to the hospital bed but were guarded by 2 plains clothes policemen. However, in the female ward the girls were not shackled, but guarded by a policewoman.

Most of the shackled children are classified as 'neglected' children under the Juvenile Justice Act 1986 and are not delinquent children. But the police justify their action in shackling kids as they claim the kids run away if they get a chance.

After spending crores of taxpayers' money and treating children in a barbaric manner, one would expect the bare minimum action would be taken to house the children at least in something which could be considered residential premises and not in a godown used formerly for storing bags of food grains and infested with rats.

In 2002, the Commissioner of Tribal & Training Institute conducted a survey which revealed that 63% of Government funds for tribal ashram schools were cornered by politician run NGOs. But even monitoring systems are politicized.

The Integrated Child Development scheme and Safe Motherhood had brought in reduction of neo-natal deaths. Now the scheme is in shambles, the neo-natal deaths account for 1/3 of infant mortality. The focus has now shifted to post-neo-natal deaths, as per a report on "state of new borns" released in Nov. 2004, by the Maharashtra Government, the state is now receding from public health. The private parties are emphasizing on curative care and not on preventive care. Consequently the poor continue to suffer.

But while the state of affairs regarding infant mortality and child welfare appears to be depressive, let us take a look at some of the disease illnesses widely prevalent in India.

1. Malaria

This is an extremely debilitating disease, at times fatal. It is spread by mosquitoes breeding in stagnant waters. Every year millions of people are affected by this deadly enfeebling disease, which is not fatal immediately, but gradually saps a person's energy. By 1955, i.e. within 10 years of independence, malaria had been brought under control and it was expected to be eradicated completely within a short time. But from 8 lac deaths in 1955, the number has jumped to more than 90 lac in 1995, and it is feared that the number may cross 120 lac by 2005.

About 50 year ago, DDT was considered to be a wonder drug and used extensively for exterminating mosquitoes, insects, etc. Subsequently the developed countries noticed extremely adverse effect on the environment and banned the manufacture and use of DDT but in India, not only are excessive reliance is put on the effectiveness and use of DDT, but also manufactured, though tests all over the world have shown the long lasting adverse toxic effects of the DDT.

Excessive dependence on occasional spraying of DDT and complete lack of preventive measures even in metros as also in other areas including rural areas, have contributed to the continual increase in the spread of malaria and other mosquito borne diseases like dengue, filaria, encephalitis, etc., a more deadly form of malaria, viz. cerebral malaria is also spreading in metros.

But malaria has been prevalent in India for decades. At one time Quinine was the common medicine prescribed and routine medical treatment was available all over India. But presently malaria is spreading all over India and getting prompt and proper treatment is becoming a problem.

A couple of years ago, the central Drug Research Institute (CDRI), Lucknow had developed a larvicide after 10 years of painstaking research. The Central Malaria Research Institute (CMRI), New Delhi had conducted extensive field trials in various parts of the country and reportedly found it to be a very cost effective larvicide. It was found to be non-toxic and without any side effects, and hence most suitable for the malaria eradication program. But this larvicide is reportedly not being used by any authority in India, all of whom continue to rely mainly on DDT, a highly toxic drug banned by all developed countries.

2. Dengue

A painful viral infection caused by the bite of the aedies mosquito which also thrives in stagnant water. The number of cases is said to be increasing every year all over India. In Delhi and areas within a radius of 15 km more than 200 cases have been reported in 2000. Unless properly treated, it can be fatal. Despite frequent occurrence of cases all over India, effective action is yet to be taken to eradicate this mosquito borne disease.

3. Cerebral Malaria

This is also a mosquito borne disease and fatal unless prompt and proper treatment is given. It is said to be widely prevalent in tribal areas, but also occurring in urban centers including metros. The basic cause is the failure to control the mosquito a menace.

4. Tuberculosis (TB)

It is another killer disease rampant in India. It does not kill an individual suddenly, but slowly weakens the victim who dies unless properly treated. The enormity of the continued spread of TB in India can be gauged from the fact that more than 1/3rd of all TB sufferers in the world are said to be in India.

Dr. R. Granich, a TB expert with WHO, has stated that TB is a serious problem for India with about 1.8 million cases every year, and about 4.5 million deaths. It is estimated that 100 million man-days are lost every year in India due to TB.

TB is a wholly preventable and curable disease. It is an enfeebling disease. Almost half the detected cases, in India, are in the age grow up of 15-45 years – normally the period when a person should be enjoying good health and making maximum contribution for the improvement of his family and indirectly the nation.

The root cause is the unhealthy living conditions coupled with inadequate nourishment. But there is lack of concerted and comprehensive efforts, including providing economical, affordable housing in clean surroundings, in urban as well as rural areas, to ensure complete eradication of this wholly preventable and curable disease.

5. Eye Diseases

India is reported to have the largest number, estimated at nine million and accounting for one-fourth of the world's blind. 90% of those blinded by preventable conditions, could have been cured. But only 21% of the blind are lucky to get their sight restored. Cataracts account for about 80% of the cases and are generally curable.

6. Polio

It is still prevalent in pockets in India. According to the Director General of WHO, the countdown for the eradication of polio from the globe by 2005 is on schedule except for India. According to the above statement made in April 2005, the epicenter of world's polio is in UP, India. 83% of the world's new cases globally are now found in India and particularly in UP.

UP has now confirmed six polio campaigns in 2005. But due to the failure of the UP Government to take simple appropriate action all these years, India will face the infamy of the few countries held up as a public health disaster along with a few backward countries in South America and Africa. It is also feared that children in developed countries will have to continue getting vaccine only because of our inability to control polio.

7. Jaundice

It is caused by contaminated water. Even in Mumbai it is quite widespread. The municipal authorities admit that water has been found to be contaminated in a number of areas. But the cause for the contamination is shocking. The authorities admit that more the 33,000 hutments have been built illegally on and around the pipelines, including the arterial pipelines bringing water from the reservoirs. But the hutments have sprung up over the water drains over a period of years. But due to political pressure from various political parties such hutments have been allowed to proliferate for decades and it is almost impossible to remove these structures, even though over 4,000 cases of jaundice were reported in 2004, excluding the unreported cases. There were also almost 100 deaths. But another major reason for the contamination of drinking water is the fact that most of these pipes laid about a century ago are rusting, and a number of them are laid near sewerage pipes which also are rusting.

Jaundice had broken out in Baramati, a modern well laid out developed area near Pune. In March 2005, more than 300 cases have been reported within 5 day and it has spread to areas in Pune. All these cases are due to drinking of contaminated water supplied through official water lines. The authorities admit that leakage in drainage lines have contaminated the drinking water supply lines that run parallel to it. But the outbreak of jaundice in 2 major cities in the vanguard of progress and better administration, underlines the dangerous situation regarding supply of essential commodity like drinking water even in the premier cities of India.

8. Fluorosis

Almost 65 million people are affected by fluorosis which affects the bony parts of the body like skeleton and teeth. This is a water-borne disease and occurs even in subsoil water. Those with low intake of calcium are more susceptible but the poor who find it difficult to get even a bowl of rice every day, attempting to increase their intake of calcium rich products is an impossibility, and so are the greatest sufferers. In Maharashtra, the most severely affected areas are 11 districts of Vidharbha, where 50% of the population, about 150 villages are affected. Mangi Pond, Yevatmal district came to prominence in the year 2000 due to the high death toll. The sharp increase in cases occurred due to drilling of large number of tube wells under the special schemes of the Maharashtra Government for tribal dominated villages. It may be noted that the safe limit of drinking water is 1.5ppm, whereas Mangi Pond village has 18 ppm. No relief has been provided to the permanently invalidated villagers so far.

9. Cancer

The number of cancer cases detected in young and old are increasing alarmingly. While it may not be possible to prevent a number of cases, yet preventable cases are rapidly increasing. The practice of chewing tobacco is widely prevalent especially in rural areas and is strongly believed to cause oral and thoracic cancer. But a more lethal form of cancer is now spreading rapidly all over the country due to large scale manufacture and widespread sale of a mixture of tobacco and harmful chemicals own as 'Gutka'. But despite being highly addictive and strongly suspected to be a cause of cancer, it is freely sold all over India.

But despite an increasing number of cases of cancer affecting even infants and children being detected in India, very little effort is being put by the Government to ascertain causes for such increase and providing proper treatment at an affordable price. Treatment of cancer is a long drawn out and expensive one.

10. Liquor

Addiction to liquor is quite widespread in urban as also rural India. Due to poverty and the need for daily consumption, such addicts consume cheap country liquor which quite often contains harmful chemicals. At times, the entire batch sold in an area may contain lethal additives, resulting in deaths of large number of consumers from those shops on a particular day. This sort of tragedy takes place frequently all over India, without being confined to any specific area- right from shops in Haryana to Kerala, and from Gujarat to Bihar and Bengal.

Apart from fatalities occurring now and then, the consumption of such harmful liquor on a daily basis not only spoils the health of the addicts themselves but has a disastrous effect on the health and economic welfare of the family members including the infants. This is because addicts spend all or the major part of the earnings on liquor, leaving nothing for their families, who, quite often, cannot feed themselves for days together. The situation is so bad, that at one time, the Maharashtra Government was thinking of paying the employee's salary to the wife of some of the employees to ensure that the family does not starve. However this is not a practical solution, as such addicts use force on their family members to extract money to satisfy their craving for hard liquor.

This is a serious health and social problem but no Government has seriously made an in-depth study to find a practical solution to ensure a safe and healthy life for not only the reformed addict but also for the dependents of such people.

It may be pertinent to note that with the advent of the Industrial Revolution in UK in the 19th century, drunkenness was a serious problem. Even children became addicted to hard liquor as child labor was rampant. But social consciousness through temperance societies and other organizations with Government support, managed to control the problem. Merely prohibiting consumption of liquor does not solve the problem.

The people and particularly the workers and their families have to be provided with decent housing and adequate and suitable recreational facilities. Providing wide open spaces with green lawns is an absolute minimum necessity. While before independence, town planning took into account the need for open spaces, subsequently the trend has been reversed and now even existing open spaces are being drastically reduced through Government action or by illegal encroachments.

The 1947 development plan for Mumbai had recommended ratio of 4 acres of open space per 1000 people, when London has 4.8/1000 and New York has 5.5/1000. Today Mumbai has barely 0.03/1000 and even this ratio is rapidly worsening. Very few open spaces now remain, but encroachments continue on the few remaining open spaces. Slums have sprung up over the last few decades with complete inaction by the authorities due to political pressures.

While open spaces are being rapidly illegaly encroached upon, leaving practically no open space for the citizens, and thus affecting adversely the health of the people, even more serious encroachment affecting the adverse health of the people continue unabated. Earlier mention has been made to the outbreak of jaundice in Mumbai and Pune due to rusting of drinking water-pipes and drain-pipes aggravated by illegal tapping of water pipes and building hutments on such water pipes including arterial pipes.

But hutments have been built even over storm water drains in some of the localities in Mumbai, and thereby prevent municipal staff from cleaning the drains. This results in overflowing of drains and flooding with filthy water in those areas. But political pressure is against removal of such illegal hutments, though a permanent source of disease.

But mention must be made of the care taken of the workers health during the early days of industrialization of Mumbai. Among the list of 12 most outstanding edifices in Mumbai chosen by a panel of international architects recently, are the Bombay Improvement Trust (BIT) chawls in Mumbai. They stated " the BIT chawls were an early application of the 19th century of the concerns for public health and sanitation and reveal successful adaptation of local conditions, both climatic and social....They seemed the ideal answer to rapid industrialization which brought thousands of workers from the hinterland to the city at the turn of the century ... it also reveals that the authorities cared to provide housing to workers".

11. Sanitation

The most important reason for the numerous diseases in India, is the lack of proper sanitation. More than a century ago, municipal corporations/councils were set up with the basic aim of ensuring the health of the populace.

But proper sanitation only means providing clean and healthy surroundings. This is a task which can and should be performed by the populace themselves for their benefit. But despite statutory backing, even the municipal bodies have failed to perform their duty. Mumbai Municipal Corporation, the oldest and largest Municipal Corporation has by and large, been unable to provide clean surroundings to the growing population over the years, and consequent increase in the solid and liquid waste. The population of Mumbai is more than 10 million, yet no effective schemes have been implemented to cope with the rapidly increasing population. The old system of collecting garbage from thousands of dumps located all over the city and trucking them to different areas and using them as landfill continues.

The city generates about 7,000 mt of garbage daily but the authorities have not succeeded in evolving any scheme for disposal of the ever increasing garbage generated by the rapidly increasing population. Heaps of garbage and overflowing garbage dumps are a common sight. In some areas even overflowing of drains is not a rare sight. But the failure of the municipal bodies to effectively discharge their duties in providing sanitation and clean surroundings in Mumbai and other metros, has compelled the local citizens to take over the task themselves. Street cleaning and garbage collection has started to be privatized in cities like Delhi, Lucknow, Mumbai, Chennai and some other cities. Locals of particular areas contribute about Rs. 20-30 each (in addition to the taxes levied by the municipal bodies) and participate in managing their own garbage collection. This has resulted in remarkably clean areas in cities where such systems are undertaken by the local citizens. It only goes to show the capacity of the citizens to rise to the occasion and provide clean and healthy surroundings, when the official bodies fail in providing the services.

The employees of BMC are well paid. A laborer gets about Rs. 7,700- p.m., clerk/teacher Rs. 8,400 p.m., top civic officials get over Rs. 25,000-pm plus all get perks like permanency of job, medical aid etc + causal leave 20 day + earned leave 33 days + annual bonus. Salaries of the staff account for over 70% of the BMC budget.

There is an urgent need to devise and implement result oriented plans without delay to ensure the health of the populace.

But the most important point to note is the need to realize that preventative measures for controlling diseases are more vital than cure. In this respect it is worthwhile referring to the steps taken by China just after the end of the long drawn out civil war. They realized that:

(i) Prevention is better than cure.

(ii) Rats, flies, mosquitoes and insects were the main cause of most of the diseases.

(iii) Proper sanitation and supply of potable water to the remotest area was necessary.

Funds were scarce, but the enthusiastic party workers fanned out all over the vast country carefully explaining the need for getting rid of pests like rats, flies, etc. and also the manner of maintaining proper sanitation. They also combined the traditional Chinese system of medicine with the Western system. Within a few years, cholera, plague, typhus, smallpox, etc. had been completely eradicated. All over the country, people understood the importance of proper sanitation and kept their surroundings clean.

The people's participation is a prime necessity in achieving the national goals. Even in India a few dedicated, sincere honest bureaucrats have also shown spectacular results can be achieved in improving the health of the nation, provided one has clear cut plan and most importantly, involvement of the people. Just a few such successful instances of overall cleaning up the city are given here. In every case, it must be realized that the cleaning up the city was not an easy task. Though the majority of the citizens desired to have clean and healthy surroundings, yet, in every case a few vested interests tried to create impediments.

Recently the Collector cleaned up the town of Thane, almost a suburb of Mumbai. He widened the streets, mainly by removing the illegal encroachments, started a campaign to clean up the lakes for which it was known till about a few decades back and made numerous other improvements resulting in not only beautification of this old city but also improved sanitation.

A similar successful job was carried out by another Collector in Surat, a prominent trading centre in Gujarat. The sanitation system had practically collapsed and it had acquired the reputation as the plague city of India. Within a short time he brought about a remarkable turnaround. The plague scare not only gave Surat a bad name, but internationally also gave India a bad name where even in the twentieth century, ancient diseases like plague flourished. But thanks to his efforts, Surat was soon declared the cleanest city in India.

One more example of tremendous changes brought about in the cleanliness and sanitation of a city is given here. Ludhiana, Punjab, was another dirty city without proper sanitation. But in 2 years, the Collector managed to install a proper sewerage system, garbage disposal system, widened the main roads, set up green belts, bus shelters, multilevel parking areas, etc.

There are numerous other bureaucrats who have tried and succeeded in making a major contribution to improvement of the people's health by improving the civic amenities of the cities within the short period they were allowed to function at that particular city. But efforts are made by vested interest to belittle their efforts and transfer such Government servants to postings considered insignificant. But luckily for India, despite hardships faced by such dedicated, honest bureaucrats, they try to continue their good work. Also more bureaucrats are coming forward to ensure that the populace does not suffer and that such actions only result in improving the health of the populace.

12. Spurious Drugs and Adulteration of Food and Beverages

There are more than 20,000 Pharmaceutical companies in India manufacturing drugs developed and patented abroad. But there are thousands of others manufacturing spurious drugs. According to World Health Organization (WHO) about 35% of all spurious pharmacy drugs are manufactured in India. Exports of Indian pharmacy products are increasing as they are cheaper than those manufactured by developed countries. Some countries like Vietnam and Myanmar import about 40% of their pharmacy requirements from India as they are cheaper. But according to WHO, about 11% of our exports of pharmacy products consists of spurious drugs. And this will have an extremely adverse impact on the reputed Indian pharma companies. The turnover of spurious drugs is about Rs. 4,000 crores. It amounts to nearly 17% of the pharmacy industry's turnover. The Mashalkar committee has recently recommended the death penalty for spurious drug manufacturers. But they have to be caught, tried and punished. But all this is only a symptom of the unbounded greed for money no matter how acquired.

The presence of spurious drugs in the market goes against the spirit and letter of law in safeguarding the health of the populace. The attitude of those in power can be seen from the fact that no investment has been made in improving the control over the pharmacy industry by the Food and Drug Administration over the last 25 years. It has only 3 intelligence offices in Maharashtra for keeping vigil on the increasing number of spurious drugs. It has only one lab for checking samples of medicines in Maharashtra.

It is not only drugs that are adulterated. Even milk water and foodstuff are adulterated in a big way.

Lack of control over the quality of food and food products should be cause for grave concern for the authorities. It may be noted that all over the world, the most stringent precautions are being enforced in all spheres to ensure that there is no danger of even accidental ingestion of harmful chemicals. There are strict regulations even regarding the quality of paint used in toys to prevent any danger to children. Even the plastic jars used for storage of food articles have to conform to the laid down safety parameters. There is world wide concern at ensuring the safety of the health of the people. But in India, there is utter lack of control over even the basic food items like milk and all types of eatables.

Now milk is a basic necessity for children particularly and one would assume that at least adulteration of milk would be dealt with severely by the authorities. But a large percentage of milk supplied all over India is invariably adulterated with water. But India probably holds the unique distinction of being the only country where not only adulterated milk is sold openly throughout the nation, but a unique product known as synthetic milk is manufactured and sold openly as milk on a large scale.

Synthetic milk is prepared with *urea detergent powder*, vegetable oil, fat and salt mixed with water. This mixture is added to natural milk –naturally the resultant mixture contains very little natural milk. The color and fat content of this mixture is similar to natural milk.

The Indian Dairy Association (IDA) has shown great concern at such 'milk' being manufactured and sold in large quantities in Delhi, UP, Haryana and Rajasthan. The association had written to the concerned ministries to take stern action against such manufacturers. Surveys by local authorities and experts of National Dairy Development Board (NDDB) have noticed large scale adulteration of milk in the Delhi region. A simultaneous raid carried out by local authorities in Kurukshetra, Haryana at four plants manufacturing synthetic milk resulted in seizure of large quantities of urea, salt, caustic soda and sugar.

Now such activities, preventable under FDA, cannot be allowed under any circumstances. There is no doubt as to its being extremely harmful to the consumers particularly children. But in India, manufacture and sale of such harmful 'milk' continues unabated.

It is interesting to recall an incident that occurred about 50 years ago in Egypt. A number of cases of people becoming paralyzed after consuming their normal food were reported from the poor and rural areas. The Egyptian authorities approached WHO for assistance in tracing the cause of the tragedy. The WHO team traced the cause to the use of cooking oil which had been adulterated with spent engine oil. The criminals responsible were traced and awarded the death penalty.

13. Cholera

Outbreaks of Cholera with resultant deaths are common in India. But such outbreaks take place not only in remote villages but also in cities and adjacent areas. The main cause of such outbreaks is the contamination of drinking water. In a number of cases the water lines pass through gutters in most of the metros and large towns.

The position of towns relying on direct water supply from the rivers is much worse. Almost all the rivers of India are heavily polluted. The towns and cities discharge their sewage and waste as also industrial effluents directly into the rivers without any treatment. The indifference exhibited by the authorities can be gauged from the fact that in Delhi, the capital of India, about 1400 mt of untreated sewage plus other industrial effluents are discharged in the Yamuna River every day. The rivers are so polluted that in some areas for example in Haryana and Delhi, the contents of the Yamuna can only be described as sludge.

Even the sub-soil water is highly polluted in a number of areas by industrial/commercial activities like dyeing works, prawn farm, etc. There are a number of areas in Bengal, Maharashtra, UP, etc. where drilling of bore wells has resulted in striking deposits of arsenic and other harmful chemicals. In the absence of alternate arrangements by the authorities, the people, amounting to lakhs in some areas, have to continue relying on such chemically harmful water for all their needs, including for drinking purposes.

In the absence of effective steps to control such pollution of water source and transmission and distribution network, the outbreak of water borne diseases will continue. There was an ambitious plan for cleaning up the Ganga but after spending hundreds of crores of rupees there is no improvement in the pollution of the Ganga.

14. Opium and Narcotics

Opium is an addictive drug extracted from the poppy plant grown mainly in Madhya Pradesh and Uttar Pradesh under Government supervision. It is greatly in demand by the international illegal narcotics trade. The local demand, even for medicinal purposes, is a fraction of the illegal demand. The British Government had encouraged cultivation of poppy in British India in the 19th century to meet their requirements for flooding China, where import and consumption of opium was prohibited, being aware of the undesirable effects of opium addiction.

MP Government is reported to have decided to ban growing of poppy and introducing new schemes to induce poppy growers to take up growing of other profitable cash crops. But certain centers in UP and even in TN have reportedly taken up growing of poppy.

India is an important link in the international illegal narcotics trade. This trade has an extremely adverse effect not only on the Indian economy but more importantly in increasing crime and corruption. Kulu Manali, Himachal Pradesh and Goa are said to be favorite haunts of international drug addicts. Unfortunately addiction to drugs and narcotics is increasing in India, affecting the younger generation particularly.

15. Mental Problems

The pace of modern life is becoming hectic very rapidly, particularly in cities. The causes are many. For centuries the citizens all over India were accustomed to a leisurely pace of life. But suddenly during the last couple of decades, the pace has accelerated very rapidly leading to increasing mental tension. The break-up of the joint family has also been contributing, to some extent, to the increasing tensions.

Today for a large number, the first and foremost worry is securing gainful employment. The job market, at present, is not keeping pace with increasing population. Even those gainfully employed for years, suddenly find themselves out of a job – and what is worse, fail to find alternative means of earning a living. In India there is no social security net to help the unemployed. For men with families, it is a big shock to find themselves in a state where they are unable to meet their family obligations.

Even when employed gainfully, the financial pressures continue to increase for a majority of the people. Getting affordable residential accommodation on rent is impossible in most cities. The compulsion to acquire a residence against a housing loan, raises the worry of meeting the loan installments on due dates during the currency of the loan.

For an ordinary person, the compulsory dependence on public transport for every occasion is again a cause of stress – as affordable, safe, dependable, reasonably priced public transport to meet the needs of rapidly increasing population is not available in the country, particularly in metros like Mumbai, Delhi, etc. Even in a city like Mumbai where a dependable, affordable, safe mass transit, rail system existed for decades, it is now almost impossible for senior citizens and handicapped persons to travel by these suburban trains. For the last few decades, the development of the mass transit systems, particularly the rail network has for various reasons not been able to make any significant improvement in the passenger carrying capacity despite the rapidly increasing population. After all, it is not only the physically fit people who are forced to travel by the mass transit systems, but also women, children and handicapped people. The inhuman and risky conditions affect the people physically but, more so, mentally.

Children's education is another major source of worry. Even to get admission in KG class has become a herculean task. Generally, children aged 2-3 years are required to appear for interview. Sometimes they even have to attend pre-admission classes. The extra financial burden as also the anxiety of actually getting admission is another source of stress. Need for attending special classes every year is another financial burden. But even after spending thousands of rupees during every year of schooling, there is no certainty of admission in the course or college of ones' choice, even after having a very good academic record and scoring over 90% in all the school and entrance exams.

Modern town planning in India does not give due attention to the need for keeping large open spaces and parks for the citizens. In a city like Mumbai, the financial capital of India, very few open spaces are left for the ordinary citizen, young or old, men, women and children to relax. Whereas till about 30 years ago, there were plenty of open spaces and even children could play open air games. Apart from destruction of open spaces, skyscrapers, anywhere between 10 to 60 stories high are being built everywhere, even in suburbs considered far away from the city. Consequently, on the one hand children have to study very hard for hours together every day, on the other hand there is no space or greenery to relax. The enormous pressure on children (and naturally on their parents also) to excel in their studies, without any open spaces to relax occasionally, is taking its toll not only on the physical health, but more importantly and sadly on their mental health.

Despite clear indications of sharply increasing number of men, women and children having psychological problems in coping with the present conditions, the authorities, by and large, have not taken any steps to improve the quality of life and thereby reduce the mental tensions. In Mumbai city and suburbs, even the reserved open spaces have been encroached upon or officially de-reserved and construction of skyscrapers permitted.

Open spaces are the lungs of the city and provide opportunity for residents, young and old, to relax in clean surroundings. Even New York has about 5.50 acres per thousand people of open space (Central Park being the largest single park in NY) as against 0.03acre/1000 in Mumbai. A recent survey by architects from the Urban Design Research institute has observed *inter-alia*, that although officially there are more than 400 garden and 233 playgrounds, the BMC could give details of only 167 grounds in its possession. 15 could not be located as they were non-existent. These included large plots of over 1,600 sq.ft.

The closure of textile mills in South and Central Mumbai could have been used to plan a huge sprawling park, something on the lines of the Maidan at Kolkata, or Hyde Park London or Central Park, New York. Instead of planning wide open spaces for the common citizens, the authorities have chosen to permit the mill owners to sell the mill lands, piece by piece and allowing most of it to be developed commercially by allowing buildings for shopping malls, skyscrapers, etc.

Mumbai is an island with a number of lovely beaches. About 70 years ago, a couple of wide promenades were built along the sea face at Marine Drive, Mahalaxmi, and Worli for the benefit of the general public. There were clean beaches for miles together. No additions have been made since then. The promenades including Marine Drive are crumbling and the beaches are being encroached upon or becoming dirty.

It is not generally known that about 70 years ago, only buildings of not more than 5 stories high were permitted along the sea face like Marine Drive, Worli or Juhu. The reason being that taller buildings would block breezes from circulating in the crowded interior parts of the city. Today skyscrapers are being built right on the sea shore without the slightest regard for the necessity of sea breezes helping ventilate the inner parts of the city. All these factors are adversely affecting the health of the people. No new promenades are being built for the citizens to enjoy the open areas and the fresh sea air.

Once a person is diagnosed as being mentally impaired, it is essential to provide proper medical care. More than a century ago, a number of hospitals were built all over India to look after the mentally impaired, at Pune, Thane, Agra, and Ranchi, etc. But during the last 50 years no new centers have been established for such people. The mental pressures on the young and old including men, women and children are increasing at a frightening pace and there is an urgent need for establishing centers where such people can get proper counselling and be treated, preferably at the incipient stage itself.

16. Pollution

The indiscriminate dumping of untreated sewage and all kinds of solid and liquid waste, including dangerous chemicals, in the life blood of the nation viz, the rivers, lakes and ponds of

India, has resulted in heavy pollution of almost all the rivers, big and small, including the mighty Ganga but water is the source of life. Life cannot exist without water. And polluted water is the cause of most of the diseases of the populace. Pollution of rivers, lakes and ponds play havoc not only with humans, but also with plants and animal life. The polluted flora and fauna enter the food chain and adversely affect the health of the populace. Such pollution tends to destruction of natures ecological balance. The penalty in the form of widespread ill health and at times death, has to be paid by the populace. A large number of diseases in India are water borne, and hence in the interest of improving the health of the nation, it is all the more necessary to take all possible steps to prevent pollution of water.

But as already mentioned, even the scheme for cleaning the heavily polluted Ganges has been given up after spending hundreds of crores of rupees including large scale foreign aid, without any results. It is interesting to recall that about 40 years ago, the Thames river near London, UK was heavily polluted, but was cleaned up in short time without resorting to foreign aid.

It is not only the rivers, lakes, ponds which are heavily polluted, but even the subsoil water is heavily polluted in large areas all over India. Even in Mumbai, the financial capital of India, there is a small river barely 15 km long. Starting from Powai Lake (Mumbai) and winds up in the Arabian sea, between Mahim and Bandra. Till about 30 year ago, it was a reasonably clean river. The survey by the Maharashtra Pollution Prevention Board survey of 2003, states "... at least 3,000 illegal industrial units spewing chemicals and solid waste on banks treat it as their personal sewerage pipe. It has become shallow with rampant encroachment and solid waste thrown in river. At places it is barely 10ft wide and is no longer a river but a filthy gutter filled with sludge unfit for any use. But it is a source of many diseases".

A project to clean the Yamuna was conceived in 1990s. The project started in 1995 and is still running in extended phase. The plan envisaged stopping of sewage draining into the river. A token amount was earmarked for Delhi to create 2 sewage treatment plants of combined capacity of 29 million litre/day and build an electric crematorium. Official estimate is that Delhi's waste water now amounts to aprox. 3,000 million litre/ day, nearly half of it is untreated. After spending approx. Rs. 500 crores over 6 years, the Yamuna remains as polluted as ever.

Nainital is a famous hill station. The vast lake in the town has started drying up and pollution is increasing rapidly. It is a source of potable water for the town and the nearby villages. Till the 1960s the lake water was pure and fish mortality was rare. But now, large numbers of fish die particularly during winter. Investigations have shown intestines of fish infested with tapeworms. School children frequently suffer from jaundice. Local sewers discharge into the lake and feaces from the sewers pollute the waters of the lake which is surrounded by steep and fragile hills. An estimated 3,500 cubic meters of silt enter the lake through small and 20 big and small storm water drains mostly during rainy season. Before 1950, there were 250 natural springs in Nainital, adequate for the needs of the town now there are only 20 such springs left.

It is not only the influx of pollutants in the rivers and lakes but far more dangerous is the indirect pollution through the use of harmful pesticides and fertilizers which enter the food chain.

A report issued in 2002 by National Institute of Occupational Health, Ahmedabad, Kasargode district, Kerala, showed growing rate of disease and deformity linked to use of Endosulfin, toxic pesticide used in cashew plantations. This is another warning against uncontrolled use of pesticides and urgent need to investigate its impact on food chain and human health, moreover foreign buyers are very strict about quality of agriculture produce. High levels were found in blood samples of children and drinking water sources.

A study by Indian Council of Medical Research in 1993 found alarming levels of benzenes hexacholoride (BHC), extremely toxic pesticide in over 2000 cow and buffalo milk samples collected from 12 states over a period of 7 years. The worst contamination was found in samples from Bihar, Andhra

Pradesh and UP. DDT residues were found in 82% of samples, with 37% exceeding tolerance limit. Maharashtra, Gujarat, AP, HP and Punjab recorded maximum DDT levels.

Organo chlorines like DDT are known to cause lymphatic cancer in rats. A study in 1993 revealed a frightening amount of DDT residues in infant milk formula bottled milk and human breast milk. High levels of residue were also found in vegetables, cereals, pulses and meat. Experts say that DDT, HCH, Aldrin, Dieldrin are proven killers. According to them, the most dangerous are Dieldrin and DDT, which have widespread effect on birds also. They belong to class of chemicals known as endocrine disrupters. The dangers of endocrine disrupters are well documented by Western researchers, the first to get affected are vultures and other birds of prey and indicated contamination in the environment. Disappearance of the American bald eagle is attributed to the effect of these chemicals.

Developed countries are now phasing out mercury. But India's consumption of mercury has doubled in the last decade – imports have increased 6 fold in last 7 years. Global use of mercury has gone down from 5,300 mt in 1990 to 2,700 in 2000. USA is the largest user of mercury at 372 mt with India at second place with 190 mt. Indian imports of organo mercury compounds like pesticides have gone up more than 1,500 times.

Smt. Sunita Narain, Director, Centre for Science and Environment (CSE) observed recently "we are rapidly becoming the dumping ground of world's mercury". Europe has decided to phase out all its chlor-alkali caustic soda plants and has 13,000 mt of mercury that it has to dispose of. In 7 years, it has sold 3,000 mt to India.

CSE has marked hotspots in India after it discovered the main user of mercury did not account for 90% of mercury they were using. Coastal areas are at maximum risk. High levels of mercury found in Mumbai, Kochi, Kolkata, etc. Mercury pollution also caused by things used everyday, like mercury cells, thermometers, pesticides, dental fillings, etc. consumption of which is increasing everyday. Consumption of button cells are up from 17 million to 91 million, mercury vapor lamps from 2,100 to 0.12 million.

Thousands of chemicals come into the Indian market without any tests for determining the toxicity. Many chemicals particularly pesticides and plasticizers are suspected endocrine disrupters.

A number of cases of severe damage to ecology and environment are the result of uncontrolled development without regard to the resultant pollution and are described in the chapter on development.

17. Sports

The best approach to develop a healthy nation is to encourage outdoor sports particularly low cost sports. Before independence, there used to be large number of open spaces in every city, town and village where football, hockey, netball, volleyball, kabbadi and host of other healthy outdoor sports. But instead of providing open spaces scattered in all parts of towns and cities in India, the authorities have been spending crores of rupees in building large sports complexes, located way outside the towns or cities, which can be used rarely.

In Mumbai, for decades, Brabourne stadium near Churchgate station, South Bombay was the venue for all international and major cricket tournaments. But about 4 decades back, the then CM got built the Wankehede stadium for cricket. Now this stadium is also in South Bombay and barely one km way from the existing Brabourne stadium. After completion of the Wankhede stadium, no more national or international cricket tournaments have been held at Brabourne stadium, though it continues to be maintained by the club owning it.

But arranging for playgrounds and maintaining open spaces is not on the priority list of any State Government or local authority. But money continues to be wasted on construction of sports complexes. At Ichalkaranji South Maharashtra, a sports complex is still incomplete after spending about Rs.3 crores over a period of 7 years.

There is tremendous interest in all types of sports/ athletics all over India but the authorities have failed in the last 50 years to encourage the sportsmen by providing them with the basic infrastructure and more importantly recognizing merit. Sports persons participate more for the love of participating and not for earning money. Cricket is the only game in India where the players officially earn lakhs of rupees. Playing the game all over the world with generous perks like stay at 5 star hotels, air travel, etc. But despite all this they are not world champions.

The Government of India, after independence has instituted a system of honoring outstanding sport person by instituting the Arjuna Award. But the selection of the awardees for these National sports awards has been politicized by the controlling authorities, the Sports Authority of India.

Three years ago, the Asian discuss throw champion, Anil Kumar had approached the court to stay the award of the year's Arjuna awards as 2 of the awardees did not have any remarkable achievements to their credit. The Delhi High Court had observed, "It is obvious the bureaucracy has taken a grip over the national awards, which should be given only to outstanding players". It was stated that the only achievement of one of the awardees was setting the second best national record in 3000 meters race in the open national athletic meet held in 1981 (i.e. more than 20 years ago). But the applicant, Anil Kumar was not given the Arjun award, despite having won the Asian discuss throw championship. Arjuna Awards lack transparency and accountability, lack of public interest and no public outrage at gross mistakes. And there is no will to change the system. But international awards are transparent and hence acclaimed. Their voting system indicates who is voting and who got how many votes. In most cases, voters are either sports writers or coaches or players themselves- all well defined electoral bodies.

Besides in sports functions (except cricket) the players are ignored and the spotlight hogged by the babus and the politicians. Just one example of such behavior of ignoring the sportspersons is given here. In Sept. 2004, National Open, an athletics championship was held at Mumbai. Surekha, 20 year old pole vaulter, improved by 0.4 cms, the National record set at 3.5 m last year. She along with the other winners had to wait for hours after the games ended, while the sports minister and the IOC head were busy giving speeches. Ultimately in the chaotic situation prevailing there, and wait for hours, the winners, about 30 in number had to be content in getting hold of their prize from one of the organizer's hand, not even from any important office bearer – let alone from the minister or the head of the IOC who was busy attending on the minister. The Vice President of Athletics Federation who was present there, reportedly non-chalantly admitted that this was a normal happening at every annual function.

The indication of the utter neglect of sports after spending hundred of crores of rupees, everything can be seen from the following:

In the Athens Olympics 2004, China ranked 2nd and got a total of 63 medals out which 32 were gold. South Korea got 30 medals including 9 gold. India ranked 65th with only 1 silver medal.

In the Sydney Games of 2000, China ranked 3rd with 59 medals including 28 gold. South Korea got nil and India ranked 70th with 1 bronze.

148 members of various sports associations, majority of them non-sportsmen went from India for the Athens Olympics, 2004, and returned with only one silver medal – but none of the office bearers of the jumbo delegation were ashamed of the performance of the Indian contingent, nor did they try to accept the blame for this sad show. Of course all this is at the taxpayers' money.

The office bearers enjoy all the perks like air travel and stay at 5 star hotels. But the real athletes do not enjoy even the minimum comforts. For instance, top athlete K Beenamol and 5 others were called to Delhi prior to departure for Athens Olympics. All 6 of them were put in a dingy room, 11' × 12' at the SAI Complex in the July sweltering heat. But the officials were put up in air conditioned rooms. Even for travel within India, national hockey teams are quite often required to travel by ordinary II class accommodation in trains.

But winning medals in international events does not help these athletes to face life cheerfully. All that they gain is momentary acclaim from the world and the personal satisfaction of having emerged victorious in the contest. The nation forgets them immediately there after. The bureaucrats have no time or the inclination to help such winners live a life of dignity.

One wonders why India the second most populous country in the world is nowhere near winning any medals in the Olympics. In the 2004 Olympics, China ranked 2nd with a tally of 63 medals including 32 gold. South Korea got 30 medals including 9 Gold. India's tally was a total of 1 silver medal and ranked 65th.

There are many factors which influence the proficiency in games. The basic ingredients are good health, fitness and athletic proficiency along with the appropriate support from the authorities and a well laid out plan. Champions cannot be created overnight. It is worthwhile looking at steps taken by some countries to produce champions.

The Soviets and the European Communist countries started competing in the Olympics from the Helsinki Games of 1952. They researched the sporting achievement of the reigning Western Champions. They studied the methods involved in the training of amateur as also professional Western athletics along with the technical and tactical skills, having made a deep study and adopted all the positive systems in their own system. Development of technical and tactical skills along with new methods of training and new scientific apparatus are needed for the development of each athletic in accordance with the skills, potentialities of each individual.

But our training systems and centers can in no way compete with the rest of the world. Even a tiny country like South Korea who had no exposure to international competition in sports can win 30 medals, including 9 gold in the Athens Olympics 2004. And South Korea is a country which came into existence barely 50 years after a bitter civil war. Germany has an Olympic training centre at Hamburg. It has equipment to churn up huge waves in the swimming pool that provide resistance training to a swimmer.

India just does not have the quantity or quality of sports persons in training at any given time. Rick Powers, a swimming coach in US, remarked during his recent visit to India that in swimming India stood no chance, as India could at the most have about 10,000 swimmers under training, which is the number of swimmers in just one town, Chicago. The total number of competitive swimmers in the US would be about 10 lac and about 5 lac in Australia. Even Indian coach S Digvikar observes that quality comes from quantity but India just does not have the infrastructure.

The poor performance in the Olympics is not the fault of the participating athlete. It is the entire system which is at fault. The system is heavily bureaucratic. The athletes are not given due importance. For instance, even at the SAI complex in Delhi, the best accommodation (A/C) will be occupied by the office bearers and those with influence leaving the real athletes to fend for themselves. The sports bodies have become fiefdoms of a group of people for decades and hence winning medals in intention events will remain a dream for Indians unless drastic changes are made in the entire system, even then results can be expected only after a decade.

But Indians love sports. Rural sports are very popular all over India but due publicity is not given to such sports and neither are they encouraged at the state level. But even in a city like Mumbai annual bullock cart race has been held since 2002 at Manori village, just off Marve (beach). The animals used are those used by the participants for their daily business and no harm is done to the animals. The race is held on the beach in the evening after the high tide recedes and is watched by about 1000 residents from the nearby villages.

But the tremendous potential in India of various skills is not being tapped properly. Schemes are started but dropped after some time due to mismanagement. For instance Bihar Government had set up a hockey centre in 1976 to train local players, as it was found that tribals of Chotanagpur plateau, particularly women had shown great ability to play hockey. It produced nearly a dozen national players but became defunct after a few years. Money meant for students never reached the students, no equipment provided. The food provided for the student sports person consisted of:

Breakfast – 2 slices of bread and a cup of tea, lunch – a bowl of rice and dal, dinner – 2 chapattis and dal. So the scheme just stopped functioning.

Facilities for healthy, low cost outdoor sports are an absolute necessity for a healthy nation. As the old proverb goes, "A healthy mind in a healthy body".

18. Public Health Care

The public health care system in India does not appear to be extending the health care which the citizens are entitled to. This sector is not considered important enough by the state as can be seen from the fact that expenditure on health care is barely 0.6% of the annual budget. Even countries like Bangladesh and China provide 1.6% and 2.0% respectively.

The authorities do not appear to realize the need for a healthy populace. Without commenting on the quality of health care provided by the state, a mere look at the expenditure on public health, even poor nations like Jordan and Belarus spend about 5% while EU countries spend about 8% of GDP.

To some extent the poor state to public health system cannot be blamed on lack of financial support. The human factor also has to be taken into account. The callousness of the hospital authorities has been indicated where even death of almost a dozen infants due to lack of oxygen is treated casually on the plea that even normally a few deaths on a particular day for whatever reason–avoidable or not is just one of the things which happen now and then all over the world. But such callousness is rarely exhibited anywhere in the world. Besides even the UNICEF has in its numerous reports indicated India for gross neglect of the health care of the infants, and put it in the same category as Eritrea and Ghana in its child development indicators.

Lip sympathy is paid by our politicians for the health of the public and particularly children but the public health system is fast crumbling and the private sector is being encouraged at a high cost to the public. One of the main reasons of the crumbling of the public health sector, is the fact that Indian politicians rush to Western countries for medical treatment and rarely go to the Government hospitals in India. If at all they avail of medical facilities in India, then it will generally be at the most expensive private hospitals.

It is worthwhile recalling that more than a century ago, the state had realized the importance of providing facilities for assisting the citizens in maintaining good health. Municipal bodies had been set up then, whose main function was to ensure the good health of the citizens. With this in view, medical facilities of the general public were set up in metros as well as some towns and cities, in the form of hospitals with the financial help from the state as well as philanthropist. Thus for instance the Sir Jamsethji Jeejibhoy group of hospitals (JJ Group of Hospitals) King Edward Memorial (KEM) Hospital, Nair Hospital, Lok Manya Tilak Hospital, Tata Memorial Hospital in Mumbai Sir, David Sassoon Hospital in Pune and a number of others all over India.

Today Mumbai has the one of the largest health care systems in the world. The Brihan Mumbai Municipal Corporation (BMC) runs 27 maternity homes, more than 170 health posts, 170 dispensaries, 16 peripheral hospitals and 5 specialized hospitals. The hospitals are run by the BMC for the urban poor who constitute more than 50% of the cities population. Funds are a serious problem. For instance the KEM hospital treats about 1.2 million out-patients in a year with a total budget of Rs. 60 crores. But the hospital makes every effort to provide quality treatment within the limited means. With the ever increasing cost of medical technologies, these hospitals are finding it difficult to provide quality treatment. They are also exploring possibilities of obtaining donations from private parties.

In 2001 BMC had allocated Rs. 548 crores for the health sector but this proved inadequate to meet the needs of the ever increasing population. One of the important factors leading to inability to provide the desired level of medical services is the fact that almost 70% of the budget provision is spent on staff salaries and other administrative expenses leaving barely 30% for the medical care as such.

More than 50 year ago, a scheme know as Employees State Insurance Schemes (ESIS) was launched as a social security cover for the workers as a joint venture with the Union, State, employers and employees contributing to a welfare fund. It covers employees earning salary below Rs. 10,000 pm. It was meant to ensure affordable health care and other cash benefits for loss in wages due to illness. On paper it caters to about 50 lac workers in Maharashtra alone which includes about 25 lac in Mumbai, which number has since reduced with the closure of many large industries in Mumbai.

The ESIS has a total of 14,000 doctors, 26,000 beds and about 45,000 paramedics. But with all this, the Union Labor Minister had admitted during the Golden Jubilee Celebration that the services were not up to the expectations of the workers. Normally one would expect workers to flock to such hospitals meant exclusively for them with services available free. But the existing hospitals present a deserted look. The workers prefer to go to private doctors though they are expensive. One of the reasons being the impracticable nature of procedures adopted in treating patients. For instance, according to workers, even the procedure for having ones blood pressure taken is very time consuming. For a routine blood pressure check, the patient has to get a form from a doctor on the ESIS panel for examination, from there the report will be sent to the hospital. After this the patient will be treated. The entire process may take weeks or months.

The fault lies in the system according to senior doctors and officials working with ESIS. The State Government has to spend on these hospitals and its services until the end of the financial year. 7/8 of the amount spent is reimbursed by ESIC. So the State Government thinks twice before spending anything. Public health comes under the State Government, so the requirements of the hospitals are routed through the state to the ESIC at Delhi, as the funding is done by ESIC.

But the functioning of the entire schemes need to be looked into, as there is tremendous wastage of funds, without any benefit to the workers. For instance, 3 hospitals constructed by ESIS funds at Bibwewadi, Chinchwad and Kolhapur have not been commissioned by the State Government. For the last 5 years 100 bed hospital built at Parel, Mumbai exclusively to cater to workers covered under ESIS is lying practically defunct as the State Government. has refused to fund health care activities. This hospital now provides employment to administrative staff.

Of course the ESIS is meant for the worker in the organized sector who are not availing the facilities as they were expected to. This continues to leave the workers in the unorganized sector, constituting about 90% of the workers, without any facilities for them. The ESIS was launched over 50 years ago with very laudable aims but over the years it has failed in its objective of providing medical care and particularly hospitalization at a nominal cost to the industrial worker. Apart from huge investment in infrastructure like hospitals being practically of little use, a large amount running to crores of rupees is spent on the maintenance and administration charges without any commensurate benefit to the workers. The Union Government is now reported to be considering plans to utilize the entire existing infrastructure profitably for the benefit of the workers particularly in the unorganized sectors.

As has been seen earlier, the standard of public health is poor in India. There are many reasons for this. An attempt has been made to briefly indicate the reasons for the same. But one of the most important factors is the lack of proper hygiene and sanitation particularly in the rural areas. It is worthwhile citing extracts from the address of President APJ Abdul Kalam at the presentation of Nirmal Gram Puraskars in New Delhi in March 2005. "... As per the 2001 census, there are nearly 2000 million dwelling units in the country of which nearly 140 million are in rural areas. Sanitation facilities are available in only about 40 million dwelling units. The lack of sanitation facilities is the greatest health hazard for our rural population. Waterborne diseases, hepatitis, leprosy, TB, etc. all are attributed to non availability of proper sanitation facilities. Hence to improve the health condition of our rural population, it is essential to hasten up the process of providing sanitation facilities to all dwelling units, schools, hospitals and community halls in rural areas. In addition there should also be a drive to convert waste to wealth." He also cited examples of successful self help by villagers.

In Cuddalore district, TN, he found that everyone of the 1,125 dwelling units in the panchayat had sanitary facilities. He also found it very interesting to find that village women had acquired masonry and plumbing skills, they not only constructed toilets in the panchayat, but also provided their skills in the neighboring villages. This provided employment opportunities for the women but resulted in the panchayat area being clean and free from diseases.

The President also gave another example of another panchayat in Vellore district, he came across. The local panchayat with the help of NGO converted the village into a clean model village. The village with 2,400 families generates about 48 mt of garbage p.a. which is converted into manure and recyclable waste generating over Rs. 3 lac in revenue p.a. The scheme provides employment to about 36 members who are paid employees of the panchayat. The salaries of these employees are covered by the sale proceeds of the manure and recyclable waste.

Accumulation of municipal solid waste in urban and rural areas is creating serious problems. Two entrepreneurs in AP have succeeded in refining of processing of waste and converting into energy. They have established two independent plants in Hyderabad and Vijaywada generating about 6 mega watts of electricity which is fed into the state grid.

So far the most vital goals of proper sanitation have remained exclusive. With the consequent ill effect on the health of the nation. Now it is being realized that hygiene and sanitation need to be recognized as behavioral issues. In many projects it has been noticed that toilet facilities remain unutilized in the absence of motivation to utilize it and absence user awareness.

It is heartening to find that the importance of sanitation is being realized in the villages for maintaining good health. That the importance is percolating all over India can be seen from a few examples from Maharashtra.

In 1997, Maharashtra Government seriously looked at the issue of sanitation with particular reference to the rural sector. It found that only 6% of villagers had access to toilets. It spent Rs. 450 crores in the next 4 years for building toilets, but found that barely 40% were used as toilets, the rest as extra rooms. It learnt an important lesson, an expensive one no doubt, that village sanitation is not merely constructing toilet but about personal hygiene, protecting water from contamination, waste management, etc. The question of motivating 42,000 villages spread over 3 lacs sq. miles was a perplexing and daunting one.

Government then launched an innovative campaign tapping into the emotional appeal of two Maharashtra icons – sant Gadge Baba and Sant Tukdoji Maharaj. Every village was told to devote the next forthnight to sanitation related activities. They were also told they would be tested, and 100 mark question paper was circulated well in advance, containing questions like habits of children including nail cutting, unconventional sources of energy, ban on use of plastics, etc.

The people exhibited enthusiasm. A team of judges paid visits and short listed 3 cleanest villages in each of the 340 talukas in the state. Next the top three were identified in each of the 33 districts, from where the 6 finalists emerged. Substantial prizes were given at each level and the statewide winning village was given Rs. 25 lac. The Government spends about Rs. 6 crores in these contests, the villagers themselves, as per World Bank, contribute cash and labor worth Rs. 200 crores and it is expected to go up every year. Competition is increasing even to score half a point extra.

Nidhal, Satara district, one of last years winner built itself an underground drainage system that would have cost the Government Rs. 1 crore. Another village conducted spate of competitions for everything that moved – from the cleanest cat to the smartest rooster. It also decided to paint their village pink, inspired by Jaipur. Now villagers and officials from Andhra Pradesh, Maharashtra, and Karnataka come to the villages to visit and learn from them. But 12,000 villages which got less than 25% points were declared dirty villages. Even families from other villages do not want to give their daughters to the dirty villages.

Kajala, district Osmanabad, is another example where even children actively participate in keeping their village clean. Every evening a bunch of children gather in the village square and ask "Do you have ideas for keeping the village clean". They also discuss about planting trees and vaccinating dogs. The awareness about cleanliness has percolated deep into the minds of the children. They automatically pick any litter on the road and put it in dustbin, gutka eating and drinking liquor is not allowed. Everyone of the 3,000 residents of Kajala is proud of their suddenly famous village. The visitors are shown solar powered lights, prettily painted houses, dustbin at convenient places, loudspeakers at every corner so that villagers can listen to panchayat and gram sabha proceedings, a major showpiece of democracy in action.

The villagers contributed Rs. 100 in cash and voluntary labor. After working in the fields they work for the village till about 10 pm. They also constructed a 2 km long pucca gutter all this the more remarkable as the village falls under constant shadow of drought, and half the villagers fall below the poverty line.

When the campaign was launched in 2000, only 6% of the more than 722 villages in Osmanabad district participated in the year. But inspired by the progress of village Kadewa almost 50% of the villages participated in the subsequent year. The villagers of Kajala were impressed by what they saw; gutka and liquor shops were closed, where they used to spend thousands of rupees, and women had taken the lead. As it bagged prizes at taluka and district levels, it adopted roof water harvesting schemes and are busy recharging wells. They also made a beginning to demolish caste barriers by constructing common crematorium.

Another success story comes from Unkahulp, district Sangli, and population 14,000. It was divided along every conceivable line, caste, religion and politics. Some move around in the latest Ford Icon cars, with about 600 families below the poverty line. Village sarpanch was not surprised when very few turned up on the first day of the campaign. But the sarpanch took the lead by picking up a broom and along with about 20 women started sweeping the roads and cleaning the gutters. Slowly women joined up. But the sarpanch realized the village was too large and diverse to be treated as one unit. So he announced cleanliness competition between various basties and gullies. Each gully has its own youth club who used to compete for the best Ganesh Mandal but now they compete for the cleanest gully. Victory at taluka level and perceptible fall in illness spurred the women for further action. Derelict public loos were pulled down and replaced with neat units, complete with running water, electricity and doors which could be closed. Acres of panchayat land which were used as open air public toilet and dumping grounds were transformed into vegetable patches. The lots were irrigated with gutter water channelised through sedimentation pits. Thus they converted waste into wealth.

To prevent complacency, it came up with another novel idea. Near every garden and newly tidied street, it displays pictures of the past showing the filth, with the remark below it "sarpanch, if you forget the past, you repeat it". But more remarkable than the physical appearance of the village and villagers, it is the change in social attitudes. The women, who would scarcely leave their house, now spend every evening in the gram panchayat office. The concept of family planning is also taking root. Even couples with only one daughter are agreeing to family planning.

Fulsare, Nandurbar district, Maharashtra, population 1,000 without a single police case for over 25 years. Though alcohol plays an important part in adivasi customs, yet it is alcohol free. Every household has its own toilet and uses it. They are mostly poor farmers and laborers but keep their village beautifully clean. It has its own water conservation techniques and herbal plantations.

Talwade, Sindhudurg district, Maharashtra a picturesque village in Sindhudurg district. There is an active women's group involved in profitable ventures like papad making and cucumber cultivation. They are also making brave attempts at bolster primary education system in their village. They also have an innovative water distribution system generating Rs. 2 lacs p.a.

The Sarpanch of Kajala attribute the success to the fact the "the Government did not thrust things upon us, but let us take the initiative we are seeing the beginning of a social revolution". The BDO of Unkahulp believes, it succeeded because there was no real money involved or any vested interest." But credit must also be given to Mr. Thakre, deputy secretary water and sanitation department for extending necessary assistance to all and having a positive approach he observed that "Winners are expected to help and inspire others to serve as a living example of health, hygiene and positive change".

The concerned villagers have realized the importance of hygiene and proper sanitation and the vital role played by these factors in the dramatic improvement in the health of residents. They have also seen the cumulative effect on the well being of all the residents. What is remarkable is the fact that this realization has dawned on them not by compulsion or force by outsiders, but through their own efforts with the help and guidance of qualified people who selflessly devote their time and energy for the betterment of the villagers and thus the nation.

The villagers have also understood, that its their right to good health and better quality of life through safe and adequate supply of water and proper sanitation without depending upon the Government but relying on self help.

Family Planning

India's population has increased at a very fast rate and now is about 2 billion. About 30 years ago, a campaign to cut down the birth rate by using incentives and in some cases even by force. Misinformation was tried out but this ended in failure and subsequently there has been a slackening in the nation wide program of family planning. From some sections of the populace there has been opposition to family planning on religious grounds. But once the women particularly, realize the benefits of family planning, it gathers momentum as has been seen even in progressive villages where women have voluntarily taken to family planning without any coercion. Unfortunately, in India the debate over family planning tends to take a communalistic hue, with a section of people attributing the sharp increase in population on the lack of birth control among Muslims. But to make matters whose, even a section of the Muslim community strongly feels that birth control goes against their religion.

A glance at the birth control practices in some of the Islamic countries gives a very illuminating insight.

In Iran, the Shah was overthrown in 1979 and the fundamentalists who came to power did away with earlier family planning programs and encouraged pro-child bearing policies. Within a decade the population rate increased by almost 40%. But the leaders realized their mistake and were bold enough to reverse their policies. They encouraged modern methods of contraception including pills, condoms and IUDs. While Iran continues to be ruled by Islamic fundamentalists, it has one of the most successful family planning programs in the world.

Tunisia gained independence from France in 1956. It is almost wholly an Islamic country. In 1956, their far sighted leader Habib Bourguiba banned polygamy by law, pointing out that the holy Quran permitted polygamy only on condition that all wives were treated equally. This is logically impossible and hence not permissible. It has a successful family planning program. This has been an important factor in empowering Tunisian women like no other women in the developing world. A high percentage of women are elected to parliament.

In Morocco, another country with almost wholly Islamic population, the annual population rate growth has come down from almost 3% to 1.6% during the last decade. The average number of children has also come down to less than 3. More than 30 Moroccan women are member of the Moroccan legislature. Beating a woman is a criminal offence in that country.

Indonesia, a country with the largest Muslim population of more than 200 million, has a very successful population control program. No coercion was used. It was the result of the

Government, convincing the religious leaders (Ulemas) of Indonesia that family planning and control were in the national interest. In 1983, the local Ulemas passed a resolution that "Islamic teachings justify family planning for the betterment of health conditions of mother and child. To make the child healthy, intelligent and devout." Passages from the holy Quran were included in the resolution of the Ulema to show that both the Quran and the Prophet justified family planning. Even the sterilization methods of male vasectomy and female tubectomy along with implants are used there. The religious leaders promote birth control.

The effect of successful implementation of birth control and family planning measures can be seen from the following figures. The population rate growth in Indonesia in 1960 was far in excess of that of India, the standard of living was far lower than that of India. Today the per capita income of India is lower than that of Indonesia while the population rate growth of India is about 2% as against 1.4% in Indonesia.

Even other Islamic countries like Bangladesh, Turkey and Egypt practice birth controls and family planning and they have been successful in controlling the growth in population. And all this without coercion; but the result of the Government to convince the Ulemas and the people, the need to control population for a healthy family and hence a healthy nation.

Transport and Communication

23

We have seen in earlier chapters that transport and communication (TC) system was quite adequate to meet the requirements in the pre-independence era till 1947. It is time to look at the extent to which the TC sector has been able to cope with the additional and varied requirements during the last fifty years since independence.

A. Railways

Indian Railways (IR) system is more than 150 years old. The earliest train was started even before 1857 in the days of the East India Company. An idea of the vastness of the rail network in India can be had from the following:

(i) More than 62,000 km of track network — one of the largest in Asia.

(ii) Carries more than 1.2 million passengers daily.

(iii) Carries over 1.0 million tones of revenue earning freight daily.

(iv) Is the largest single employer in the country with staff strength of over 1.6 million.

(v) Wage bill and miscellaneous expenses on staff amount to Rs.10,000 crores per annum.

The railway network in the pre-independence era was built by private joint stock companies and was based on techno commercial viability, but also took into account the strategic requirements of the Government. The network covered not only British India, but also some of the Princely Indian states. There were a number of joint stock companies which were nationalized after independence and formed one organization known as Indian Railways (IR).

Even after independence, the IR used to run profitably and contributed by way of dividend to the general revenues of the Government of India. But for the last few decades, internal resources are only 23% of its requirements. Market borrowings are now in excess of 30% with increased dependence every year on capital transfer from general exchequer.

But railways continue to function as an independent ministry. But such independence has not resulted in making the IR an efficient organization. The entire operations of IR have been politicized. Every incumbent minister for the last few decades considers his accountability only to his perceived political constituencies and not to the safety of passengers/property or running the railways in the interest of the nation.

New lines have been announced by every incoming Railway Minister for years without any techno-economic survey. But such projects are never completed as individual Railway Minister demits office at short intervals — and the new Minister has his own ideas and has no interest in implementing projects initiated by his predecessor. Projects initiated in 1970, i.e. over 30 years ago, with nominal initial investment continue to languish in an incomplete stage.

For almost last three decades, the railways have proved to be the least safe mode of travel in India, notwithstanding its safety record for over a century in the pre-independence era. The rail network extending over 62,000 km covers 7,000 stations but it is most ill-equipped in terms of telecom and signaling systems. Even track circuiting system, a vital instrument for monitoring tracks on busy routes, is said to function properly on barely 3,000 stations. But every Railway Minister has been introducing more super fast trains without the slightest consideration for the safety of the passengers. The number of accidents and deaths keep on increasing alarmingly. From 1986 to 2000, the IR set up a record of approximately 400 accidents on the average every year, resulting in more than 6,000 deaths and maiming thousands of passengers. But such accidents and tragic loss of lives has not forced any Railway Minister to give priority to ensuring safety of passengers. Some of the major rail disasters during the period 1989 to 2002 are given below:

Feb 1989	near Lalitpur, CR	over 69 dead	derailments
April 1990	near Patna, Bihar	over 70 charred to death	
June 1990	near Golluguda, AP	over 36 dead	collision
June 1990	near Manjra, Bihar	over 60 dead	collision
Nov 1990	near Sakaldih, Bihar	over 50 dead	derailment
Sep 1992	near Raigarh, MP	over 41 dead	collision
June 1993	near Darbhanga, Bihar	over 60 dead	collision
Sep 1993	near Chadra, Raj	over 71 dead	collision
June 1995	near Kabibastan, WB	over 57 dead	collision
Aug 1995	near Ferozabad, UP	over 500 dead	collision
April 1996	near Gorakhpur, UP	over 60 dead	collision
Sep 1997	near Korba, MP	over 100 dead	express falls from bridge
Nov 1998	near Khanna, Punjab	over 200 dead	collision
Aug 1999	near Ghaisal, WB	over 250 dead	collision
June 2001	near Kozikode, Kerala	over 62 dead	train falls from bridge
Sep 2002	near Rafigunj, Bihar	over 120 dead	train falls from bridge

As per official statistics two thirds of the accidents are due to human errors. Official expert group in Railway Ministry estimate railways need minimum of Rs. 130,000 crores for low growth scenario entailing network expansion, rolling stock, safety requirements, line augmentation, technological upgradation, etc. High rate of growth scenario providing modernization in terms of speed and quality, organizational restructuring, etc. would need about Rs. 200,000 crores.The dismal financial performance over last few years, causes serious concern particularly when additional resources are needed.

But despite increasing number of accidents and needless loss of lives and injury to passengers, no priority has been accorded to ensuring safety of passengers over the last few decades. Instead of improving safety measures, one Minister ordered that all existing rail lines should be of one gauge only viz. broad gauge. He also bought an aeroplane for the railways on the plea that the minister could rush fast to the site of rail accidents. Thus he diverted all resources for such projects at the cost of all other requirements including safety requirements.

No minister appears to be concerned with the new challenges faced on account of alternate means of transport like road and air. The rail finances continue to deteriorate. The lack of concern for the safety of the rail passengers has been pointed out by the Justice Garg commission report on 1998 Khanna rail tragedy killing over 200 people and maiming hundreds of others. Important points from the report are given below:

"I would hold the Directorate of Track Procurement to be primarily responsible for not ensuring production of quality rails, for granting relaxation in production of quality rail steels and rails and for not making available USFD machine for a long time to staff."

Report details how Railway Board casually continued to give relaxation on quality specification set by itself- " putting on tracks such substandard or defective rails would endanger safety of traveling public". R.K. Singh who ordered purchase of such tracks later superceded dozens of other officers to become the Chairman of the Railway Board in 2003. Copies of letters signed by Singh granting relaxation to public sector Bhilai Steel Plant annexed to report. Railway tried to pinpoint reasons for increasing accidents due to cracks in rails and decided in 1996 that permissible limits of hydrogen content in steel rails be brought down to 3 ppml from 6 ppml.

By 1997, issue of bad rails had become a matter of great concern to IR. The purchase of rails having high hydrogen content was stopped only after the Khanna tragedy of 1998. But there are other reasons for frequent accidents, some of them are:

(i) Almost 15,000 km of track needs renewal.

(ii) Track maintenance system using antiquated crowbars, shovels instead of welded track, concrete sleepers, and laser based track recording cars used in all developed countries.

(iii) Low quality of materials – average life span of rail track in India said to be 15 years against 45 years in other countries.

(iv) No premium on quality.

(v) Inspection procedures faulty.

(vi) Most of staff manning safety positions are said to be incapable of reading rules in safety manuals as literacy is hardly a criterion for employment at lower levels.

(vii) Over 50,000 bridges said to be over 100 years old-rule of thumb of structural engineers that trains should not run across bridges over 100 years old.

More accidents like the one at Kozikode in June 2001, where the train fell into the river on account of the collapse of the bridge are likely.

The history of the bridge is interesting. It was meant to be a temporary one built on a screw pile foundation, which cannot withstand running of heavy or fast trains for long. The British had built a number of bridges during 1880-90 on screw pile foundation as they could reportedly be built within about seven days. The country was affected by a severe drought and the British needed some kind of rail network urgently to expedite relief operations. The Bridge rehabilitation committee of 1989 had listed about 25 bridges built on screw pile foundation and had strongly recommended that they be eliminated on priority basis within 4 years. But even after 15 years of these recommendations such bridges continue to be used.

Numerous committees have been set up in the past after every accident but their reports continue to gather dust. After the Ferozabad tragedy of August 1995 killing more than 500 passengers, the Kaw committee had, *inter alia*, recommended:

(i) Making locomotive and station staff more accountable. Studies by railway show that about 70 % of all rail accidents are caused by inattentive staff like stationmaster, guard and callous running staff.

(ii) More funds need to be allocated for development. Barely 2% of development funds are spent by railways on safety, whereas USA and Japan spend at least 20%.

But scarce funds continue to be wasted on projects without any techno economic feasibility study. For instance, one Railway Minister had insisted on importing more than 30 ABB locomotives for speeding up freight and passenger traffic and had signed a transfer of technology of the new 6000 HP locomotives over a period of 10 years. The Parliamentary standing committee headed by Shri Somnath Chatterji felt that fixing 10 year period for transfer of technology was not based on any in-depth study particularly when technology was rapidly changing. It went on to state "It is incomprehensible to the committee as to how it would be possible for the railways to move increased level of freight as well as passenger traffic with the present pace of electrification and with reduced projection for locomotives. The committee therefore, reiterated their earlier recommendations that the railways should arrange their strategies taking into account the present pace of electrification and the resources available at their disposal for procurement of rolling stock, etc."

A study conducted by the railways showed that incompetence and inefficiency on the part of the railway staff accounted for almost 600 accidents out of 800 that occurred in 1994-95. Yet the IR has done practically nothing to motivate its staff and increase efficiency. But the extent of indiscipline can be seen from the one incident given below.

It is reported that in Aug 1996, a railway porter, Solanki, had been deputed as Guard on the Super fast Rajdhani Express to Delhi by the allocation staff at Mumbai Central instead of a qualified Guard as the Guard who was on duty "did not feel like doing his duty because the train was rescheduled from 16.55 hrs to 21.55 hrs. It is also reported that the Divisional Safety Officer (DSO) had warned the porter for committing similar offence the previous month and that the DSO had issued caution notices to all running staff on all Mail/Express trains about Solanki's practice and had asked them to disallow it.

Two deputy station masters posted at Mumbai Central had been chargesheeted under SF 5, said to be for most serious offences. It is reported that in earlier cases the station master had been held responsible for any mistake or offence by any employee under his control. But in this case neither the station master nor the porter has been chargesheeted. Strangely no action has been taken against the porter who reportedly made it a practice to work as a guard.

Recently, in March 2005, the railway board has decreed that no gazetted railway officer in the country may be arrested or detained by the Railway Protection Force (RPF) without the permission of the divisional railway manager and the General Manager. This is a fall out of the arrest of two booking clerks and two others for encashing forged tickets. The booking staff implicated Senior Divisional Commercial Manager (SDCM), the Divisional Commercial Manager (DCM) and Divisional Commercial Inspector (DCI). In January 2005, the DCM and DCI were arrested, followed by the arrest of SDCM in Feb. 2005. This circular appears to be issued immediately after the rejection by a Vadodra sessions court of the bail application made by SDCM.

The RPF is reported to be upset by this sudden circular as they feel it is arbitrary and contrary to law. The duties of RPF were recently broadened in July 2004 to include law and order functions related to minor railway offences. However, they claim that this scam involves the faking of cancelled tickets and appropriation of refunds and falls within their jurisdiction under the Railway Property (Unlawful Possession) Act 1966. Since then some officers of RPF including investigating officers have been transferred.

The action of the Railway Board in putting restrictions on the arrest or detention by the RPF of any gazetted railway officer is bound to adversely affect the discipline in the IR and functioning of RPF.

The functioning of short distance local trains (suburban trains) in Mumbai has come under grave threat from the thousands of encroachers who have built pucca structures on railway land abutting the rail track and also between two sets of tracks. Children play and men, women sit and chat while local and other trains pass by. The presence of thousands of encroachers has resulted in the slowing down of the trains to prevent mishaps. Consequently this result in cutting down the number of trips a rake can make and the number passengers carried. Besides, the train drivers are under constant tension of having to be constantly on high alert for children are playing on the tracks and people carrying on normal life on railway tracks. The situation is so alarming that the Commissioner of Railway Safety (CRS) has declared in a letter to the Maharashtra Government that the Sewri-Mahim chord of the Harbor Line was unsafe, adding that the unauthorized hutments along the tracks posed grave threat to the rail commuters. He had called for the Harbor line services to be shut down to avoid any security problems in the future. The letter also gives Central Railway (CR) legal sanction to shutdown the service at any time. " Due to the impunity of encroachments along the Mahim chord, which have already assumed menacing proportions, the CR may approach the Railway Board to permit the withdrawal of services between Wadala and Mahim by invoking section 25 of the Railway Act."

The Railways have stated that it has no policy for rehabilitation of unauthorized occupants keeping in mind the interest of over 6 million daily commuters. The Mumbai High Court has stated that there is no need to have a Resettlement and Rehabilitation (RR) policy to clear hutments in the safety zone. But so far no attempt has been made to remove the unauthorized occupants under political pressure and millions of commuters, men, women and children continue to suffer.

Having seen the abysmal performance of IR and increasing number of accidents, it is worthwhile having a glimpse at a few performance indicators of some countries.

A comparison with China with reference to the progress since 1950 is instructive:

	Year	Indian Railway	Chinese Railway
Rail track -	1950	54,000 km	22,000 km
Rail track -	2003	63,000 km	73,000 km
Passengers- billions	1950	63	21
Passengers- billions	2003	515	479
Freight- bn tonnes	1950	44	39
Freight- bn tonnes	2003	356	1724

China has now introduced market principles in running its railways. Non-core activities have been divested. New technologies are being inducted. In 1986-92, Chinese Railway (CR) made profit on transport but started losing in 1993. Former Prime Minister proposed separation of Government from passenger and freight enterprises, reduction of staff, increased efficiency. This converted loss into profit between 1998-2001. China started reforms immediately by forming 5 major autonomous corporations for: (i) rolling stock, (ii) railway construction, (iii) goods and materials, (iv) civil engineering and (v) signaling and telecommunications.

Number of passenger and freight transport companies started to operate on competitive basis. Chinese Railway welcomes foreign capital and joint ventures process of rationalization started with urgency. 40 stations and 18 power supply depots were closed by 1998. It has also decided that railway workforce not to exceed the 1991 figure of 23.4 million.

Chinese Railway expanded fast. In the 9th Plan (1996-2000) it added 5,600 km of new rail lines. In the 10th plan (2001-05) it envisages investment of $ 42 billion on rail modernization and construction, tracks for high speed trains being re-laid, bridges being strengthened, level crossings being replaced by over bridges, curves/gradients being straightened/flattened. Plans drawn up to accelerate express trains on 3 major North/South lines- TGV (levitation) will connect Beijing/Shanghai; Beijing/Guangzhou will have another 350 kph service.

Chinese Railway envisages vast rail network between 30 major cities for bulk and containerized traffic. In contrast, the performance of Indian railways continues to be dismal without any apparent planning to meet not only the emerging challenges but even to provide safe transport to the passengers.

A few instances of progress made by some countries in the 2 years since 2000 are given here:

	Miles	Stops
Bangkok	23	24
Manila	17	10
Teheran	41	10
Shanghai	17	12
Guangzhou	18	16
Inchon (Korea)	22	22

Even USA is now going in for building more metro rail links due to ever increasing automobile traffic resulting in congested roads and increased pollution. Boston, Chicago, New York and Washington DC already have metros. But now Denver, Phoenix, Seattle and Salt Lake City are also going in for metro rail.

Las Vegas (USA) is probably the most popular tourist destination in the world attracting more than 35 million tourists each year. (Incidentally, India attracts about 2 million tourists) and the population has more than doubled in the period 1990-2000. The city leaders are worried over the increasing traffic congestion, driving away tourists. So a project for building a 14 mile long metro rail is under way. The project is estimated to cost $ 650 million and to be built within a year. It will be funded entirely with private money raised through tax free bonds.

So, while the rest of the world is trying to improve its existing first class rail network, in India working and planning of the entire IR depends on the ideas of the incumbent Railway Minister without being hampered by techno-economic feasibility studies or even considering the safety of the rail passengers.

B. Aviation

The aviation industry had its beginning in Europe and USA in the 1920s. But India did not lag behind, thanks to the pioneering spirit and vision of the late JRD Tata who piloted the maiden flight in India between Bombay and Karachi in 1932, i.e. 15 years before independence. This was just 5 years after Lindberg's historic transatlantic flight in 1927. After independence Tata started an international airline known as Air India International (AII) whose punctuality was praised even by Westerners who value punctuality. In the meantime after 1947, a number of private operators had been licensed to fly within the country. But by late 1950s, all these private internal as also AII had been nationalized resulting in Air India (AI) to fly internationally and Indian Airlines (IA) to fly within the country.

But over the years, AI has drastically reduced its flights to many international destinations and also surrendered its flying rights. Despite reduction/stoppage of flights to numerous destinations, it continues to maintain offices all over the world including, reportedly, 25 in Europe alone. During the past three decades, AI have dropped destinations like Cairo, Geneva, Rome, Sydney, Amesterdam, etc. though it has about 70 air bilateral agreements lying unused. But foreign airlines like Lufthansa, BA, etc. have gained new points in India like Kochi, Bangalore, and Kolkata, etc. However, I A which was meant as a carrier over domestic routes has flights to many foreign destinations. Today, a number of domestic private carriers have been recently licensed to fly not only within India, but also internationally.

But the performance of AI over the last few decades has been unsatisfactory. It is reported to have accumulated losses of over Rs 1200 crores during 1996-97 to 2000-01. Some of the reasons are indicated below. Even now it is said to have rights to fly to about 100 destinations – but it flies to barely 20. Another 20 routes are being served through code sharing or joint operations. This means a foreign airline flies on AI quota and shares revenues.

Some of the important comparative data for a few international airlines is given below:

Airline	Number of Aircraft	Average Age in Year's	Utilization Hours/Day	Staff per Aircraft
Air France	209	9.0	12.5	277
British Airways	282	10.1	13.3	227
Cathay Pacific	62	6.2	11.4	170
Emirates	32	4.9	-	176
Lufthansa	289	6.7	12.3	185
Japan Airlines	136	10.0	11.4	146
Malaysian	93	4.1	9.3	170
Singapore	94	5.0	10.0	341
Air India	23	14.1	8.5	750

It can be seen that AI:

(i) Is the smallest in fleet size.

(ii) Has the oldest fleet, average age being 14 years.

(iii) Has the least average utilization of fleet at 8.5 hrs.

(iv) Has an unusually large staff strength of 750 per plane.

AI is supposed to be an autonomous corporation unlike Indian Railways which is part of the Central Government. It's very autonomy should have resulted in continuing it's growth and profitability after it's nationalization in 1950s. The Indian Railways are not autonomous and are a part of the Government but the Railway Minister exercises practically unfettered powers on all matters, whether it concerns long term investments of thousands of crores of rupees in purchase of dozens of locomotives at a time of untried technology or introducing new lines or converting all rail lines to broad gauge without any techno-economic feasibility studies.

But for some reason AI has been unable to upgrade its ageing fleet. For a long established international airline to have barely two dozen aircraft is a reflection on the unsatisfactory state of affairs. Even this fleet is over aged with average age of 14 years and some even 20 years old, leading to mounting repairs and maintenance charges, which in turn affect adversely the operational performance and ultimately its profitability and safety. But even the small fleet is not utilized profitably. According to aviation experts, large aircraft like JUMBO 747 (with passenger capacity of about 400) need to be used upto 10 hours on any route to optimize performance. But most AI flights to Gulf or East Asian destinations are only of about 4 hours and hence the average utilization is 8.5 hrs which is below the optimal usage and far less than the other airlines mentioned above.

While the fleet strength and average utilization is the smallest, the staff strength per aircraft at 750 is extremely high. It means that staff strength is far in excess of that warranted by the fleet strength. Perhaps an increase in the fleet without increase in staff strength could improve the ratio. But the ever increasing wage bill without corresponding increase in revenues is also a cause for concern. The annual wage bill has risen from Rs 289 crores in 1992-93 to Rs 762 crores in 1999-2000 and is still rising. Staff costs account for about 25% of AI's total expenditure.

But Human Resources Management (HRM) seems to be in need of immediate attention. It has reportedly only 8 assistant managers against 90 sanctioned posts in India and abroad. It is also reported that it has only one security officer to cover 5 stations in USA including New York, Newark, Chicago and Los Angeles. Senior personnel were compelled to approach the court for filling up more than 125 higher and middle management posts, though interviews and group discussions had been conducted more than 2 years ago in 2000. AI flies over 200 untrained crew without a single day training on 400 seater Jumbo 747 which has 12 doors and each exit has to be manned in an emergency. Senior flight crew claimed having undergone 6 months training in safety and charged management of cutting costs in flying untrained staff which was contrary to Aircraft Act, AI's own guidelines and International convention. However, the Supreme Court has permitted it on certain conditions.

It is reported that some of the staff at times indulge in restrictive trade practices. But only one example of an extremely glaring restrictive trade practice is given here. The cabin crew insisted on flying back to base only by the particular type of aircraft by which they had flown out, e.g. if the cabin crew flew on duty to Hong Kong on Jumbo 747, they spent, at times as long as one week at Hong Kong(without any duties) till they could return by another Jumbo 747. Besides, it had to confirm to their flight and duty time limitations. This is reported to have cost AI about Rs. 15 crores additional every year.

Recently at New York, USA, itself in May 2005, the toilets stopped functioning in a fully loaded Jumbo 747 on New York-Paris- Mumbai flight. Passengers were not allowed to deplane at Paris during the 2 hour halt at Paris. The toilets were not repaired at Paris as it is reported that: (i) engineers did not have spares and (ii) their aircraft was required at Mumbai. The Public Relations Director clarified that five toilets could not be used from New York. Later on five more toilets could not be used as they were overused. Passengers in Economy also were allowed to use two toilets each in First and Executive class, resulting in inconveniencing high paying First and Executive class passengers.

But recently in May 2005, the starting of the Mumbai-Frankfurt-Los Angeles was delayed at Mumbai by about half an hour as the Executive class toilets were stinking—and this was the sate of affairs at the start of the flight from Mumbai, the Head quarters of AI. Apparently even the cleanliness of toilets is not checked at the starting point. These few illustrative cases indicate the lack of attention to customer services. While the Singapore Airlines normally is rated annually the best airline every year, it is difficult to imagine AI anywhere near the top.

In 1992, IA was permitted to fly to Gulf destinations which were the most profitable destination for AI. The idea was for AI and IA to capture the maximum share of the large and profitable Gulf traffic. But instead of complementing each other on this route, the two Indian carriers AI and IA, started competing with each other, thus adversely affecting AI's profitability.

AI came to the conclusion that its routes to Europe/Far-East were not profitable and hence cut down its flights to these destinations. But these routes were inherently profitable, as other airlines like Lufthansa, BA, etc. increased frequency of India/Europe/Far-East to daily ones and keep on increasing frequency of flights from India. But by withdrawing from these routes, AI has put itself in an awkward spot, as attracting passengers back is a difficult task. But now that AI is likely to sign an agreement soon with Boeing for 50 new planes, it will have to aggressively market itself and increase its revenues manifold, just to stay in the race. But despite the deal between AI and Boeing having been practically signed for 50 Boeing planes, the implementation is being inordinately delayed. Any further delay in procuring new aircraft by AI will have extremely serious consequences on the operations of the nation's international flag carrier.

But such delays are hampering the operations of IA also. Three years ago the Board of IA had cleared the proposal to purchase 43 Airbus aircraft. It had also entered into an agreement with International Aviation Corporation, London (IAC) for training its pilots on the new Airbus to be acquired. The contract included sending 66 pilots for training, out of which only 10 pilots have been sent so far by IA. Now IAC has moved the High Court in London seeking damages of Pounds 0.5 million for breach of contract in failing to send pilots for training. Though the Board of Indian Airlines had approved the contract 3 years ago, the Government of India has not yet given the final clearance. The delay in clearance may also result in IA having to suffer from delays in delivery by Airbus Industries. This inordinately long delay by the Government of India in clearing the proposal for acquiring badly needed new additional aircraft will adversely affect the working of IA – more so when private Indian carriers have also been licensed to operate within the country and also internationally.

Successful airliners always ensure having a young fleet with no aircraft aged over 10 years. Acquiring aircraft, particularly long haul aircraft for international routes is a highly complex and long drawn out process. It is, therefore, all the more necessary for the Government of India to lay down for Air India and Indian Airlines clear cut guidelines for acquiring aircraft keeping in view that both are autonomous corporations and national flag carriers.

(a) Airports

After the hijacking of the Indian Airlines aircraft to Kandahar, a high powered official committee was set up under Justice RC Jain to study the management and security of airports in the country. It submitted its report to the Union Civil Aviation Ministry in December 2000. The highlights of the report are:

(i) Airports suffer from outdated technology and lack adequate security equipment.

(ii) At least 33 airports in the country lack baggage X-ray machines, resulting in baggage not being screened.

(iii) Existing equipment not being maintained properly.

(iv) Staff lack professional training.

(v) Airport security divided among 4 agencies- state police, airport security unit, airport watch and ward staff and airlines security—leading to overlapping of functions and lack of clarity.

(vi) Airport Authority of India (AAI) is not functioning as a cohesive unit. It suffers from lack of realistic long-term planning, an indifferent project management, an inefficient maintenance regime and a dysfunctional delegation of administrative technical and financial powers.

(vii) Airports in the country are ill planned, lack co-ordination, are porous and need complete overhaul in management.

Surprise checks carried out by Bureau of Civil Aviation Security (BCAS) seven months after hijacking of IA plane to Kandahar has shown practically no improvement in airport security. A BCAS official was able to plant dummy explosive under the pilot's seat in Jet Airways aircraft without anybody noticing it at Mumbai airport. The airport officials gave several reasons for lax in security.

Officials admitted that it was virtually impossible to guard all aircraft when several departures were scheduled within a short space of time. The local policemen have now been replaced by the Central Industrial Security Force (CISF) so far at 18 out of the country's 66 airports. But the success of the CISF remains to be seen as those now deployed at airports were considered surplus by CISF. Besides, working of the CISF personnel at airports will be monitored by three agencies, viz. (i) functionally under the aegis of the AAI, (ii) follow policies of BCAS and (iii) administratively report to CISF HQ at Delhi. This will cause a lot of confusion. The BCAS has repeatedly been calling for a dedicated aviation security service but repeatedly shot down by the authorities on the plea of shortage of funds - no matter if the security of the nation is at stake. The BCAS has no power to enforce rules or even to initiate punitive action against defaulters.

(i) Mumbai Airport

But the induction of the CISF to provide even minimum security to airport property and installation is open to doubt. In Dec 2004, expensive and vital equipment known as localizers, energized and fixed firmly to the ground, were stolen in broad daylight from runway no. 27 which is the main runway at

Mumbai airport. The localizers radiate electro magnetic waves and are an integral part of the Instrument Landing System (ILS). Each localizer is about 2 feet to 3 feet in length and about 1.5 inches in diameter. The stolen localizers were functioning at the busiest runway in India. The entire ILS system stopped functioning for 2 days due to the theft, forcing aircraft to use alternate runway resulting in huge financial losses to the airlines, disruption of schedules, apart from affecting the safety of the aircrafts.

This theft brings into focus lack of effective security system even after spending crores of rupees. A CISF guard is posted barely 20 feet from the localizer. In addition, an observation post is located at a vantage point barely 70 feet away overlooking the localizers. In view of the above, it is incredible that a functioning localizer, part of the ILS , could be stolen in broad daylight from the busiest runway in India.

But Mumbai airport security is easily breached. But the greatest danger is from over 100,000 slums/shanties who have illegally encroached upon AAI land causing serious concern for the take off and landing of planes. Though no construction is permitted internationally within 100 meters of the perimeter of any international airport, in Mumbai some of the slums actually touch the perimeter walls. Besides there are mounds of rotting garbage abutting the perimeter walls. These garbage dumps attract dogs and birds posing serious danger to planes, so much so that guards are employed to shoot stray dogs prowling on the runway. But shooting dogs is also risky as they approach in the path of a plane taking off or landing. It may be noted that mention here is made of shooting dogs, in the 21st century, prowling on the main runway of the busiest runway of Mumbai, the financial capital of India and not that of a runway in a remote jungle. This busy airport reportedly sees about 500 landings/take offs in a day.

Once a plane misses its turn to land due to presence of dogs/ birds, it has to go back to the end of the queue in line for landing. This results in a cascading effect. A bird hit may cost the airline crores of rupees if the engine is damaged – not to mention the fear of heavy loss of life if the plane crashes.

It is only a couple of local politicians who have not only prevented the removal of illegal slum dwellers, but also reportedly brought in new comers merely to favor their vote bank, no matter what the cost to the nation in terms of money, prestige or the potential loss of lives in case of a crash. But then for more than 20 years the authorities have continued to pander to the desires of a couple of local politicians despite all these factors. After all it has become a political problem involving only a couple of local politicians and their few voters. But it is only the lack of political will in making Mumbai airport a normal safe one. In case, necessary steps are not taken expeditiously to ensure the safety of the premier airport in India, it will not be surprising if foreign airlines stop flying to Mumbai, citing unacceptable risks. Mumbai airport has only one runway for both landing and takeoff, unlike foreign airports which have separate runways. At present, pilots have to backtrack from intersection, go to beginning and take off, involving waste of time and fuel in the process.

The continuing inaction for decades against illegal slum dwellers and anti-social elements has emboldened them to almost lay siege to the nearby AAI colony housing about 600 families of AAI. The colony is exclusively meant for staff of AAI and Air Traffic Controllers (ATC), on whom depends the safety of air travel over the Mumbai skies. The colony is now practically surrounded on three sides by illegal slums with boundary walls being broken in many places.

The official staff residents are scared for themselves and their families. Some of the quarters are reported to have been abandoned after several attacks by vandals. The staff claims that the crime level has reached intolerably high levels. The AAI has reportedly claimed that necessary support from the local police is not forthcoming. The ladies and children of the AAI staff are said to be afraid to walk freely in their own colony. The staff of AAI, including ATCs on whom depends the safety of the skies over Mumbai, is always frightened about the safety of their families, when they are on duty, particularly night duty. The slum dwellers and anti-social elements are getting bolder due to complete inaction by the authorities. But the AAI staff, working in shifts, are now trying desperately to find a way to break the siege of the slum dwellers and slumlords inside the AAI colony near the Mumbai International Airport.

The general upkeep of the airports in India leaves much to be desired. India is reported to have about 125 airports and 300 landing strips. The Naresh chandra report has stated "AAI has large reserves of cash merely because they have not ploughed back in modernization and expansion...but kept on raising charges exorbitantly at regular intervals...absence of even one airport with parallel runways is a sad comment on the monolithic management of runways". Some airports were originally built by erstwhile Rulers of Princely States, a few were airstrips built during World War II (1939-45), but expenses and income of a few are given below to show the inability to utilize such assets and the huge waste of money:

(i) Kandla, Gujarat: first major port to be built after independence and first free trade zone—but lacks air link with the rest of the country.

(ii) Bhuj, Gujarat: just 60 kms from Kandla , has new airport, but most passengers on Mumbai – Bhuj are for Kandla, Gandhidham area—has 20 member staff.

(iii) Keshod, Gujarat: originally built before independence by the then ruler of Junagadh State—has everything including equipment and staff of 10—but no work in the absence of any flights.

(iv) Kota, Rajasthan: built before independence by Kota's Royal family and taken over in 1951 by IA—spread over 150 acres—idle staff- gates are always locked—cattle graze freely and children use it as playground.

(v) Kanpur, UP: one time industrial hub of UP- expense about Rs. 1.3 crores for upkeep but income less than Rs. 2 lac p.a.

(vi) Dehradun, Uttaranchal: upkeep about Rs. 2.5 crores p.a— income less than Rs. 9 lac p.a.

(vii) Pantnagar, Uttaranchal: upkeep about Rs. 80 lac p.a. – revenue Rs. 5 lac p.a.

(viii) Behala, Kolkata: upkeep Rs. 1.7 lac p.a.—income negligible.

But the authorities have to move fast and implement plan for proper utilization of such a large number of airports/ airstrips. The need of the hour, with rapidly increasing air travel is to have airports of international standards. But politicians/ bureaucrats fail to understand the necessity for having national outlook and not narrow parochial or party outlook. A classic case is that of the proposed new Bangalore airport where personal ego and greed overcomes the interest of the state and the nation.

(ii) Bangalore Airport

Idea of the first greenfield airport at Bangalore was first conceived in early 1993, the promoters being Karnataka State Industrial and Investment Corporation, L & T Corporation and Siemens. The starting date was postponed six times with completion date 33 months from date of starting. But in 2004, there were assembly elections in Karnataka. Though the Congress returned to power, the incumbent Chief Minister, Shri S.M. Krishna who had taken keen interest in expediting the building of the new airport along with the entire latest infrastructure, was replaced by Shri Dharamsinh also a Congressman. The entire project had been examined in detail by the earlier Government with Shri Krishna as CM and the work was going on at a very fast pace. But the new CM insisted on a thorough review of the entire project. Consequently, the entire project has come to a standstill for months. It may be noted that both Shri Dharmsinh and Shri Krishna both belong to the same Congress party which even now commands the majority in the Karnataka assembly, besides the Prime Minister of India also belongs to the same Congress party which is an important constituent of the coalition at the Centre.

Considering the growing importance of Bangalore as an Information Technology (IT) centre of international importance, the Karnataka Government under the leadership of Shri Krishna as CM had taken urgent steps to revamp the entire Bangalore city and its infrastructure. The task of revamping had been entrusted to a civil servant Shri J. Jerome who successfully carried out:

(i) In 8 months completed project of 6 laning about 60 km of outer ring road connecting all major highways and roads – incidentally all this was stuck for a decade earlier.

(ii) Built 4 flyovers including India's longest interchange.

(iii) Rejuvenated lakes.

(iv) Within a 4 year period 2000 to 2004, could sell 50,000 sites in colonies formed by Bangalore Development Authority (BDA), when it could sell only 3,400 sites over a period of 10 years earlier.

(v) Collected over Rs. 900 crores as initial deposit alone by tenders for BDA's largest development project involving distribution of 20,000 house sites.

(vi) Converted BDA which had been slated earlier for closure into a cash rich cow with a surplus of Rs. 1,600 crores to fight the land mafia which was grabbing all the land – also recovered land from the grabbers and still fighting cases against the land mafia.

(vii) Finalization of plans for peripheral roads which could permanently keep trucks from the city and a 10 km long high-tech corridor which could be a vast base for the high-tech industry and relocate smaller IT firms now in residential areas.

The new CM immediately shifted Shri Jerome to an insignificant post. The development work of Bangalore airport and infrastructure has come to a standstill for almost a year. Now leading IT companies have officially advised the Karnataka Government of their intention to shift to other states which are offering excellent facilities. But Karnataka Government has yet to initiate any action not only to retain existing business, let alone attract new ones. Shri Devegowda, who was the Prime Minister of India for a very short time and who belongs to Karnataka and is permanent resident of Bangalore has strongly opposed the entire project of new airport and improving the infrastructure and is firm on not allowing any such project. So development of Bangalore airport and infrastructure has come to a standstill

But the Karnataka Government has apparently not realized that IT industry can relocate staff anywhere in India but the sufferers will be the common people of Karnataka, like drivers, taxi operators, waiters, etc. and businesses like hotels, shops, restaurants, transporters, travel agents, etc. This is another example where personal ego and greed of politicians overcomes the interest of the common people, the state and the nation.

The needless delay has kept on escalating the cost of the project and with the vehement opposition from Shri Devegowda, it is doubtful when the project will fructify and at what cost.

The Karnataka High Court in its judgment of May 2005 passed severe strictures against the Karnataka Government for its shortsightedness in delaying the building of the planned infrastructure including airport. The High Court (HC) is very clear that the four lanes Bangalore – Mysore highway is in the interest of the state. It needs to be recalled that the agreement was signed 8 years ago and Bangalore has been rapidly growing as a very important IT centre for the last few years and so under no circumstances should it be delayed. The court displayed its unhappiness at the tactics employed by the Government to delay the project by making some false allegations. The HC has stated that the state's Chief Secretary and another bureaucrat should be prosecuted for perjury and trying to mislead the court. But the Government, unmindful of the national or state interest, is said to be considering challenging the HC verdict and thereby further delay the project.

(b) New Aviation Challenges

India is emerging as one of the fastest growing markets in Aviation. 35 airlines wanted to enter Indian market in 2001, which went up to 51 in 2003. Over 100 applications were pending in 2004. But infrastructure needs to be upgraded fast to international standards. But one cannot help feeling apprehensive at the ability to meet the challenges, looking at the present state of affairs in India. China has realized that first rate airports act as multiplier for growth. Even Thailand and Malaysia are busy building world class infrastructure. All of them realize that first rate airports and increased air traffic ultimately results in better life for its citizens. But Indian politicians/bureaucrats dragging their feet and engaged in needless and endless debates. One former Prime Minister of India had in June 2005 called the development of airlines in India as "anti poor".

(c) Helicopters

About 10 years ago , there were about 60 helicopters in India, today there are about 120 registered helicopters and about 60 small winged aircraft. These form the backbone of the non-scheduled aviation sector. In the last decade, there have been over a dozen helicopter crashes. But for about 2 years from 2001, the post of Flight Operations Inspector (FOI) lay vacant. This is a very vital post as the FOI is expected to: (i) regular inspection of copters, (ii) conduct safety audits and (iii) suggest changes to improve safety. Despite crashes and lack of FOI for about 2 years, the Director General of Civil Aviation (DGCA) feels the sector is well regulated. The post of FOI was hurriedly filled up by appointing a pilot from Pawan Hans, after the copter crash killing 25 ONGC personnel near Mumbai High.

USA is one of the world's busiest hubs with more than 11,000 copters. It has fixed copter routes over the entire airspace as copters fly at reduced speed, short path and low altitude.

There is no such provision in India. It means that in off course locations, the copters, as a rule, have little or no knowledge of weather conditions due to lack of ATC support and the same applies to night flying. Only basic helicopter training for pilots and engineers provided at Bangalore. There are no other specialized courses. Even some of the mandatory international tests are not held in India. For instance, international standards require helicopter crew member to pass "Helicopter Underwater Escape Training Test" (HUET), where a candidate has to come out of a helicopter trapped under water and come out within a specified time frame. This test is not mandatory in India and there is no provision for such a test.

All pilots and aircraft maintenance engineers have to be endorsed by DGCA. But big operators like Pawan Hans with 30 copters have their own tests, but small operators go by DGCA Certificate and Work Experience.

C. Sea Ports

During the first half of the 20th century, passengers and cargo traffic between India and the rest of the world depended upon steamers. Air traffic was in its infancy. But with the development of large aircraft capable of carrying 300-400 passengers and separate freighter aircraft capable of carrying tonnes of cargo, there was a complete change in the role of steamers in the world's passenger and cargo traffic. There was a tremendous increase in the number of passengers, particularly intercontinental passengers but as air travel was very quick, the aviation industry got a tremendous boost. The international travel between countries also increased many fold. But instead of using crates of varying sizes, the traders preferred to use large containers of standard size internationally. The steamers as well as the seaports had to modify their handling procedures to cope with the containers. New ports had to be built with appropriate infrastructure, including linkages by rail/road to the hinterland. Today, all new seaports deal exclusively with containerized cargo, which is the international practice. Even in India, a new port, Jawaharlal Nehru Port was built near Mumbai exclusively for container traffic. It is barely 5 miles across the sea, as the crow flies, from the existing Mumbai port. Containerization has completely revolutionized sea borne trade, and to some extent air/road cargo.

The existing seaports are old and not suitable for containerized traffic. Kochi, (Kerala) is one of the 12 existing major ports in India. But it is planning to enlarge and develop the role of Kochi as an international transshipment container terminal to overcome the lack of adequate facilities in Indian ports, leading to substantial amount of such traffic being diverted to Colombo, Dubai, and Salalah, Singapore, etc.

Kochi is an all weather port close to the major sea routes from Europe to Far East and Australia. The Singapore – Gulf sea route passes barely 11 nautical miles from Kochi. Hence it expects to gain substantially when the new sea port is ready. Besides the project is planned as a self-contained compact port that will not depend upon the existing Kochi city for anything but on the contrary is planned to provide amenities to the city as it will have a captive power plant, a desalination plant, a garbage treatment plant and direct access to national highway.

It can be seen that Indians are alive to the fast changing international scenario in sea transport. In addition, the Government is alive to the need for building seaports to meet the special needs of the developing fishing industry. These seaports are expected to have all the infrastructure like cold storage and telecom facilities, linkages to markets, etc. necessary for a modern sea going ocean fleet.

D. Highways

The road network was quite adequate to meet the needs of the populace in pre-independence period. It was expected that immediately after independence, the existing network would be expanded rapidly to meet the growing aspirations of the populace particularly the rural sector who constitute more than half the total population and whose socio-economic betterment needed to be improved rapidly.

But for almost half a century after independence, very little attention was paid at the state level as also the centre for improving the linkages between the rural sector and the rest. Consequently, though claims continued to be made regarding increase in foodgrain production and making the country self sufficient in food grains, yet the benefits did not percolate to the rural sector which made such self sufficiency in food possible through their hard work. But the basic linkages between villages and towns were not developed. Even the linking of the four metros (Delhi, Mumbai, Chennai and Kolkata)which carry extremely heavy passenger and freight traffic, were not improved upon . These are the main trunk or arterial routes. Incidentally, it may be recalled that the broad arterial road from Peshawar to Kolkata was built centuries ago by Sher Shah Suri and is known as the Grand Trunk Road.

About 3 years ago, a plan was drawn up to strengthen the all India road network by broadening the existing network. The basic plan laid stress on the linking up of the 4 metros, Delhi, Mumbai, Kolkata and Chennai by means of super highways and popularly known as Golden Quadrilateral. The plan also envisaged connecting villages and the hinterland with the national highway so as to provide adequate and necessary linkages with all the villages and provide an impetus to rural development. It is said that in the initial period about 11 kms of roads were built per day but the latest figures are not available and said to be very much less than the previous performance.

The importance of a good road network in fighting extreme poverty is not realized. Lack of roads leads to isolation of communities with no access to food, medical services, etc.The dramatic change in the health and life style can be seen where communities have been linked to a good roads network. Generally the worst poverty stricken communities can be seen in hamlets and tribal areas which do not have roads connecting such areas to other towns.

It is not generally realized that any slow down in the implementation of plan for building arterials and trunk roads will adversely affect the people below the poverty line living in the villages and tribal hamlets. So it is all the more necessary to ensure implementation of road building programme at a fast pace.

E. Telecommunications

During the last 2 decades the telecom industry has shown phenomenal progress all over the country, including rural areas. The number of cell phones (mobile phones) is increasing in millions every year. This coupled with rapid developments in the computer industry is bringing in changes in all spheres including medical and agro industries at a speed undreamt of even a decade earlier. It has varied applications, too numerous to list out. For instance, the income tax administration shows considerable improvement based as it is now on computerization of tax deducted at source. It permits checking of statements submitted by assessee of tax deducted at source with amount of such tax deposited in bank. This reduces scope for corruption and improves tax collection and naturally cuts down the laborious and time consuming efforts of the tax department. Besides paper forms are being replaced by online information at Tax Information Network centers. Similarly, consultation with renowned doctors and specialists can now be made available within seconds from almost anywhere in the country. The scope for availing the ever widening network of information technology is increasing rapidly in India.

F. Power

Fantastic developments are taking place all over India, thanks to the revolution in IT. But it depends entirely on the availability of guaranteed power of requisite quality for all 24 hours throughout India. There is acute shortage of power in metros like Delhi and Kolkata. Even Maharashtra suffers from shortage of power to the extent of about 4000 mw resulting in power cuts of 2 to 8 hours daily in most parts of the state except Mumbai city. No new power generating plants were set up during the last decade though the demand was rapidly increasing. Some years back an ambitious plan was drawn up to set up a power plant by Enron at Dabhol, Maharashtra, at a cost of $3 billion. But for various reasons the project lies incomplete and involved in disputes for years. Enron, the largest shareholder in the project has been declared bankrupt and alleged to be involved in criminal practices in the USA. The World Bank had appraised the project in 1993 and had reportedly declared it to be economically not viable and would be an unbearable burden for Maharashtra. Incidentally it is reported that a project identical to the Enron was completed within the same time frame and at less than one third of the cost in South Korea. The shortage of power all over is alarming. Even hospitals in small towns do not get uninterrupted power of the required quality and voltage. Small towns and villages are now trying to harness wind/solar/biogas power to the extent possible. But this is an area needing immediate attention as the progress of the nation depends on adequate and uninterrupted supply of the right quality of power, not only in cities and towns but also in villages. And this is a problem with no overnight solutions, as planning, installing of power plants and proper distribution is spread over a time frame extending over months if not years.

But merely increasing generation of electricity is not the solution. The greatest problem is abnormally high Transmission and Distribution (TD) losses all over the country. In Maharashtra TD losses amount to about 35% of power generated.

A study conducted between April 2004 and Feb 2005 by the Maharashtra State Electricity Board (MSEB), as per the directives of the Maharashtra Energy Regulatory Commission (MERC) came out with some unusual figures. In Western Maharashtra, Baramati taluka, (near Pune) along with rural Ahmednagar taluka tops the list of power thefts with 48% of electricity "vanishing", among the six districts of the region. The third place, after these two, is taken by Sangamner at 47% power thefts; Pimpri (near Pune) is close behind at 41%. Minimum power theft at 22% reported by Kothrud, mainly middle class residential suburb of Pune. Incidentally, Baramati is the home taluka of Shri Sharad Pawar, presently the Union Agriculture Minister and an erstwhile Chief Minister of Maharashtra in the recent past.

The study also states that power is commonly stolen in rural parts by using "crude apparatus and political connections". Satara and Sholapur reported 35%, but the lowest in Western Maharashtra was 26% in Kolhapur. While technically a small percentage, say about 7% may be accounted for by genuine TD losses, the unusually high percentage of loss is attributed to large extent to thefts of power. So the root cause of inadequate power all over India is unacceptable levels of TD losses including theft of power on a large scale. Effective steps need to be taken immediately to curb TD losses. Otherwise any additional generation of power will only result in increase of TD losses. But putting an end to power thefts and bringing down TD losses is more of a political problem than a technical one.

At a meeting of energy experts gathered in Mumbai in May 2005, at a review meeting on "Indian Power and Construction Energy", speakers dealt with various factors hampering the power sector. The Chairman of the UP Electricity Regulatory

Commission (UPERC) was of the opinion that the lack of political will was responsible for the current state of affairs in the power sector. He said incessant power cuts have been applied for years in UP and have become a way of life. Besides, the overdue bills of Public Sector Undertakings (PSU) to various Electricity Boards were in excess of Rs 50,000 crores. But the Government has not taken any action.

It is for the politicians to take a firm stand in the national interest on giving whole hearted support to the Electricity Board staff in cutting down TD losses and theft of power rather divert scarce resources in investing thousands of crores of rupees in generating additional power.

In conclusion, the transport and communication sector on the whole has failed to keep pace with the needs of the rapidly expanding and diversifying economy. But the telecom sector particularly the IT sector is growing and spreading its network at a very fast pace throughout the country including the rural areas. And that gives hope for optimism that the entire transport and communication sector will also develop at a fast pace and help the national economy grow and simultaneously ensure the distribution of such national growth to every citizen of the country.

Banks and other Financial Institutions

24

Economic development and continued well being of the nation depends upon the smooth functioning of the financial system providing money and credit facilities to the deserving sectors of the populace. A well regulated banking system capable of providing need based, timely and reasonably priced credit flow to all sectors of the national economy is the prime requisite for the continued economic growth of a nation. Naturally this casts a duty on the banking system to ensure proper pre-sanction appraisal of the needs of the borrower and subsequent monitoring of the credit extended. Failure by the borrower to repay as per the terms of the sanction, the credit facilities extended by the bank, results in such lending being considered as bad or doubtful debt, or in today's terminology as Non-Performing Asset (NPA).

It is necessary to look at the banks and other financial institutions as to the extent to which they have helped and continue to assist the national economy in providing need based, adequate and timely financial assistance to all sectors of the national economy. The major types of financial institutions providing credit are:

A. Public Sector Banks (PSB)

B. Co-operative Banks

C. Regional Rural Banks (RRB)/ Grameen Bank

D. Branches in India of foreign banks

E. Private sector banks

F. Non-Banking Finance Companies (NBFC).

The above, except NBFC, are commercial banks and basically engaged in meeting the needs of the borrower for short-term credit facilities. For instance, a trader needs funds to buy and hold stocks in his shop, a farmer needs to buy seeds, pesticides, etc. In other words, the commercial banks provide working capital to the entire gamut of economic activity including agriculture, trade, industry, etc.

But funds for acquiring fixed assets are provided by means of term loans repayable over a long-term period extending over years. Normally commercial banks are supposed to confine their activities to working capital as term loans are provided by specialized institutions like Industrial Development Bank of India (IDBI), Industrial Finance Corporation of India (IFCI), Unit Trust of India (UTI), etc. But at present commercial banks also extend term loans to a limited extent.

A. Public Sector Banks (PSB)

Each of the PSB has thousands of branches spread over India. As such extending credit to a borrower anywhere in India should be no problem, as they would have gathered adequate expertise in extending all types of credit facilities to their diversified borrowers through their wide network of branches. The PSB came into existence in 1969 on the nationalization of some of the larger existing private sector banks. As such the PSB have more than 30 years experience in dealing with the credit requirements of a wide and varied clientele spread over India. Having financed the entire spectrum of economic activity all over India for over 30 years, one would expect PSB to have built up expertise to handle safely and expeditiously the varied and diversified credit requirements of the borrowers.

But the large amount of NPA is an indicator of the failure of the banks to monitor effectively the credit facilities extended to borrowers. According to the All India Bank Employees Association (AIBEA), the total amount of bad loans in the banking sector at the end of March 2004 stood at Rs. 96,084 crores out of which PSB Rs. 52,100 crores, Private sector and foreign banks with stressed accounts of Rs. 22, 300 crores.

Besides, about 60% of Indians are said to live in villages. It is the rural sector which needs a credit delivery system which can meet their requirements for credit in an inexpensive and expeditious manner. It is the farmer for whom timely and adequate credit at reasonable cost is of crucial importance.

India has adopted the British system of branch banking with each PSB having thousands of branches. This system of branch banking may be appropriate for traders/industrialists operating on a national scale but has its drawbacks in regard to developing rural India.

In USA, unit banks (with one branch) were set up and helped develop the economy. Even today unit banking is the norm in USA and continue to perform a useful role in the economic development. In the 1970s, a large number of such banks, generally known as Savings and Loan Associations went bankrupt, mainly due to mismatch between the lending rates which were fixed and borrowing rates which were variable. There was no criminal intent or action on their part, but only commercial folly of mismatched interest rates. The range of operations is confined to one or maximum two nearby towns in the same state and are found to be adequate to serve the credit needs of the entire community. Being unitary organizations, they are flexible and in the constant knowledge of the local conditions. Hence they are able to provide timely assistance at economic rates.

But the branch of any PSB lack in flexibility being a part of a large all India organization bound by rules and regulations. So a rural branch of a PSB necessarily has a built in high cost structure as the manning pattern and establishment charges are based on the all India pattern. But a bank has to recover all its charges from its all India operations. Hence there is a limit below which such banks cannot bring down the cost of extending credit facilities to rural areas.

Does this mean that the rural sector has to live with high cost and at times delayed credit facilities provided by commercial banks? Before the advent of the British and latest development of widespread branch banking, the rural sector was served by the 'Unit bank', viz. the indigenous village banker who even today continues to perform a useful service in meeting expeditiously and without bureaucratic hassles, the credit needs of the rural community consisting not only of farmers but also small traders and small industries. But charges of exploiting the borrowers have been leveled against such indigenous bankers. Now, on the one hand it is evident that he performs a valuable function in providing much needed credit expeditiously but on the other hand he is accused of exploiting his position by charging high rate of interest.

He conducts all his 'banking' operations from one room single handedly, but at times levies charges generally considered extremely high. Indigenous bankers have played and continue to play an important part in the rural economy. Such bankers have been dealing in hundies (bills of exchange) for centuries. In the early days, the Imperial Bank of India (predecessor of State Bank of India), could even offer them rediscounting facilities without cumbersome procedures. The Imperial Bank of India (IBI) could even influence the rate of interest to be charged to the borrower by the indigenous banker. Today the State Bank of India (SBI) has the largest branch network in India and could conveniently arrange for rediscounting trade bills covering trade, agriculture and industries financed by the indigenous banker in the villages. Only Reserve Bank of India (RBI) or the controlling monetary authority would have to lay down guidelines and ensure that interest charged to borrowers is within permissible limits. This would enable the rural sector access to a flexible and expeditious system of credit availability at a rate much lower than that charged by commercial banks. It would also enable PSBs to cut down direct establishment costs of running such rural branches and costs of monitoring operations of such branches.

With adequate safeguards, such system would be of immense help in recognizing the importance of the role played by indigenous bankers in the rural sector which covers over half a million villages and almost 50 % of India's total population.

Looking at the quantum of NPAs, the capacity of commercial banks to assess and monitor credit facilities remains debatable. It needs to be mentioned that the work force of these banks consists of extremely well paid staff who are not only academically highly qualified but also undergo periodical training courses in various banking areas, particularly credit assessment and credit monitoring. Hence commercial banks should be in a position to expedite credit appraisal and monitoring, and thereby bring down the quantum of NPAs. Besides, de-linking of rural financing from normal commercial activities could enable such banks to concentrate on core activities like financing, trade and industry, both of which are diversifying into new areas requiring special approach to extending credit facilities, taking into account the globalization of trade with consequent international currency ramifications.

The mounting NPAs are evidence of the need for improving the operational efficiency and running these banks on purely business lines. But it appears that non-banking considerations have an important role in the functioning of these banks. A glaring example is given below of a PSB viz, Indian Bank, Chennai, where bad advances wiped off the entire net worth of this old established bank.

At the end of 1995-96, the bank registered a huge loss of Rs.1336 crores and had its entire net worth wiped out. Reports indicate that during the period 1991-96, Indian Bank, blatantly ignored RBI guidelines and reportedly distributed over Rs. 10 crores to various institutes, departments, trusts, etc. But the monitoring authority, RBI, is said to have kept silent during this period when the Bank was said to be ignoring RBI guidelines.

In view of the huge amounts stuck in NPAs of various banks, the Government set up special tribunals for ensuring expeditious adjudication and speedy recovery of claims of banks and financial institutions after the enactment of the Recovery of Debts due to Banks and Financial Institutions Act 1993. All the claims above Rs. 10 lakhs automatically get transferred to these Tribunals from the High Court.

These tribunals are known as Debt Recovery Tribunals (DRT). After judgment is passed by DRT, the recovery officers have to execute them. But even after passing judgment expeditiously, there is a tremendous delay in execution due to shortage of recovery officers. This is a cause of serious concern.

About Rs. 24,000 crores involving about 4000 cases is stuck in DRTs. It is estimated that an equal amount is stuck in cases where order has been passed but not executed.

Three DRTs have been set up in Mumbai to deal with cases above Rs. 10 lakhs from Mumbai and certain regions of Maharashtra. Each tribunal is supposed to have 2 recovery officers. But DRT - I and DRT - II are functioning with just one officer each. But there are some major lacunae leading to delays. The first being the lack of permanent staff for these DRT. All the officers and staff are on deputation from other tribunals and courts for a tenure not exceeding 3 years. The officers and staff need accounting qualifications and banking knowledge, apart from possessing knowledge of banking law and practice to handle the technical complexities involved. Besides the quantum of staff provided is grossly inadequate. About 60 claims get filed every month with about 40 to 50 cases being heard everyday at each tribunal. But the staff strength is fixed at only 30 employees including section officers and presiding officers.

Merely setting up DRTs without providing the necessary infrastructure has not helped at all. The pending cases are piling up. Cases are decided but orders are not executed due to shortage of staff. It is therefore all the more necessary for the authorities to rectify the lacunae at the earliest as it would result in providing relief to PSBs by reducing existing NPAs in their books and release locked up funds which could assist in providing credit to genuine borrowers.

B. Co-operative Banks

The co-operative movement was started in Maharashtra over 70 years ago and by now has been successful in forming a number of co-operative organizations engaged in a wide variety of activities. A number of co-operative Banks are functioning all over India particularly in Maharashtra and Gujarat. Besides a large number of co-operative sugar factories have been set up in Western Maharashtra. Perhaps one of the main reasons for the popularity of co-operative organizations is the fact that each member has one vote irrespective of his shareholding. This is in sharp contrast to joint stock companies where the voting strength of a member depends on the number of shares he holds. Hence the co-operative sector naturally attracts the ordinary person who may hold only one share but his voting power is the same as that of any other person with larger share holding.

Co-operative banks are of various sizes - from small village banks involved in micro-financing of rural women to large district, state level and urban co-operative banks with vast network of branches.

But large co-operative banks occupy a politically and economically sensitive sector and generally enjoy strong political backing. Reserve Bank of India (RBI) has noticed increasing frauds/failures in such banks. According to RBI, almost 144 out of 370 district co-operative banks are making huge losses on account of increasing bad debts arising out of lack of proper supervision. RBI identified several weak banks fit for liquidation but unable to act due to diffused control and to a large extent on account of the political clout enjoyed by such banks.

A large number of multicrore rupee scams are coming to light with greater frequency indicating lack of control in their working. The urban co-operative banks are said to be regulated by RBI and the Registrar of Co-operative Societies (RCS) while the District and State Co-operative Banks are said to be regulated by RBI and NABARD.

RBI has stated that state co-operative department gives licenses to start co-operative banks without any intimation to RBI. Most of these banks are highly politicized and wield enormous clout particularly during election times. Hence they can reportedly get away after flouting all rules and can generally depend on bail out by the Government.

While RBI is reportedly trying to go for unifying and tightening controls, the politically strong banks want loosening of controls. The Maharashtra Urban Co-operative Bank Federation controls over Rs. 55,000 crores of deposits and reportedly lobbying hard to water down regulations. But it is not only the multi branch banks which are in serious trouble. For instance, Jai Hind Co-operative Bank Ltd, Mumbai with a single branch crashed in 2003 after its Directors reportedly took loans amounting to Rs 27 crores out of total deposits of Rs. 53 crores. The loans have reportedly turned sticky and unpaid.

But despite numerous scams involving thousands of crores, it appears that no positive and firm action has been taken by the authorities: (i) to recover even a part of the thousands of crores defrauded through banks, (ii) to severely punish the perpetrators and (iii) implement well thought out positive action to prevent such occurrences where ultimately the poor depositor ultimately loses hard earned savings. But the failure of the co-operative banks forces the farmer and the small borrower to go back to the village money lender who is quick to respond but at a high rate of interest. The failure of the authorities in effectively supervising and controlling the co-operative banks not only results in unnecessary hardship to the farmer and the small borrower but actually tightens the grip of the local money lender on such people thereby defeating the very purpose of launching the co-operative movement.

But the rules are broken with impunity, e.g. only a chairman of a district co-operative bank can be the Chairman of the Maharashtra State Co-operative Bank Ltd (MSCB) but board of the Wardha Dist Co-operative Bank (WDCB) Ltd was dissolved, the chairman of dissolved WDCB continued to be chairman of MSCB.

This does not mean that all co-operative banks have unsatisfactory records. A number of them are doing commendable work and greatly assisting in the growth of the co-operative movement. A few such examples are given below.

Mahila Sahakari Bank Ltd, Mhaswad, Satara district, Maharashtra has been successful in micro financing and assisting rural women. They have more than 2000 members with shareholding of Rs. 24 lakhs. But what is noteworthy is their loan recovery rate of 98%. They realized that before they could uplift women through improved health and education, they had to tackle migration from their drought prone Satara district. They were inspired by SEWA. Their main hurdle was to provide collateral demanded by the Bank for any loan. Women have for long been marginalized from ownership of land or any means of production. So they prevailed upon their husbands to be co-parcenors of property. This move effectively challenged the centuries old feudal structure of society.. Women now have assets in their own names. They are also given identity cards to make them socially and economically viable.

Self help groups have taken loans from Mahila Bank to buy cows and buffaloes and formed Mahila dairies. Marginal women can thus earn a regular income while landless women and laborers can buy sheep and goats on credit. These loans are given on the advice of the entire group. This has a very important effect. Upper caste women wanting loan must seek approval from the group which includes lower caste women. This naturally influences the local power structure. Self help groups (not necessarily legally co-operative organizations but based on co-operative principles) are making rapid strides in Maharashtra, e.g. village of Manewadi was facing water problem for years. As no action was taken for years, the self help group of women went to district headquarters at Satara and organized a dharma in front of Collectors office. They negotiated with local MLA until water supply was set up. Soon thereafter women's candidate was elected unopposed to the local panchayat.

Shri. Vishvas Thakre, 35 years old, founder chairman of Vishvas Co-operative Bank Ltd, Nashik, Maharashtra, feels that by and large the co-operative banking sector is doing good work but because of the glaring misdeeds of about a dozen banks, the entire sector gets a bad name and people fail to realize the good work being done by all other banks, big and small. Vishvas Bank is a profitable bank established in 1997, effectively engaged in funding self help women's groups, but also training them for manufacturing brooms, candles, phenol, chalk, etc. and has a tie up with the Nashik Municipal Corporation which shell out 50% of total capital investment for needy women. He strongly feels that "we are trustees of the farmers' hard earned money and are committed to his social and economic upliftment. Bank managements have to sink their party differences and work towards a larger goal. Failure of a co-operative bank results in a poor farmer being deprived of credit and the poor depositor will lose his deposit, the perpetrator of the fraud normally escapes and the person who has wrongfully managed to get funds of crores of rupees by manipulating bank officials, keeps the entire loot without any pressure on him to return the ill-gotten gains".

C. Regional Rural Banks/Grameen Banks

To improve the credit delivery system particularly to the economically weaker sectors in the rural areas, almost 200 specialized banks known as Grameen Banks (Regional Rural Banks) were set up a few decades ago. Their operations were confined to a restricted area, normally a district. But the overall performance of such RRBs has not been upto expectations.

As seen in earlier chapters, Grameen Bank of Bangladesh is a highly successful bank in providing microfinance to the rural sector and has made significant contribution to the upliftment of women, most of whom are illiterate or barely literate. So it was held up as role model, but the Gurgaon Grameen Bank, UP has also shown that Grameen banks can be successful even in India provided they get the right type of leadership.

The Gurgaon Grameen Bank (GGB) has more than a hundred branches in the area with business of Rs. 830 crores in 2002. The GGB had NPA OF 8.4% in March 1999. Subsequently an officer was deputed from Syndicate Bank (a PSB) as chairman. Within 3 years he has brought down NPAs to barely 2% and deposits up by 44%.

He gave special attention to human resources development of his bank. All his staff including peon were sent to training institutes. Good performers was rewarded. Staffs were felicitated at public functions for high recovery rates of loans and also deposit mobilization. The concept of societal pressure used by Grameen Bank of Bangladesh was also successfully implemented by him. Women particularly from the weaker section now patronize the GGB in large numbers. About 1500 self help groups of women have been set up for micro credit schemes like making simple things like bags, etc. and helping some of them to earn upto Rs. 1000 per month. So it can be seen that the right type of leadership is a prime requisite for running any successful organization including Grameen Bank, and thereby play an important role in the economic upliftment of the economically weaker sections of society.

FINANCIAL INSTITUTIONS

This is with special reference to specialized financial institutions like the Industrial Development Bank of India (IDBI), Industrial Finance Corporation of India (IFCI), etc. set up by the Government of India to provide long term credit to industrial organizations needing large quantum of funds to assist in industrialization of the country. As the repayment is spread over a number of years and quantum of funds needed is large, the appraisal of such loan proposals and constant monitoring of loans extended, cast a duty on such term lending institutions to be extra vigilant. For this purpose each such institution employs a large number of qualified well paid staff. But for more than a year the Government of India did not appoint a regular fulltime Chairman for IDBI.

But despite all this, these institutions are stuck with thousands of crores of bad advances. The quantum of bad loans given by IFCI (formed under the IFCI Act 1948) is so large that the only way out is for its merger with a healthy financial institution or PSB. The Government of India (GoI) has already given Rs. 5000 crores to IFCI to tackle its NPAs. IFCI had accumulated losses exceeding Rs. 2000 crores as on Dec 2003. Its net worth (NW) is negative and has set a record for loss made by any financial institutions. It has also defaulted in external payment of $ 100 million, besides default in payment of interest to Employees Provident Fund Organization (EPFO) which had parked some of its investments in IFCI.

But despite the large organizational set up of all the leading financial institutions like IDBI, IFCI, UTI, etc. the performance continues to be unsatisfactory. The Central Bureau of Investigation (CBI) has alleged in a case filed in 2002 that Usha (Rai) group had floated nearly 250 fictitious companies and defrauded financial institutions like IDBI, IFCI, UTI, GIC, etc.

CBI has also filed chargesheet against Vinay Rai (Usha group) and others including Executive Director and other officers of IFCI for defrauding financial institutions of Rs. 20 crores.

Financial institutions have lent Rs. 35,000 crores to the steel industry and still waiting for repayment to commence. But companies like Essar, Jindal, and Ispat, etc. have approached financial institutions for concessions like reduction in interest rates, increase in tenure of loan and conversion of rupee loans into cheaper foreign currency loans. Shares of all these companies are being quoted at less than Rs. 5 against face value of Rs. 10.

The Financial Institutions (FI) continue to bailout these companies. For instance, it is reported that Lloyds group (which includes Lloyds Steel, Lloyds Metal, Lloyds Finance) has defaulted to the extent of about Rs. 900 crores to banks and FIs. But Lloyds Steels is reported to have been given substantial concessions by FIs in May 2005. The institutional loans will be converted into equity. The company will issue redeemable preference shares (RPS) worth Rs. 235 crores on private placement basis. Those shares would be redeemed with a premium of 11.5% in six annual installments commencing 2016 and will not carry any right to dividend. The capital base of the company is Rs. 118 crores and negative reserves at Rs. 700 crores (March 2005). Thus the defaulting company will be the gainer at the cost of IDBI whose financial position is not very sound.

But the attitude of banks and FIs towards corporate defaulters is in sharp contrast to that exhibited by these organizations towards farmers and small borrowers. An example is given above how a big defaulter like Lloyds has been given such generous terms and allowed to convert loan into equity. But a small farmer/borrower is hounded by banks for repayment of even a small amount of a few hundred rupees. Even their pots and pans of very little value are taken away. A large number of these borrowers all over India, commit suicide unable to bear the stigma of defaulting on their commitments. This is in sharp contrast to the large corporate borrowers who not only continue individually to commit defaults of hundreds of crores of rupees, and yet manage to get more credit facilities from banks and FIs. It needs to be pointed that the farmer has practically no control over inputs and no control whatsoever over the weather. He is at the mercy of the trader for the sale price of his produce.

Perhaps the farmer should follow the example of corporate defaulters who are not in the least bothered about defaults, but insists on getting more credit facilities from banks and FIs, notwithstanding large defaults.

D. Branches in India of Foreign Banks

A number of foreign banks, Citibank, ABN AMRO, Bank of Japan, American Express, and HSBC, etc. have been operating in India for about five decades. Such branches are expected to be fully conversant with Indian laws, rules and regulations for carrying on banking operations imposed by the banking regulatory authorities. Besides they are fully aware of the severity with which such regulatory laws/rules/regulations are enforced in their own country. So one expects that such banks will share their expertise, particularly foreign currency transactions, financing of large projects as well as an international trade. They operate mainly in metros and large cities and normally confine their operations to assisting large borrowers' mainly corporate borrowers, in financing large projects and international trade.

Recently they have been aggressively participating in extending housing loans and issuance of credit cards. But direct financing of agricultural sector or the small borrower is practically non-existent. In view of their expertise in foreign exchange transactions and having more than 50 years experience of the requirements of the banking regulatory authorities in India, it is extremely surprising to find some of these banks having been alleged to have been involved in some very large scale transactions considered to be highly irregular and contrary to Banking regulations.

In 1992, it came to the notice of the Enforcement Directorate of the Government of India that Vostro account of banks had been used to transfer illegally large rupee amounts through vostro accounts in foreign banks. Now Vostro account is simply an account in Indian rupees maintained by a bank abroad with bank in India. For example, Citibank, NY, maintains an account in Indian rupees with Citibank, Mumbai, it is known as Vostro account in the books of Citibank, Mumbai. Such accounts known as Vostro account maintained in local currency, i.e., Indian rupees to facilitate trade and business transactions. Naturally the local exchange control authorities specify strict rules and regulations governing the conduct of such Vostro accounts. It is the duty of the bank in India to maintaining such account to verify the genuineness of the transaction and naturally complying with the exchange control regulations.

In 1991-92, the country was passing through severe foreign exchange crisis. Now it was at this time that the Vostro account at some banks like Stanchart, Indian Overseas Bank was being used to transfer funds abroad in complete violation of exchange control regulations. It must be remembered that Vostro account is meant to be used only for settlement of trade and business transactions within the country and not for remittance abroad.

Some Indians were charged with violation of Foreign Exchange Regulation Act (FERA) for alleged involvement in illegal transactions of more than Rs. 140 crores through Vostro account to UK. This was the simplest way of transferring funds abroad and that too through banking channels particularly through Stanchart, ANZ bank.

So it can be seen that one's expectations that foreign banks, used to strict compliance with the banking laws in their home countries, would exhibit the same spirit in conduct of their business in India, seems to be belied by their conduct particularly in vostro account management involving almost Rs. 150 crores over a period of about a year.

But the fault also lies with the Reserve Bank of India (RBI), the controlling and monetary authority for not detecting such large quantum of illegal transactions in the space of about a year. No punitive action was taken against any foreign bank though the authorities are even empowered to cancel the license of the defaulting bank. But investigating havala transactions is an extremely touchy issue. And controlling and investigating authorities are extremely reluctant to take strong action against suspected perpetrators of such offences as generally there is suspected to be a link between political fixers, politicians, bureaucrats and of all links and alliances.

In regard to a case in 1995 which was filed to prevent the CBI hushing up havala payoffs made by some political fixers to politicians, bureaucrats, and journalists of all hues, Justice J. S. Verma, of the Supreme Court had said " all you need is courage, enough to be a criminal of the highest order and say I can get away doing anything. If we are meant only for punishing people for petty offenses and allow those who spend lakhs of rupees on birthdays to go scot free, we had better then close down the courts".

But the havala , share scams, etc. are in the past, and atleast it is hoped that no more scams are perpetrated. While foreign banks may not be participating in direct financing to farmers, they are contributing to development of the national economy particularly in project financing and international trade.

E. Private Sector Banks

Most of the private sector banks like Bank of Rajasthan, United Western Bank were started more than 50 years ago. In the last decade some more banks like ICICI Bank, UTI Bank, IDBI Bank, etc. have come up. Some of the banks have a focus on rendering banking services within a specific area. Over the years the scale of operations has expanded, but none of them have the vast network of branches like the PSBs.

The large private sector banks like ICICI Bank, UTI Bank, IDBI Bank, came up only during the last 2 decades with the opening of the economy. But some of them already have substantial NPAs. Till June 2003 private sector banks had already filed suits aggregating to more than Rs. 6000 crores but it is a cause of concern that out of this amount , the major part was accounted for by ICICI Bank, at about Rs. 3500 crores and Indusind Bank about Rs. 1000 crores.

Such big private banks confine their activities to the urban areas and are mainly engaged in project financing and assisting large scale trade, national and international.

F. Term Lending Institutions

Immediately after independence the Government of India realizing the need for rapidly industrializing the country, had set up a committee, and popularly known as the AD Shroff committee, to look into how best to arrange for finance for setting up industries in the private sector. Soon after submission of the committees report, the GoI set up the IFCI (under the IFCI Act, 1948) for extending long-term finance to private entrepreneurs. Subsequently IDBI was also set for assisting industrial growth in India.

Such organizations were of immense help in setting up the industrial organizations. But over the years some major shortcomings crept into the working of these organizations, resulting in large scale blocking of funds in bad and doubtful debts.

The working of IFCI deteriorated in recent years resulting in record loss of Rs. 3220 crores with NPAs of Rs. 3860 crores in 2004. The net worth also turned negative. So the GoI has been forced to consider merging it with a healthy PSB or Institution.

The working of IDBI has also become unsatisfactory during recent years with NPAs estimated at about Rs. 9000 crores. One of the reasons contributing to the unsatisfactory performance has been the lack of leadership at the top. For reasons not known, the Government did not appoint a Chairman for over a year.

IDBI has advanced large amounts to co-operative textile and co-operative sugar mills and guaranteed by the Central Government. The tendency of IDBI seems to be to rely more on the guarantee of the Government rather than on the intrinsic merit of the credit proposal. There have been large scale defaults in these sectors and IDBI invoked the guarantee in some cases but the Government is said to have failed to respond. Besides it is reported that the IDBI cannot file suit against the Central Government as it is said that they cannot take over property which has been guaranteed by the Central Government.

There are a number of other institutions like UTI, GIC, etc. who extend term loans. But a large number of such loans are turning sticky particularly in the steel sector.

There is no dearth of financial institutions extending term loans. Besides the capital market has also developed tremendously. Hence Indian industry has a number of sources to tap for long term finance.

G. Non-Banking Finance Companies (NBFC)

Promoters have started a number of companies known as NBFCs inviting deposits from the general public, quite often, offering very attractive rates on deposits. The high rate of interest offered is higher in some cases than that offered by established or well managed companies, sometimes such companies even offer to double the investment within a year. This extremely high, but financially exorbitant and impractical rate of interest attracts millions of people from all over India and enables such companies to collect thousands of crores of rupees.

One of the most prominent persons involved in running such a company is one Shri C. R. Bhansali. It is interesting to have a look at the extent to which he could spread his financial empire without any solid foundation. He floated more than 130 subsidiaries and unlisted companies and managed to collect thousands of crores of rupees during the period 1992-96 from the public through Fixed Deposits, Bonds, and Debentures, etc. Some of the particulars of the major deposits raised by him are given below:

(i) CRB Capital Markets (CRB's flagship) went public in 1992 and raised Rs. 176 crores in 1992-95.

(ii) CRB Mutual Fund raised Rs. 280 crores.

(iii) CRB Corporation Rs. 84 crores in 1993-95.

(iv) CRB Share Custodial Services raised Rs. 100 crores in 1995.

CRB had also managed to get an "in principle " banking license from RBI in 1996. SEBI had banned CRB Mutual Fund from floating any new schemes. In 1997, RBI banned CRB from accepting fresh deposits from investors. Shri C. R. Bhansali spent 3 months in jail but was released on bail subsequently. Thousands of depositors are still waiting to get even a part of their deposit or interest.

But there are a number of NBFCs who are conducting their business within the framework of the rules and regulations laid down by the regulatory authorities.

Another common method is collecting huge amounts from the gullible investors is by inviting people to subscribe to shares of new companies. The promoters paint a very rosy picture of generous dividends and large capital appreciation of shares in the near future. After collecting large amounts, the promoters vanish and the depositors lose their investment.

SEBI has been set up as a regulatory authority and keep a watchful eye on such activities and also on the manipulation of share prices by interested parties. The manipulators manage to raise the share prices of selected shares, leading to large scale entry of buyers at high prices. Subsequently, the manipulators suddenly and quietly sell their shares leading to a crash in the prices of these shares but after having made huge profits by inflating the share prices. Later on neither the company nor the promoters are normally traceable and the investors are left high and dry having lost their money. At times SEBI has taken action against such manipulators but it apparently has very little effect. Just two instances are cited here showing how action taken by SEBI has had no effect.

SEBI had banned promoters of Aftek for allegedly facilitating price manipulation in Aftek scrip during 1999-2000 in collusion with Triumph International Finance (controlled by Ketan Parekh–one time Big Bull). But the Securities Appellate Tribunal (SAT) set aside the order of SEBI on a technicality.

The case of VLS Finance Ltd is very interesting. During the stock market boom of 1994-95, VLS F Ltd had come out with a public issue of Rs. 10 per share at a premium of Rs. 390 to raise Rs. 147 crores. Promoters had also given undertaking to subscribe to one crore shares @ Rs. 400 each through optionally convertible non-transferable warrants (CNTW) convertible within

5 years of date of allotment of warrants. But company refused to carry out its commitment as shares prices crashed to Rs 8.50 in 1999. In 2002, SEBI debarred company from accessing capital market for 5 years. But SAT set aside SEBI order. Subsequently SEBI filed an appeal in the Supreme Court.

After running for 10 years from pillar to post, now investors have approached Delhi High Court to direct CBI to investigate the issue and prosecute the promoters for cheating investors of Rs. 167 crores. During search and seizure operations in 1998, Income Tax Department came across financial irregularities to the tune of Rs. 198 crores and wanted to appoint auditors in 2000 to assess the extent of tax evasion. But company got a stay order from the court. So far out of the 16 hearings, 14 had to be adjourned as the Government counsel was absent. During the recent hearing in Feb. 2005, the case was adjourned as the lawyer from the Income Tax Department was absent.

It can be seen that the legal machinery has failed to give any relief to the investors after 10 years. Even the investigation by the Income Tax Department has been stalled as the promoters got a stay order from the Court.

Scams involving thousands of crores of rupees keep on occurring with great frequency. The promoters keep the loot and the investors can only take recourse to court. But investigations will drag on for years. Even if the matter comes to the trial stage, the court proceedings will drag on for decades as the scamsters have no shortage of money to avail of the most expensive legal talent. In the process, the regulatory authorities and investigative bodies have to spend large amounts of taxpayers' money in trying to prosecute the scamsters. The investors have very little money to fight such cases as the scamsters have already deprived them of their money. Scams continue and scamsters continue to flourish. One cannot help feeling that at present in India, "crime pays provided you do it on a big enough scale".

Just auctioning Harshad Mehta's securities took over a decade and auctioning the other assets will take longer involving much more expenditure by the authorities with no end in sight of possible litigation.

SEBI had imposed monetary penalties in a number of cases, but SAT drastically reduced the monetary penalties on the grounds that SEBI had reportedly overlooked the "ability to pay" clause as defined by the Supreme Court. This naturally has effectively curbed SEBI's powers to control and regulate market operations. This is quite opposite to the practice in USA where the justice system believes that imposing monetary penalties much larger than the profit from the financial scam acts as a bigger deterrent than prison sentences. Individual's brokers/ scamsters can be sent to prison but not corporate organizations.

For instance, in the major scandal involving Boesky and Milken for insider trading in the mid 1980s, Boesky was fined $ 100 million and Milken fined $ 600 million and also sent to prison as part of criminal settlement. Even by US standards the amount was very high - even bigger than the annual budget of the SEC. The total fees, including those paid by other employees of Drexel Burnham Lambert amounted to $ 1.3 billion.

In March 2005, Bernard Ebbers, former Chief Executive Officer (CEO) of World Com was found guilty by a Federal Court in USA of orchestrating a record $ 11 billion fraud symbolizing the telecom bubble of the 1990s. A jury deliberated for over 8 days and convicted him of securities fraud, conspiracy and 7 counts of filing false reports with regulators – each count carrying a sentence of 5 to 10 years. Jury was not convinced that such executives were unaware of securities and accounting crimes were committed in their office.

Ebbers came from a modest background with little schooling and knowledge of technology or accounting. But he turned around a small reseller of long distance phone services into a Global telecom giant. He was widely hailed in US for his vision during late 1980s and early 1990s and was said to be worth $ 1 billion. His company grew, through acquisitions, made possible through the rising prices in the booming stock market. Ebbers resigned in 2002 and inflated earnings by $ 3.8 billion. SEC accused World Com of fraud and action was taken against him. This led to the filing of the largest corporate bankruptcy in history of USA. But Wall Street firms have agreed to pay more than $ 6 billion World Com investors. Even in the case of JP Morgan Chase they have agreed to pay $2 billion to investors.

In 2001 Enron went into bankruptcy. But Enron's biggest lenders, J.P.Morgan Chase and Citigroup reached a settlement to pay Enron investors $ 2.2 billion and $ 2 billion respectively. Investors in Enron had lost billions of $ when Enron went into bankruptcy. But a number of settlements like the one above have made a pool of $ 4.7 billion and expected to exceed $ 6 billion for the benefit of the investors.

One more US case cited here as it is a rather unusual one. The case arose out of a deal with Perelman and Sunbeam Inc in 1998. Perelmen later contended that Morgan Stanly covered up state of Sunbeam's risky finances to close the deal and hence the investment bank (Morgan Stanley) defrauded him. No major regulatory infraction and misfeasance was cited. The general feeling is that the matter could have been settled, but somehow landed in court. Florida jury awarded $ 604 million in damages to Perelmen. But the total amount could go upto $ 2.4 billion if the jury agrees to the total punitive award that Perelmen is seeking through his lawyers.

Having seen the SEC and the US courts in action, let us look at the Indian scene. A few examples are given above of the manner in which the SEC discharges its duties by taking action against the biggest companies in US. It also shows the judiciary imposing fines amounting to billions of dollars in individual cases and also awarding prison sentences.

In India, fines, if at all imposed are for insignificant amounts and other punishments, if imposed, are of no consequence as they are perceived to be token punishments. The glaring contrast between the functioning of the SEC and the SEBI can be seen by the instances given below. SEBI imposed a fine of Rs. one lakh (about $ 2,000.) on Sterlite Ind Ltd for violating the take over code while making preferential allotment to its promoter group Twinstar Holding Ltd in 2001.

One more case is cited here showing the standards of Indian regulators, in this case the RBI, in imposing penalties. RBI had found that the Dutch bank, INGVyasa Bank had not deducted full amount of unamortized VRS expenditure violating RBI instructions and resulting in overstating TIER I Capital and CRAR in the disclosures in the Balance Sheet for 31 March 2004.

(i) It had not even provided for outstanding debit entries in Interbranch accounts pending for more than 6 months as required by RBI, thereby impacting profits for 2003-04.

(ii) The bank had also contravened RBI guidelines in matters such as financing promoter's contribution.

(iii) Offering interest concession to borrowers availing of insurance products floated by its group companies, depriving it's customers choice in availing of insurance from any company.

(iv) Classifying ineligible advances under Priority sector credit.

In view of these contraventions which RBI found substantial, it imposed a penalty of Rs. 5 lakhs (approx $ 10,000.) under provisions of Sec 47 A (i) (b) of Banking Regulation Act, 1949.

ING Vyasa Bank's total income was Rs. 128 crores and had posted a profit of Rs. 59 crores in 2003-04.

But it was doubtful if the regulators (SEBI/SAT/RBI, etc,) can ever change their mental make up and realize that a mere delicate gentle slap on the wrist is adequate punishment even if crores of investors are cheated out of their hard earned money. It is high time that the regulators gave serious thought of implementing a plan for making such promoters disgorge their ill-gotten gains and compensate the investors within a short time.

A brief look at the Banking and Financial sector indicates the need for a review of the working with a view to strengthening the entire system including the safety of depositors and investors.

It is felt that the working of the PSBs needs to be reviewed particularly their role in meeting the credit requirements of the rural sector. Perhaps PSBs may concentrate on improving the performance in providing credit to trade and industry. With increasing globalization, the PSBs will have to meet the rapidly changing economic scenario calling for developing new flexible and adequate credit facilities in quality and quantity to entrepreneurs in India.

The co-operative banks even today play and will continue to play a significant role in the overall development particularly with the rural sector poised for development in the coming decades. There have been a few cases of huge NPAs in some of these banks. But it is for the regulatory authorities to devise and implement appropriate systems to ensure the proper functioning of these banks without endangering the safety of depositors' funds.

The specialized Grameen Banks (RRBs) have not been able really to achieve the aims for which they were set up. An indepth study is needed to assess if the role at present assigned to them in rural development can be better served by other means.

Branches of foreign banks in India have an important role to play in the new economic scenario rapidly unfolding in India with India also affected by the globalization of trade and industry. Their bases abroad should assist them in easy access to cheaper funds abroad. Besides the vast varied exposure to trade and industry all over the world they should be of tremendous advantage in extending their expertise to Indian entrepreneurs setting up large greenfield projects and financing international trade.

Non-Banking Finance Companies (NBFCs) also have an important part to play. Thousands of small and big NBFCs have been carrying on business for decades. But during the last decade or so, during the stock exchange boom, a number of fly by night operators entered the scene and duped millions of depositors and thereby giving all NBFCs a bad name. But intrinsically such companies play a vital role in gathering the deposits of the community. But stricter and more efficient control is needed to protect the depositors.

The stock markets all over India have expanded tremendously

during the last few decades. So have the number of companies incorporated. Market prices of shares listed on the stock exchanges do move up and down within a narrow range practically everyday. But sudden or significant upsurge and down swing in market is a cause for concern. SEBI is supposed to keep a careful watch on stock market operations and take remedial action without delay. An appellate tribunal (SAT) has also been set up for benefit of the people aggrieved by the orders of SEBI. The orders issued by SEBI are considered far milder than those of SEC (the US body overseeing market operations). But even then a number of orders of SEBI have been overruled by SAT giving the benefit to the party appealing against the order of SEBI. It is also reported that the Supreme Court has introduced the concept of the "the ability to pay "in cases where duping of depositors/investors has been alleged. In other words, a promoter/scamster who has been proved to have duped thousands of depositors/investors of their hard earned money will be liable to a penalty dependent upon the ' ability to pay ' of such promoters/scamsters, no matter if the amount involved in each individual case runs into hundreds of thousands of crores of rupees. This is in complete contrast to the US judicial system where heavy penalties running into billions of dollars and prison sentences have been announced in a number of cases.

So, it is all the more necessary to ensure that scamsters are punished expeditiously and more importantly they are made to disgorge their ill-gotten gains, and duped depositors/investors are recompensed their losses without delay.

Defence

25

The first and foremost duty of any Government is to protect the territorial integrity and economic stability of the country for which purpose countries maintain adequate defence forces. The size and composition of the armed forces depends upon the threat perception of each country and this perception changes from time to time.

In 1950, India became a sovereign democratic republic and the entire task of protecting the territorial integrity was cast on the Indian Government. But maintaining the territorial integrity does not consist only of posting the army on the land frontiers or the navy to protect the nation from any attacks from the sea frontier or ensuring the safety of the skies over the country.

Now wars are fought mainly for economic gains like access to resources like oil, gas, minerals, etc. Though countries maintain adequate armed forces, they are mainly for defensive purposes. Instead of directly attacking in the conventional manner by using its armed forces, war is now normally waged through unconventional means like economic measures and politically destabilizing activities. Normally the aim is to weaken the country so that it can offer no resistance to the policies and actions of the targeting country and/or its allies. In some rare cases, acquiring additional territory could also be the aim.

In the Indian context, the most important factor to be kept in mind is the fact that the Indian subcontinent forming British India was partitioned into two parts, viz. India and Pakistan. But the partition was based solely on basis of religion. The demand by the Muslims of British India for a separate Muslim homeland was met by the creation of Pakistan. Hundreds of thousands of Muslims from British India migrated to the newly formed state of Pakistan simultaneously millions of Hindus migrated to India from the areas now designated as Pakistan. But Pakistan consisted of 2 parts- one part, viz. West Pakistan carved out of Punjab and Sind, while the other wing, viz. East Pakistan carved out of Bengal. Punjabi Mussalmans constituted the bulk of the population of West Pakistan, while East Pakistan consisted of Bengali Muslims. There was very little cultural affinity between the two and the common Islamic religion was the only bond between the two wings of Pakistan. East Pakistan had practically no industry and its main agricultural crops were jute and rice. The fertile Punjab was divided with West Pakistan getting significant part of the fertile wheat growing areas.

With the creation of Pakistan, the demand of the Muslims of India for a separate Muslim homeland was met. Hindus from what was to become Pakistan, migrated in large numbers to India but a large number of Muslims preferred to stay in India, rather than migrate to the newly created Pakistan. The transfer of population was effected among horrors of violence and butchery never seen before and hoping never to be repeated again.

It was expected that Muslims having achieved their aim of a Muslim state by partitioning the Indian subcontinent, there would be no more communal violence. But such hopes have been belied.

In 1971, East Pakistan separated after a violent struggle where India played a significant role in assisting the Bangladeshis against West Pakistan. It declared itself a new state of Bangladesh. After this, Pakistan consisted of only that part which was originally West Pakistan. The creation of Bangladesh thus resulted in the creation of two separate independent Muslim states on either side of India. There was great jubilation in India when Pakistan broke up and Bangladesh came into existence. India offered all assistance to Bangladesh in its developmental activities.

But there were a few voices which expressed concern at the break up of Pakistan. According to them, Pakistan could not be a serious threat with 2 wings separated by more than a 1000 miles. Besides almost 100,000 troops were stationed in East Pakistan as the relations between the East wing and West wing continued to deteriorate culminating in the creation of Bangladesh in 1971. It was felt that prior to 1971 West Pakistan would be preoccupied with maintaining peace in the East wing and thus could not pose a serious threat to India. But with the creation of Bangladesh, Pakistan could concentrate its entire armed forces on India's western borders. In the general euphoria in 1971, over the break up of Pakistan, such strategic aspects were not considered. One of the most important persons to comment on the breakup of Pakistan and creation of Bangladesh was Henry Kissinger, former Secy of State, USA. He was of the view that breaking up of Pakistan was not in India's interest.

Today, a large part of India's armed forces are tied up in maintaining a strong defensive position all along the western border, right from the Rann of Kutch to the Siachin glacier. It also has to maintain strong defensive front all along the India/ Bangladesh border, which is an extremely porous and largely unfenced and undemarcated border. Large scale infiltration from Bangladesh into India has been going on for years creating very serious problems for the *safety and integrity of the Indian nation*.

The partition of the Indian subcontinent and the emergence of Bangladesh have created immense problems for India. To make things worse, some elements in Pakistan are not happy with the economic and social progress made by India since 1947 and particularly since 1990s. This is in contrast to conditions in Pakistan. Such elements are trying to destabilize India by weakening India's democratic and social structure. Hence it's all the more necessary for the Indian authorities to take steps - whether it's maintaining the defence forces ready for any eventualities or strengthening the internal security systems and prevent infiltration of foreign nationals. But how far is the Indian Government successful in achieving these aims?

Bangladesh is now an Islamic state but economically very weak and poor. India's expectations that it would become a secular state and eschew politics based on religion have been belied. Very little economic development coupled with increasing population is placing an immense burden on the scarce resources including land.

Ever since creation of Bangladesh, there has been large scale illegal influx of Bangladeshis into India, particularly the areas bordering Bangladesh. Numerous official reports have given data which clearly indicates the increasing influx of Bangladeshis, changing the entire demographic constitution of these areas. Some of the data is given below.

T. V. Rajeshwar, former chief of the Intelligence Bureau (IB), when Governor of West Bengal had repeatedly sent reports to successive Governments at Centre and also to the President and Prime Minister warning that a IIIrd Islamic republic (I & II being Pakistan and Bangladesh) would be carved out in the subcontinent in view of the rapidly changing demographic constitution of districts bordering Bangladesh.

A few tables in support are given below:

WEST BENGAL

Table 1: Percentage growth of population between 1991-2001 in districts of WB

District	Muslim	Non-Muslim	Total
South 24 Parganas	34.2	11.5	20.8
North 24 Parganas	23	22.6	22.7
Nadia	22	18.8	19.5
Murshidabad	28.4	16.4	23.8
Malda	30.7	19.4	24.7
Kolkata	19	0.7	4.0
South & North Dinajpur	32	22.7	26
Jalpaiguri	31.3	20.4	21.5
Coochbehar	18.5	12.8	14.2

Table 2: Muslims as per cent of total population

District	1991	2001
South 24 Parganas	30	33.2
North 24 Parganas	24.2	24.2
Nadia	24.9	25.4
Murshidabad	61.4	63.7
Malda	47.5	49.7
Kolkata	17.7	20.3
S & N Dinajpur	37	38
Jalpaiguri	10	11
Coochbehar	23	24

It can be seen from Table 2 that Muslims as per cent of total population of WB has increased in every district over the decade 1991-2001. Table 1 also shows that percentage growth of Muslims in districts of WB between 1991 and 2001 was significantly higher than that of non-Muslims.

ASSAM

Table 3: Growth of population between 1991-2001 in districts bordering Bangladesh

District	Muslims	Non-Muslims	Total
Dhubri	29	17	23
Goalpara	32	14	23
Hailakandi	27	13	21
Karimganj	29	14	22
Cachar	25	16	19

Table 4: Percentage growth of population between 1991-2001 in other districts

District	Muslims	Non-Muslims	Total
Barpeta	26	10	19
Naogaon	32	11	22
Marigaon	27	16	21
Darrang	29	10	16

Table 5: Muslims as per cent of population in districts bordering Bangladesh

District	1991	2001
Dhubri	70	74
Hailakandi	55	58
Goalpara	50	54
Cachar	35	36

Table 6: Muslims as % of population in other districts

District	1991	2001
Barpeta	56	59
Naogaon	47	52
Marigaon	46	46
Darrang	32	36

BIHAR

Table 7: Percentage growth of population between 1991-2001

District	Muslims	Non-Muslims	Total
Kishanganj	35	25	32
Araria	36	32	34
Purnea	44	31	35
Katihar	40	26	32

Table 8: Muslims as per cent of population

District	1991	2001
Kishanganj	66	67
Araria	40	41
Purnea	34	37
Katihar	40	42

What are the reasons for the differences in growth of Muslim and non-Muslim population? Are the Muslims of these regions exceptionally fecund? Are non-Muslims suddenly embracing Islam? Are Muslims from other parts of India flooding these areas which are not prosperous? Or is natural growth being topped by inundation from Bangladesh?

In November 1998, Gen. Sinha, then Governor of Assam had sent to the President of India " Report on illegal migration into Assam". Just like T.V. Rajeshwar, Governor of West Bengal, he also drew attention to differential decadal growth of non-Muslims and Muslims in Assam.

(in per cent)

	1950-61	196-71	1981-91
Non-Muslims	34	37	42
Muslims	38	31	77

Till 1971 the rate of growth of population of non-Muslims and Muslims was more or less steady. But after 1971, the non-Muslim rate of growth increased by 42%, but the Muslim growth rate more than doubled to 77%.

Extracts from Gen. Sinha's report quoted in subsequent paras:

"By 1991, 4 districts, Dhubri, Goalpara, Barpeta and Hailakundi have become Muslim majority districts.... Growth of Muslim population emphasized to show extent of illegal Bangladeshi migration. It poses *grave threat to identity of Assamese people and to our national security.*" Threat to reduce local Assamese to minority status as has happened in Sikkim and local original Buddhist and Christians in Tripura. He further states "entire land mass of North-East can be severed from the rest of India — a long cherished dream of Bangladesh. East Pakistan. The demographic balance changed in favor of Muslims in border districts and process is still continuing. This demographic invasion of Assam may result *in loss of geostrategically vital districts of Assam.* Bangladesh has discarded secularism and is an Islamic state". The above are extracts from official reports by a retired Army General when he was posted as Governor of Assam.

Apparently no action was taken on this report or on the earlier report of T. V. Rajeshwar then Governor of West Bengal.

In 1992, Hiteshwar Saikia, Chief Minister of Assam had declared in the Assam Assembly that there were about three million illegal Bangladeshi immigrants in the state. But he had to capitulate to the demand of the Muslim United Front leaders and withdraw his statement within 48 hours. So a responsible and duly elected Chief Minster had to withdraw within 48 hours an official statement made by him in the state Assembly about the large scale illegal influx of Bangladeshis in the state under the pressure of a Muslim organization though this continuing huge influx was affecting not only all aspects of the state's well being but also a *matter of national security*.

In 1993, the Home Minster of India had officially replied to a question that he was not in a position to give the number of illegal migrants from Bangladesh, as "we are not able to count them". In 1997, late Inderjit Gupta, when Home Minister of India, had stated that there were about 10 million (1 crore) illegal immigrants from Bangladesh. But no action was taken or contemplated even after acknowledging above. So about 1% of India's population consists of illegal Bangladeshis.

The Director Generals (DG) of Police met in a conference at Delhi in 1994. The Intelligence Bureau (IB) presented a detailed note *on Bangladesh being a continuing haven for terrorists striking at India and constituted a grave danger to national security, an accretion to security threats from Bangladesh* particularly after formation of BNP led Government in 2001.The IB report further stated that "Bangladesh provides shelter to insurgent groups and assists in carrying out raids in our border states. Arms are also reported to be supplied by Bangladesh. There has been a growth of radical Islamic groups and also Madrassas reported to be teaching hatred against India as also efforts said to be going on to subvert section of India's border states. IB also stated that the continuing inflow of illegal immigrants *resulting in demographical distortion and growing political clout of such illegal* particularly in Border States, such illegals have *assumed serious security implications*. Lakhs of illegals are already in Delhi, Maharashtra, Gujarat, UP, etc. In Nagaland illegals have increased from 20,000 (1991) to 75,000 (2001)".

It is widely reported that Indian citizens particularly those affiliated to political parties, assist illegals in getting ration cards and enrolling as voters and indirectly help in getting Indian citizenship. "In Assam, already illegals have managed to influence in 50 out of 126 assembly constituencies. Naturally there is strong resentment, often involving violence in Assam and Nagaland. The North East Students Organization (NESO) has taken up issue of illegals and repeal of IMDT act. Already there is steady growth in Bangladesh of Wahabi type of Islam which encourages 'jehadi terrorism'. Islamic organizations in Bangladesh distributing anti India and fundamentalist propaganda in North East (NE)."

In November 2002 , calendars depicting Osama Bin Laden found widely circulated in Karimganj district, Assam. Large number of CDs and audio cassettes containing anti-India inflammatory speeches seized in Tezpur and Karimganj. Now there is talk in Bangladesh, of Lebensraum in NE to cope with increasing population. Few people in India remember that World War II started with talk by Hitler of Lebensraum and hence marched into Czechoslovakia thereby leading to the horrific World War II.

All the above points were made at the DG conference held in Oct 2004 at Delhi. Usual resolutions were passed, papers distributed, but no action was taken as Central Government was unwilling to pay the slightest attention or take action against more than a million Bangladeshi infiltrators to *safeguard the integrity of the nation despite particularly the reports* at the DGs conference and also reports of former Governors of Assam and West Bengal .

The facts in regard to the political developments in Assam since 1978 are as follows. All Assam Students Union Organization (AASUO) and All Assam Gana Samgram Parishad (AAGSP) agitated from 1979 to 1985 against large scale influx of foreigners in state and were apprehensive of being swamped by them. Rajiv Gandhi as Prime Minister took the initiative leading to the signing of the Assam Accord where it was agreed:

(1) For of detection of foreigners, January 1966 to be the base date and those who came on or after the base date

and upto 24 March 1971 shall be detected and their names deleted from electoral roll.

(2) Those coming after 25 March 1971 shall be detected and expelled.

The IMDT Act was enacted to detect and deport foreigners in view of the Rajiv Accord. But it has proved ineffective and tilted in favor of illegal as:

(i) Every application made against any person to be accompanied by affidavit sworn by not less than 2 persons residing within jurisdiction of the same police station.

(ii) Application to be made with prescribed fees.

(iii) Onus shall lie with complainant.

Unlike Foreigners Act, it took away powers of issuing Quit India notices, arrest, interrogation, etc. from *the police and put the burden of proof on the police.*

So detection and deportation was extremely slow and cumbersome procedure. IMDT Act was labeled as Black Law and discriminated against Assam as rest of India governed by Foreigners Act which made deportation relatively easy. But IMDT Act made deportation practically impossible as:

(i) Onus of proving nationality put on citizen making complaint.

(ii) So encouraged illegal migrants from other states to Assam from where it was practically impossible to deport him.

India now has 2 different laws dealing with immigration. All over the world any country has only one law dealing with migrants. Former Assam Gana Parishad (AGP) Government of Assam went to Supreme Court for abrogation of the IMDT Act, NE states also filed affidavits in SC. The SC expressed concern over unabated immigration of Bangladeshis to NE states and asked the Centre to make 'strict and serious 'attempts to stop the influx. Division Bench of the SC said "this influx *of Bangladeshis was posing danger to region's demography*". But the present Government in Assam made a complete volte face and filed an affidavit that IMDT Act "was adequate to detect and deport illegal immigrants and that it did not protect interest of Bangladeshis". Affidavit admitted that so far only 1494 persons declared illegal migrants could be deported. 1494 was not even 0.03% of the number of illegal Bangladeshis in Assam alone.

The NE is a very important part of India. The huge influx of Bangladeshis in Assam and other states bordering Bangladesh is a dangerous portend for the safety and integrity of India. Nagaland has been demanding independence for decades. So it is all the necessary to ensure the development of all the border states. Forces inimical to India are only too eager to foment trouble with a view to destabilize India.

Manipur is a small state on the international border touching 2 countries. So, strategically it is an important part of India. It has a distinct cultural and political identity. In the 19th century, the British took Manipur as its Protectorate. Subsequently, it became a part of India. The Manipuris are basically honest and easy-going and carefree, because of the fertile Imphal Valley and natural beauty. The growth in population which is educated has not been matched by outlets for their talents. The Centre has failed to provide an administrative and political structure to encourage the people. Large amounts have been provided by the Centre but it has reportedly landed mostly with corrupt politicians or the venal bureaucrats. Most of the all India cadre of bureaucrats are said to consider this as a punishment posting and do not exhibit any inclination to perform their duty in developing the state. But this dissatisfaction is rapidly increasingly erupting in violence. With the Centre maintaining a strong army presence and treating it is a law and order problem and apparently not realizing that the occasional violence is only the sign of the easy going carefree and basically honest Manipuris yearning for good governance and getting rid of corrupt politicians and bureaucrats. The most important aspect the Centre has to keep constantly in mind is that Manipur state is very strategically situated and the people which are well inclined towards India of which they are a part. Rather than keep on pouring funds for 'development' which do not result in development of the people as a whole and maintaining a large army presence, it is essential to take urgent steps to root out corruption and simultaneously build up a prosperous and contented Manipur which is *essential for the defence of India*, otherwise forces inimical to India will use Manipur as one more base to further their objective of destabilizing India.

WEST BENGAL

In WB, the almost 2,200 km border with Bangladesh (BD) runs along 10 border districts. According to intelligence branch and also census reports, the demographic profile of border district has dramatically changed over the last 3 decades with the growth of Muslim population far in excess of that of non-Muslim and turning some of the districts into Muslim majority districts.

Shri R.N. Bhattacharya topped the West Bengal Civil Service exam in 1965 and joined the Indian Police Service (IPS) in 1966. He has extensive experience. He served in Tripura which has a 1000 km border with Bangladesh. Besides he has served as in charge of both the North and South Bengal border in 1993-96. It can be seen that he has extensive experience in Bengal and Tripura. He was subsequently Inspector General (IG) Border Security Force (BSF) in charge of South Bengal border. During this period he had made in 1998, a number of vital and worrisome points.

He estimated the total influx of Bangladeshis to be about 1 crore out of which 50% settled in WB, so every 15th resident of WB is a Bangladeshi. But Bangladeshis have also spread all over India, including Delhi, Gujarat, Maharashtra, Rajasthan and even Tamil Nadu. One of the reasons for the huge influx could be the extreme poverty in Bangladesh.

According to him almost all these infiltrators are harbored by locals. Lakhs of them work as domestic servants. About 75% of rikshawalas in Siliguri are Bangladeshis. He also states that about 25 % of the 11 million population of Greater Kolkata is Bangladeshi. But the BSF faces many problems in preventing the influx. The land border is only 750 km out of the total international border in South Bengal of 1150 km, the rest is either a river line or a "fluid" border which means an imaginary line across the centre of the river which keeps on changing its course constantly. The task of identifying infiltrators is difficult as: (i) common language and social customs, (ii) invariably there is an outcry when a known smuggler or tout is caught red-handed with BSF and are quite often manhandled or beaten up and (iii) most of the BSF personnel are non-Bengali. According to him the Dhaka/Kolkata axis has become a golden route for the ISI and WB a safe haven for spies.

But the contrast in handling of infiltrators by the two countries is glaring. India merely pushes them across the border, and then the Bangladeshis simply cross into again at some other place or after some time. The BSF in West Bengal is not permitted to shoot at illegal intruders, whereas in the Western Sector, J & K, Gujarat, Rajasthan, the intruders can be shot. If at all an intruder is arrested in India, the maximum punishment is 6 months, whereas in Bangladesh, an illegal Indian will have to undergo 13 years rigorous imprisonment.

In July 1999, there was a blast at New Jalpaiguri station (West Bengal) near Siliguri which killed 10 and wounded over 80 persons. An estimate by the IB reportedly puts the increase in the population of Siliguri and adjoining areas at 150 % against 30% to 40% in other Muslim dominated areas in WB. The Siliguri corridor (known as chicken's neck) is barely 30 miles wide. *It is the only link between rest of India and the North East.* So this is an extremely important area from the strategic angle. The *sole rail connection between rest of India and NE states passes through this narrow corridor.*

The intelligence agencies, including army intelligence are said to be extremely worried about the safety of this narrow Siliguri corridor, more so because army intelligence has reportedly identified villages in and around Siliguri with a curious population mix as havens for ISI operations. Chopra, about 50 km from Siliguri with a population of 25,000 is said to be the nerve centre for illegal border trade and fake currency rackets. Another village, Islampur, 70 km from Siliguri has a peculiar population mix. About 2000 Poshtu, Baluch settlers engaged in money lending and are suspected ISI activities. There are also about 6000 Iranians settled since 1960s, all reportedly without valid documents. But the reasons for such a mix of non-Indians settling in and around the strategic Siliguri-corridor are not known.

Shri Buddhadeb Bhattacharya, erstwhile Home Minister, now C.M. WB, has been getting hundreds of official reports from various intelligence agencies about the alarming influx of Bangladeshis in the state and the increasing activities of the ISI. But it was only in 1999 that after a visit to Murshidabad, he reportedly commented "there are a lot of ISI operatives here". Debabrata Bandopadhyay, the Director, Intelligence branch was said to be more specific by stating "This region has become a fertile ground for ISI".

The unending influx of illegal Bangladeshis with already more than 1.5 crores estimated to have settled in India is creating serious security and severe economic problems for India. But the problem mainly involves enclaves and 'adverse possessions'. According to some officials, the border dispute could have been resolved long ago as the Indira- Mujib accord clearly stipulates that all enclaves will merge with the country within which they are located and the population living there having the option of shifting out or joining the country they are in. Similar guidelines were also laid down regarding "adverse possession". There are 11 exchangeable Indian enclaves in Bangladesh with an area of 17,150 acres. Similarly, there are 51 exchangeable enclaves in India. There are 43 pieces of Indian land under Bangladesh and 447 pieces of Bangladesh under India's "adverse possession".

Regarding the dispute on undemarcated land, it arises from original land documents, with India relying on 1914 land records and Bangladesh on 1937 documents. The responsibility in Bangladesh for fixing land boundary rests on the Home Ministry but in India with the Ministry of External Affairs (MEA) and not Home Ministry. It is the MEA which has the task of any survey or change to be effected on the international border. But the reasons reportedly given by MEA for keeping the border problem festering since 1974 and creating serious security and economic problems, apart from the deaths of thousands of Indians, is "demarcation of border has not been completed yet".

It is high time the Central Government took firm steps to implement the Indira-Mujib Accord of 1974 and straightened out the porous border. That will go a long way in controlling the influx which has assumed alarming proportions and pose a serious threat to the integrity and economic stability of India. The Centre had appointed a Task Force on Border Management (TFBM) under Shri Godbole, Home Secy, Government of India, in the wake of the Kargil conflict. It made a number of observations and recommendations. Some of the reported observations are stated below.

It emphatically recommended that IMDT Act be repealed and action be taken uniformly throughout India under the Foreigners Act. The NDA Government had introduced a bill in the Lok Sabha to repeal the IMDT Act but the House was dissolved and the Bill lapsed.

All these years the WB Government did not take strong action to prevent infiltration. It was only in 2004 that Buddhadeb Bhattacharya, the new Chief Minister of WB, who acknowledged that infiltration across the border, had become a drain on the state's resources.

According to the TFBM , since 1970s over 64,000 killed in extremist violence related to Islamic Fundamentalists and Naxalite violence. In Oct 2003, 55 districts in 9 states affected by Naxalite violence. In Oct 2004, it had increased to 158 districts in 13 states as per official figures. Only 4 districts affected by Maoist violence in Dec 2001. This had increased to 75 districts.

It is only through well informed and vigilant public opinion that national security can be strengthened. Excessive and undue secrecy in such matters can be counter productive. TFBM drew pointed attention to danger of large scale immigration by Bangladeshis. 18% of WB and 32% of Assam assembly constituencies can be influenced by Bangladeshis. A study showed 96% of alleged Bangladeshis took active part in electoral politics in Kishanganj, Bihar in running of administration, police and influencing legislation. Emerging danger of future subversion can be clearly seen. Detailed steps to be taken to prevent subversion given in the report, but no action has said to have been taken.

Passport, ration card and registration as voter have been obtained easily by such immigrants, and that too very cheaply for a few hundred rupees. How much cheaper can obtaining citizenship of a country by an illegal means can be? Thanks to politicians and venal bureaucracy at all levels. Illegal Bangladeshis have spread all over India including Delhi, Mumbai and even remote areas of Kutch, etc.

Madrassas are rapidly increasing in sensitive border areas. In Terai region (Indo-Nepal border) there has been fourfold increase in Muslim population. On Indian side, there are over 340 mosques and 300 madarsas within 10 km of border. There are more than 280 mosques and 180 madarsas on the Nepal side. On the Rajasthan border, there are 130 madarsas registered with Wakf Board plus large number of unregistered madarsas on border itself. Growth of madarsas on border and strategic areas like Pokhran, Jaisalmer are higher than other areas and are centres of fundamentalists' activities.

There is a more startling and menacing and most rapid growth on Indo-Bangladesh border. There are about 1,000 mosques and 500 madarsas in close proximity to border on Indian side. An equal number in close proximity to border on Bangladesh side. Economic backwardness and sparse population falsifies claim of construction of these mosques and madarsas with local support. TFBM also forcefully brings out dissimilarities in visa system in India vis-à-vis Pakistan. India is very liberal, Pakistan is not. There is no control in India on Pakistanis who overstay and disappear. Officially the cumulative number of Pakistanis overstaying was over 11,000 (1999), of these 3,000 have gone underground. It may be recalled that Pak national responsible for hijacking plane to Khandahar had entered India on valid visa and gone underground.

Ministry of Home Affairs (MHA) is unable to give any information to TF about 11,000 Pakistanis who have just disappeared. Growing incidence of drug abuse have been in

Manipur, Mizoram, Arunachal Pradesh and other border areas of Assam , mostly through Morek in Manipur. Narcotic Control Board (NCB), the nodal national agency has regional office in Imphal with jurisdiction over 7 states with staff of 11. It has no roadworthy vehicle, no communication system. Regional officer does not even have a phone at his residence. There is: (i) no institutionalized arrangement for sharing of intelligence between NCB and other concerned agencies and (ii) no arrangement even for exchanging information on matters of mutual interest. Army and paramilitary forces (CPMF) are not even aware that any central agency is responsible for taking action against drug traffickers located in NE states. Working of NCB has been severely handicapped for lack of vehicles, equipment/gadgets, secret service funds to develop network of informants. NCB as constituted now and functioning now—incapable of playing role of an apex central co-ordinating agency for which it was constituted – only results in providing ISI easy entry points.

RBI had issued instructions in 1994 to all commercial banks to provide particulars regarding receipt of foreign contributions. But as per RBI, the MHA is not even receiving quarterly statements of foreign contributions received by foreign associations. The non-chalant attitude towards large scale foreign contributions being used for terrorist activities in India can be seen from the following statement by MHA in 2000 that "the situation same as in 1994 and had no idea of actual quantum of receipts which could be very much larger, we share RAW observation that most of foreign contribution received under Foreign Exchange Regulation Act (FERA) are being diverted for funding terrorist organizations".

Directorate of Enforcement (DE) unable to detect linkages between activities of havala operators and subversive elements, as no mechanism exists in DE to collate required information from IB, RAW, Special Branch (SB), etc. "Each organization working its own watertight compartment and urges MHA to organize co-ordination between all concerned agencies."

Now, money laundering (ML) is a vital means of promoting terrorism and other subversive and illegal activities in a country. Naturally, it has a significant effect on the *stability of a nation*.

But no effective measures appear to have been taken so far to curb this menace. The reaction of the Government agencies to ML is reported to be:

(i) Department of Revenue, Ministry of Finance, states that no system exists for detecting ML and apparently aware of the problem.

(ii) Income tax authorities claim to be concerned with collection of taxes and not source.

(iii) Directorate of Enforcement (DE) apparently not concerned as money received through banking channels.

(iv) Revenue intelligence and customs department apparently not concerned unless linked with invoice manipulation.

Another device used by ISI to destabilize the Indian economy is by trying to flood India with fake currency notes. Official sources confirm widespread network particularly in Gujarat, Maharashtra and some other states to pump forged Indian currency (FIC) into Indian economy. But as official statement of total FIC seized was not available, RBI confirmed that no system at all for all seizure of FIC being reported to designated Central agency. Incidentally, it is worth recalling that Germany had tried to flood UK with forged British currency notes during World War II but were not successful as quick and appropriate action was taken by British authorities to catch and imprison all persons trying to circulate such notes.

It appears that Intelligence Bureau (IB) had submitted a detailed report in June 2002 to Home Minster/Dy PM showing the magnitude of the problem and listed out persons holding key positions in various banks, where they facilitated conversion of fake currency and other transactions, and detailed the nexus between fake currency notes smugglers, terrorists and bank officials. But it appears that no effective action was taken on the IB report.

DEFENCE SERVICES —ARMY/NAVY/AIR FORCE

The function of India's Defence Forces is basically defensive and meant to deter and not attack. But even the Cabinet Ministers on the Cabinet Committee on National Security

(CCNS) are hardly aware of this fact and that the size of the armed forces, their quality and type and quantity of their equipment are meant for deterrence and to face a potential threat if deterrence fails. Naturally, this is related to the expenditure on defence the country has to bear.

The most important function of the CCNS is to periodically post itself with a professional threat assessment against which the country's armed forces have to be prepared. But neither the CCNS nor the top civilian bureaucracy manage to do so and do not keep the Parliament adequately informed. The failure of the CCNS to obtain a comprehensive threat assessment results in each service chief relying on his own threat assessment and naturally demands equipment as per his own threat assessment without taking into account the threat perceptions made by the other Service Chiefs. Each of the three Service Chief works thus in isolation with nobody to collate all the views in the absence of a single comprehensive threat assessment. Such reports are prepared in mature democracies like UK, USA by civilians of course with the aid of the armed forces chiefs, as these reports are a vital factor in maintaining civilian control.

But in India, even the elementary Joint Intelligence Committee has not been able to function. One of the main reasons being the inability of the Parliamentarians to grasp the broader picture of National security. In recent years, Parliamentarians are preoccupied with criticizing defence deals and thereby delaying by decades badly needed comprehensive modernizing of the entire armed services including weaponry.

Out of the entire Defence budget of Rs. 42,000 thousand crores, barely 10% is available for new equipment and modernization. To ensure optimal utilization of such meager resources, it is vital that the demands from the 3 services be carefully considered and sanctioned so as to get the maximum benefit to the 3 services from the same resources. At present each service chief presses his demands for his own service without considering the other two.

But a balanced view needs to be taken of the total requirements of the 3 services and optimize the use of scarce funds. This could very well be achieved by having a Chairman of Chief of Staff committee, like other countries. But for reasons unknown, this is not being done. It is ultimately the CCNS which has to manage the entire defence portfolio. The Defence Minister leaves it to the bureaucracy. But these are generalists and are incapable of providing modern, upto date, and specialized knowledge in the field of defence services.

This seems to have resulted in the creation of a defence bureaucracy with a vested interest and Parliamentarians who take active and vociferous part in criticizing old or proposed deals for acquiring modern weaponery. But today there has to be a common understanding of threat perceptions over at least 10 year time span by the three wings of the armed forces as also the political analysis in the MoD and the ruling Government. This entire process can be summed up as defence planning which determines the national security goals. It also determines formulation of policies and strategies which will govern:

(i) Allocation of funds.

(ii) Building of capabilities which have to be deployed for achieving these objectives.

It is obvious that not only is the planning a time consuming process, but there is bound to be a substantial time lag between formulation of defence plan and implementation thereof. The factors in implementation can be briefly considered as follows:

(i) First stage acquisition indigenously or by import of the weaponry (includes guns, ships, planes, etc.).

(ii) Revision of tactics and procedures in terms of new weaponry.

(iii) Training at all levels to operate the weapons.

(iv) Ensure adequate and proper maintenance capabilities - men and materials.

Weapons of any sort cannot be bought off the shelf and given to troops without ensuring compliance with the aspects briefly indicated above. So the importance of the overall time factor has to be kept in mind when considering defence preparedness. It must also be remembered that the cost of purchasing/acquisition of any weapon will also be normally be staggered over a period of years. Hence a thorough evaluation of any weaponry to be acquired has to be gone through – which itself is a time consuming process extending over a period of may be 5 years.

The process of deciding upon the purchase of each and every item is subjected to a thorough and rigorous scrutiny, right from considering the necessity of acquiring such a weapon. As explained by knowledgeable sources, within the army, 5 departments independently analyze and comment on each and every case. Only after completion of this process, do the three seniormost army chiefs, viz. Deputy Chief, Vice Chief and the Chief give their approval. But this is not the end. It is thereafter subjected to a detailed review in the MoD. Differences, if any, have to be reconciled. Only then does the case get cleared for procurement.

The process is long and tortuous. It involves not only the technical/financial details, but also other options. As this process takes a couple of years, the officers who initiated the process rarely continue in the same post over the entire period involved in the evaluation process.

But this detailed procedure leads to inordinate delays. During this period, the supplier may change the prices/delivery terms/technical specifications, so while the procedure has certain advantages, it also leads to delayed supplies which could have very serious adverse consequences for the nation. In the light of rapidly changing threat perceptions, it is necessary to have a close look at the antiquated systems and procedures for procurement of defence requirements and ensure a permanent state of preparedness. This also involves a study of the entire process of defence planning and also the ability of the Indian industry to meet a substantial part, if not the whole, of the vital needs of the armed forces and thereby reduce dependence on foreign suppliers who can always hold the country to ransom.

Some years ago the defence budget used to be passed without any debate, probably because the MPs realized their ignorance about defence matters. Today the pendulum has swung to the other extreme. Not only have the MPs become vociferous but even the media is active in unearthing 'scams' or suspected scams. This has resulted in almost a complete lack of decisions being taken on defence matters though the need is for expeditious action to bolster our defences. For over 2 decades, since the HDW/Bofors controversy, decision taking has come to almost a standstill.

The lack of decisiveness in procurement can be seen from the fact that Defence Ministry surrendered Rs. 6,000 crores (2001/02) and Rs. 9,000 crores (2002/03) marked for procurement. The army badly needs self propelled guns and a deal was underway with Denel of South Africa. But in May 2005, the Government of India has referred 38 defence deals to the Central Bureau of Investigation (CBI) for investigation. Now no official will take any decision on any of the defence deals, thus completely upsetting the army's modernization plans. The Government had looked at South Africa, France and Israel as Russia had reportedly delayed supplying arms and spares. But it's the nation's security which suffers from such delays.

Some of the weapons procurement which will be indefinitely delayed is listed below:

(i) Scorpene submarines from France.

(ii) Heron unmanned aerial vehicles (UAVs) from Israel, proposal said to be lying with CCNS since January 2005.

(iii) Tracked self propelled guns – Denel's G6 self-propelled guns were to be fitted on Indian chassis.

(iv) Multirole combat aircraft to replace 30-year-old MIG 21 (dubbed as coffin makers) – 4 foreign companies have submitted offers.

(v) Wheeled self-propelled guns from Denel approved in Jan 2004. India has the 4th largest army in the world but does not have such wheeled guns.

(vi) 155 mm towed guns—400 were to be procured and the balance of about 1100 were to be manufactured locally under transfer of technology.

Even procurement of bulletproof jackets badly needed in anti-insurgency operations particularly, are delayed. Troops lack over 200,000 such jacketes, but still not completed though process started over a decade ago. The Standing Committee on Defence had noted with concern in 2003 the underutilization of funds earmarked for capital expenditure. One of the reasons for lapsing or underutilization of funds for modernization appears to be the process of annual budgets but purchase and delivery of any contracted item normally is spread over a number of years. Hence the need for changing system of annual budgeting for a modified roll over budget. It has weakened the process of modernization of the forces. The 10th defence plan has not been finalized even though the first 2 years of the projected plan are already over in 2003. This is a repetition of earlier similar mistakes in the defence planning process and is indicative of adhocism and non-serious approach which seems to prevail, notwithstanding, the trauma of Kargil and other assaults on national security.

Currently the defence budget is about Rs. 45,000 crores which sounds impressive but in reality only about 10% is available for modernization. More than 50% is taken up by pay and allowances.

The bulk of the army's equipment consists of outdated equipments. It is reported that out the total of 3,000 tanks, almost half (1200) are Vijayanta tanks of 1965 vintage and another 800 are of 1970 vintage. Even the main weapon for infantry, viz. 7.62 mm self-loading rifles (SLR) are 30 years old. The process of modernizing has only recently started with Indian small arms system 5.5 mm rifles. The army does not have battlefield surveillance radars, which help troops to locate opposition's artillery guns and assists in directing accurate counter bombardment. The list is large including winter equipment (especially for Siachin, the coldest place in the world) reliable communication sets, night vision equipment, self-propelled guns, etc.

There is a tendency to believe that the armed forces have to depend entirely on imported equipment, despite the fact of India having a well equipped Defence Research and Development Organization (DRDO) engaged for decades in cutting edge technologies essential mainly for guided missiles and other high tech equipments like Light Combat Aircraft (LCA) or air borne early warning aircraft. But the Kargil conflict has shown that the maximum and urgent need is for less hi-tech products but of maximum utility, like night vision glasses, fail safe communication systems in the most rugged terrain, synthetic aperture radar (SAR), etc. This does not mean that DRDO cut out its ongoing research and involvement in cutting technologies. But DRDO needs to collaborate with Indian industry to reduce and preferably cut out India's dependence on imported weaponry.

It is reported that India uses remote sensing satellites for flood control or crop estimates, etc. Such equipment does not appear to be used by the armed forces for reasons unknown. DRDO could have assisted the army in utilizing such SARs or modified SARs in locating enemy troop movements/camps/helipads, etc. It is said that Pakistan built 13 helipads in the Kargil sector without being noticed by the Indians. Numerous Indian lives could have been saved had such SARs, night vision glasses, periscopes, etc. been provided to the Indian troops.

The ignorance of most of the Parliamentarians about modern warfare and their inability to grasp the necessity for a well thoughtof strategic forward looking defence plan projected over a time span of at least 10 years is adversely affecting the national's security. But even with the adoption of such a plan with list of agreed weaponry, it is doubtful if it benefits the nation as the bureaucracy and the Parliament would keep on discussing the financial aspects without understanding the need for quick and firm decisions when technology changes rapidly and strategies have to keep pace with changing geo-political scenario.

ORDNANCE DEPOTS

Armed forces necessarily have to store large quantities of arms and ammunitions to meet the potential requirement in case of need. These have to be stored at scattered ordnance depots all over India at strategic locations. A Parliamentary panel had stated that security measures and storage methods had not changed since 1760s, though the type of ammunition keeps on changing.

There are 7 Central Ordnance Depots (COD) and all of them badly need modernization as these were constructed during World War II (1939-45), i.e. almost 70 years ago. In all, there are 40 main central and regional depots – all of them require modernization. But only Kanpur COD is being modernized at a cost of about Rs. 200 crores. Though all CODs are supposed to be modernized at a cost of about Rs. 300 crores each. Yet, getting such large amounts sanctioned seems to be an almost impossible task even though the losses through fires at depots in the last 5 years are huge as stated below:

	Depot	Loss-Rs. crores
March 2005	Pulgaon Central	22
July 2004	IAF Amla	28
May 2001	Bridwel field	375
April 2001	Manion field	28
April 2000	Bharatpur	393

A report after fire at Pulgaon in 1989 had *inter alia*, recommended not letting elephant grass in the vicinity of depots. A fire at Jabalpur was of such intensity that it raged for 3 days.

As regards Bharatpur fire of 2000 the Defence Minister told Parliament that loss including infrastructural damage of about Rs. 13 crores and 12,000 tonnes of ammunition was about Rs. 390 crores. The cost of ammunition used in Kargil conflict was almost half of that at about Rs. 200 crores. Over the years, the Army's requests for modernization of ordnance depots have been reportedly been ignored by the bureaucracy and the Ministry of Defence. A Standing Committee of Parliament had about 5 years back highlighted the fact that modernization of at least 7 principal CODs around the country, has despite reminders over the years, been stalled by the MoD /Finance Ministry on the plea of lack of funds – the result of this attitude can be seen in the huge financial and strategic loss of ammunition periodically in frequent fires.

Ordnance depots necessarily have to be spread over a large area. The largest depot at Pulgaon (Maharashtra) is bigger in size than the average town. The army has sent teams abroad to study methods of storing ammunition. In NATO countries, ammunition is stored in box like structures with not a blade of grass allowed to grow in the vicinity and installation of state of the art fire fighting equipment. The structures are practical to implement and cost effective.

Every investigative team in India has made one very simple recommendation among others, viz. not letting elephant grass grow in the vicinity of depots. But somehow, for reasons not stated, such grass is allowed to grow and this helps the fire to spread very rapidly.

The proper storage of ordnances is very important but so is the inventory management for such large diversified army spread out over a variety of terrain. But according to a report on "Review of Inventory Management in Ordnance Services" tabled in Parliament by the Comptroller and Auditor General (CAG), the inventory management policies, practices and procedure currently in vogue are essentially based on World War II experiences. No comprehensive review has been carried out, though modified from time to time.

Army established a college of material management at Jabalpur to improve the inventory management system. Despite advances in computerization including development of indigenous super computer, major activity at all ordnance depots are still being done manually with few exceptions.

The present system of inventory control at ordnance depots is evidently extremely unsatisfactory. Just one example is given here which makes one apprehensive of the inadequacy of controls and checks over the inventory of such explosives. In Sept 2000, the Railway police found 130 boxes in a sealed wagon lying for over 2 years in the railway yard at Bhayandar (near Mumbai). On opening one of the boxes, the police found naval ammunition in it. The railway records indicated the sealed wagon containing ammunition was dispatched from Jabalpur ordnance depot to Uran (near Mumbai but away from Bhayandar and on a different railway line) ammunition depot. Neither the Jabalpur depot nor the naval authorities ever bothered to ascertain the whereabouts of a wagon load of ammunition for 2 years. It only shows that even wagon loads of ammunition can disappear without anybody knowing or bothering about it.

Numerous audit reports by Controller of Defence Accounts (CDA) have reported serious shortages in inventory as also stock registers missing. In Sept, 2000, some Naxalites arrested at Warangal, Andhra Pradesh had a few boxes of ammunition which had full details of originating Indian ordnance factory including batch number. But serious deficiencies continue as per CDA.

So, it is high time the Army improved its inventory control to a level befitting the fourth largest army in the world in a country which is the leader in Information Technology (IT) and most importantly ensured that it not fall into anti-national hands.

A. Army Jawans

A contented security force is a necessity for the safety of the country. The army depends to a large extent on the jawans, the non-officer class . Even when the Kargil conflict raged, the MoD showed its apathy towards the fighting jawans by issuing its directive where monthly pensions of officers were increased by about 12 to 24%, the personnel below officer rank (PBOR), the jawans would get no increment.

Pension rules are such that about 40 lakhs PBORs will get no benefit under the new directive of MoD. A PBOR has to put in 33 years service to get 50% of pay as pension. But PBORS retire after about 10 years service as the armed forces need young PBORs to fight. If a jawan retires after about 17 years service, it is felt that he should get at least 50% of pay. Presuming he joins at 18 and retires after 17 years active service, he will be only about 35 years old and in the prime of life, but with no job and a meager pension on which he as to support his family and dependents as Government does not provide him an alternative job or means of earning. Even a sepoy or a peon in a Public Sector Bank without any risk to his life, works till the age of 60 years and spends his entire life with his family. But a jawan's life is always at risk and almost his entire life is spent away from his family. Even after retiring , he is forced to take up a job away from his village and family, to earn a meager amount to maintain his family. But it is manifestly unfair to make a jawan suffer even after retirement, and the position of the injured is pitiable. But the nation has still to learn to honour those who undergo and are ready to sacrifice their lives in the interest of the nation.

B. Navy

India has a coastline of over 8,000 miles. India consists not only of mainland India whose Western border touches Pakistan and Bangladesh more or less on its South Eastern border. Besides it also consists of archipelago of Lakshwadeep as also the Andaman and Nicobar islands. Each of the archipelagos consists of hundreds of islands. The Andaman and Nicobar islands are almost a thousand miles from the mainland India in the Bay of Bengal but some of the islands in the archipelago are barely 100 miles from Myanmar or about 150 miles from Thailand or Indonesia. While Lakshwadeep islands are about 150 miles in the Arabian Sea off Kochi. The Bombay High oil fields lie about 100 miles off the West coast of India. India is heavily dependent on fuel oil from West Asian countries like UAE, Saudia, etc. so the sea lanes bringing fuel also have to be protected.

So all this requires a well equipped Navy. But how far is the Navy equipped to discharge its duty particularly in case of hostilities breaking one.

Jane's Fighting Ships are the most authoritative source for information regarding navies of the entire world. A comparison of India's navy with Japan's, even in 1980, as per data given in Jane's Fighting Ships (JFS) is quite interesting:

	India	Japan
Destroyers	-	31
Cruisers	2	-
Frigates	25	15
Submarines	8	15
Fast attack craft	16	5
Minesweepers	8	29
Aircraft carrier	1	-
Total	60	95
Personnel	46,000	42,200

India had in 1980, 4 frigates with a range 4,500 miles @ 12 knots and 3 other frigates with range of 7,500 miles @ 16 knots. The carrier Vikrant could do 12,000 miles @ 16 knots or 6,200 miles @ 23 knots.

The entire Japanese fleet is indigenous armed with an average range of 7,000 miles @ 20 knots. It has to be remembered that after World War II , the build up of a modern well equipped Navy goes on despite Article 9 of the Japanese constitution stipulating that Japan forever renounces making war on anyone. It assigns barely 1% of its GNP to national defence. The Navy accounts for over 20% of its military budget. But with the increasing GNP, the budget for defence also keeps on increasing.

There has been a slight increase in the Indian navy. It had in 1995, 2 carriers, 18 submarines, 5 destroyers, 16 frigates, 18 corvettes, 20 fast attack craft and 22 minesweepers plus 11 naval air squadrons with a total of 101 ships and 56,000 personnel. India has shipyards at Goa, Kolkata, Vizag and Mumbai but they could manufacture only a few Godavari class frigates, Kukri class corvette and a few Tarantula class fast attack craft. All the other ships of the Indian navy particularly aircraft carriers, cruisers, submarines, etc. are imported.

The entire Japanese fleet (as also Airforce) is indigenously designed and manufactured ever since World War II. But even today India lacks plans to indigenize planning and manufacture of naval/army/airforce requirements and is dependent on foreign suppliers. But this is not due to lack of local talent.

JFS of 1995-96 makes some startling statements. "In 1990 there was a vibrant indigenous building programme, a stream of new construction, acquisition from Russia, the lease of a nuclear submarine and designs for new aircraft carriers. This was the force that was going to dominate the Indian Ocean, ready to challenge even superpower incursions. But since 1990 no order has been placed for warships for 5 years. Ships under construction are running years behind schedule, those in service suffer from lack of spares, refits and updates are being postponed. There also appears to have been no strategic review of requirements for many years leading to adhoc decisions replacing planning priorities based on a coherent policy. This is still a powerful regional navy, but without more Government support, block obsolescence of ships going to catch up in a few years time. Comparatively speaking, Pakistan's navy is doing better, with real growth included in the budget, gas turbine frigates replacing steam driven ships and a new order placed for French submarines."

About 20 years back, the East yard at Mazagon Dock, Mumbai had been specially constructed at a cost of about Rs. 50 crores. It made only 2 submarines, the Shalki in 1992 and the Shankul in 1994. Since then the only work done at the specially constructed dockyard at a cost of Rs. 50 crores was the refitting of 2 German submarines acquired earlier. The entire investment of Rs. 50 crores is unutilized, the specially trained labor force has either left or just idle since 1994.

India and France completed negotiations in early 2004 to assemble six 2000 tonne displacement Scorpene submarines at Mumbai with full technology transfer. The deal is estimated at about 7 billion Euros. Though the deal has been cleared by the Navy and the MoD, the CCS has not yet cleared the deal. According to the deal, each year a submarine would be assembled at Mazagon Dock after signing the contract.

In May 2005, the Chief of the Navy expressed his unhappiness by terming the inordinate delay as regrettable in the decision making level at the political level. The delay will have an adverse impact on the Navy's operational capability. Submarines cannot be replaced overnight. It takes 6 to 7 years to make a submarine. Pakistan and some of the neighboring countries are already making or acquiring the most modern submarines and India will be the one with practically no submarines as the older ones will have to be phased out soon and become outdated for modern warfare.

The lack of funding and a coherent long term planning was hampering the Navy's operational capability particularly with an ageing fleet. The entire process ensures avoidable delays extending over years. A senior Navy officer stated how inordinate delays take place. The Scorpene project was finalized twice over after answering each and every question - once to the NDA Government and then to the subsequent UPA Government. And now the file is lying with the CCS. As a result of the delay in the final sanction, it is reported that the German HDW is making a bid for this same submarine contract. If the HDW is allowed to compete at this late stage, it could delay the entire project by at least another 4 years. In the mean while, Pakistan has started manufacturing the French Augusta 90 B submarine, armed with Harpoon and Exocet missiles. With India not even having finalized the Scorpene, deal after so many years and CCS still not approving the deal, and inspite of having a special yard for making submarines, the Navy is in a tough spot.

India has to learn fast to become self-sufficient in every sphere. It cannot afford national defence to be at the mercy of foreign suppliers. All that is required is the political will to face self-reliance as a goal as there is no lack of indigenous talent in every field. Despite having so many steel plants, yet more than 10,000 tonnes of high strength steel had to be imported for making the stealth warships.

So, the inordinate delay in finalizing the deal to acquire Scorpene submarines is going to have a serious effect on the national security. But there is no sign of the bureaucracy or the politicians waking up to the need for systemizing and institutionalizing the defence planning and ensuring the availability of necessary weaponry on an ongoing basis.

C. Air Force

The Air force plays an extremely vital role in modern warfare, both in the defensive as well as offensive aspect. The Indian Air Force (IAF) has always played a very important role both in peace time as well as war time. But it is known for the needless deaths of hundreds of young and brave pilots.

It has cost the lives of more than 160 young pilots and over 300 supersonic fighter planes since 1971. According to the statement made in Parliament about 5 years ago, the IAF admitted having lost more than 80 trained young pilots and 185 supersonic fighter planes – in financial terms, it means a loss of about Rs 7,000 crores being the cost of the planes. This loss of planes is said to amount a squadron a year or almost 25 % of the entire fleet of planes during the decade ending 1990. The losses continue to mount.

Almost 60% of the losses are accounted for by the ageing MiG 21 which are about 30 to 40 years old. They constitute 22 of the 35 squadrons of the IAF. But even newly acquired Jaguar has crashed - almost 20 Jaguars out of the 4 Jaguar squadrons in the force. One of the main reasons for these crashes is the lack of proper training for the pilots of this supersonic jet fighter. The AJT is a prime necessity for any modern air force. India has not been able to acquire even a single AJT though supersonic fighters have been inducted all these years over the last 4 decades. It means that pilots are being made to fly supersonic fighters without proper training.

IAF has been repeatedly asking for AJTs, but the bureaucrats have been delaying it on some pretext or the other for the last so many decades- no matter if hundreds of pilots needlessly lose their lives and continue to lose their lives. The Parliamentarians also have not shown the slightest interest over the last so many decades in making any effort to ensure that obtaining the AJTs are expedited and lives of young pilots are saved. Even the loss of planes in financial terms exceeds Rs 10,000 crores. But then, what is this insurmountable factor which prevents India from acquiring these badly needed AJTs over the last so many decades.

It appears that the delay is occasioned solely on account of the price factor. The IAF had complained to the Defence Minister about 5 years back that the bureaucrats of MoD were needlessly delaying the acquisition. So the Minister introduced an innovation by making a senior Air Marshal as Chairman of the Price Negotiation Committee (PNC). But this has also not resulted in the acquisition of AJTs. It is said that after several rounds of negotiations, British Aerospace (BAe) made their final offer of $ 15.5 million per AJT Hawk but a MoD official in the PNC insisted on a reduction in the price to $ 11.9 million which BAe did not accept.

But again the inept handling by the bureaucrats of the MoD brings out the vital fact that the MoD fails to realise the needless loss of young lives and also the adverse effect on the nation's security. Let alone acquisition of latest planes and equipment, even routine maintenance is badly affected leading to unusually high number of crashes. But even Parliament has not taken any steps to expedite building up and modernising the Air Force.

One of the functions of the Air Force is to protect the skies with the help of other civilian agencies. On the night of 17 Dec. 1995, a huge cache of arms and ammunitions including AK assault rifles, anti-tank boosters, rocket launchers and rocket propelled grenades, etc. was dropped in Joypur and Jhalda villages in Purulia district, West Bengal. The air drop was not an accident but a deliberate one. The Centre had admitted having prior information of this arms drop, but claimed having quickly informed the State Government. The top secret intelligence inputs were received by the Home Ministry, Delhi and were put in a note form by the then Joint Secretary at the Home Ministry's Internal Security Department. This note was sent in a letter by registered post to State Government of Bengal and Bihar. The Central Government justified the action of sending such urgent information by registered post as it was in accordance with existing instructions for handling of secret and top secret matters.

Shri Inderjit Gupta (CPI) submitted his resignation as chairman of Parliament's standing committee on defence to protest against the chinks in national security which permitted the dropping of arms at Purulia. He went on to say "... the incident had rudely shaken the nation's confidence... it shows the plight of our defence system and intelligence set-up.... How can public be assured that more flights have not been carried out undetected in the past, and that enemy planes cannot penetrate deep into our space for aggressive purposes?... the whole thing not only exposes our national security system but makes us an object of international ridicule". He further states "Under the circumstances, his continuance as Chairman of the Parliamentary Standing Committee on Defence has become meaningless and totally ineffective as the committee is treated with indifference and even contempt by the Government...since the committee is not taken into confidence on such crucial matters as the violation of our air borders and is thereby subjected to a humiliation which I, for one, am not prepared to tolerate".

There is a big airforce base near Purulia at Kalaikunda (West Bengal) which has radar. But the air force authorities explained that it was not meant for surveillance, but for providing training.

The AN 26 aircraft took off from Varanasi without prior air defence clearance and reached Calcutta 3 hours later – a flight which should have taken only 45 minutes. Nobody bothered to ask why the plane took 3 hours and where it was all that time. Many questions were raised about the safety of our skies at that time but it is not known if adequate measures have been taken to plug all the loopholes and ensure the safety of our skies.

The IAF is fully aware of the need for expeditiously updating its overaged aircraft and acquire new weaponry. But it remains to be seen whether the clumsy, outdated, time-consuming weapons acquisition system can rise to the occasion and ensure the safety of our skies.

All the three wings of the Defence Services, viz. Army, Navy and Air Force are doing a wonderful job within the constraints they have to operate. It is high time the people of India took an active part in ensuring a change of the outdated and inordinately delaying system of defence planning and weapons procurement thereby render the needed support to the gallant defence forces.

Development

26

Since becoming independent in 1947, the measurement of cost-benefit analysis in financial terms has been the main consideration in project evaluation. Development has been linked to consumption of natural resources without regard to protecting the environment for the benefit of future generations.

On the one hand there is a sense of national pride in the large number of new industries, mega dam projects, large mining ventures, etc. set up during the last 50 years since independence. But on the other hand, it is only recently that the consequent degradation of the environment and the adverse effects on the health of the citizens and the loss to the nation as a whole on account of polluted rivers, lakes, soil, subsoil water, and even the seas and the atmosphere is receiving due attention.

Disregard and degradation of the environment can only result in untold suffering for the citizens in the years to come. While degradation of environment can be a quick process, reversing it is a long drawn out costly process which is not always successful even after spending crores of rupees over a period of years. Cutting down forest covering hundreds of acres can be achieved in a few days but regeneration of forests and grasslands takes years. Degradation of the environment is not merely a theoretical concept. The practical effect is the untold and wholly avoidable adverse effects not only on the flora and fauna, but also the citizens.

A glance at some of the sectors of development brings out the adverse effects of such development without a human face. A few examples of such environmental degradation are cited here.

The setting up of new industries all over India is cited as a noteworthy achievement in the progress of the nation. The process of manufacture of any product always results in adversely affecting the environment to some extent. But a number of industrial units have been and continue to be a source of dangerous and harmful pollutants. A few examples are cited here though the number of polluting units run into hundreds of thousands. Perhaps it would not be incorrect to say that almost no effective action has been taken to curb pollution by industries big or small. That is not to say that the problem has not been recognized or that attempts to curb pollution are not made by the authorities. But the very fact of the continuing and increasing problem clearly indicates the lack of will to curb pollution on the part of the industries and the authorities.

An official report released by the Government of Gujarat in Nov 2000 is frank enough to admit that prosperity among the people brought about by industrialization has been achieved at high cost in environmental degradation and human suffering. It also admits that the degree of industrialization of the state has resulted in its being one of the most polluted states in India.

Unlike Maharashtra, where majority of the industries are less polluting like mechanical/electrical engineering and electronic, in Gujarat, almost 65% of large and medium industries and almost 50% of Small Scale Industries (SSI) are engaged in petrochemicals , drugs, pharmaceuticals, chemical fertilizers – all of which are highly polluting industries. Even the number of vehicles has increased from about 5 lakhs to more than 50 lakhs in 2 decades and continues to increase rapidly.

Several studies have shown that people in the highly industrialized corridor, extending from Vapi to Mehasana, complain of respiratory problems, itching of eyes and skin, cancer, perforation of wall separating the nostrils and a number of health problems. A lot of domestic sewage and industrial wastes are dumped in the rivers without any treatment. Though sewage treatment plants have been set up in a number of places, yet the utilization due to various reasons is extremely low. Indiscriminate dumping of industrial waste by various units without taking any precaution to prevent misuse or even warning regarding serious ill effects is also another major cause of serious health problems. Just one example is given to indicate the serious health problems arising out of such reckless dumping. In Vadodara district, local citizens have been using chromium waste for over 20 years, dumped by a chemical manufacturing unit for building their houses. Today, the locals are suffering from lung cancer, skin ulcers, and nasal perforations, etc. due to the use of chromium waste.

It is not only the small units which ignore safety measures, but also large industrial units. The IPCL unit at Vadodara dumps its waste in a semi open space just outside its factory. The waste includes organic acids, hydrocarbons, acrylonitride and other harmful chemicals. With the slightest rainfall, this chemical and harmful waste is carried downhill into the river.

In Vapi area alone, there are more than 600 chemical plants. Gujarat Government had taken steps in attempting to control pollution. But the extent of sincerity in reducing pollution can be seen from the following. A common effluent treatment plant (CETP) has been set where effluents from more than 600 industries are collected. The effluent treatment plant is controlled by the Vapi Waste and Effluent Management Company Ltd (VWEMC). The waste flowing in from the industries is not monitored. But the efficacy of the pollution treatment plant can be gauged from the fact that the effluents discharged from this plant into the Damanganga river is destroying marine ecology, including fish and thereby destroying the livelihood of hundreds of fishermen. But demonstrations by hundreds of affected people along with activists and meetings with Government authorities has only brought out the fact that during a meeting in the presence of all the various authorities concerned viz, CETP, VWEMC, Gujarat Pollution Control Board, Vapi Industries Association, even a simple question as to who the CETP is accountable to, or reasons for poisonous effluents being allowed to flow into the river, could not elicit any answer. In the meanwhile pollution of the entire area and also the Damanganga river with consequent destruction of marine ecology and livelihood of fisher folk continues unabated in the name of industrial development.

But this is not an isolated instance of pollution of environment by industries. Now, an example is given from an economically advanced state, viz. Maharashtra. The Government of Maharashtra set up through the Maharashtra Industrial Development Corporation (MIDC) the MIDC, Lote industrial area in 1981. There are more than 110 industrial units, mainly of chemicals in the area. Only 10 units treat the effluents they generate, the others release all mercury, copper, zinc, cadmium, chromium, etc. directly into the nearby creek. There are 50 odd villages situated on the creek. The chemical effluents from the creek have killed the fish. More than 2000 fishermen, who for generations depended upon the fishing have been reduced to penury with no source of livelihood. The villagers have only one demand viz, set up a Common Effluent Treatment (CET) plant and control pollution. But despite repeated protests by the villagers, no steps have been taken to put up a CET plant and enable more than 2000 fishermen to carry on their traditional activity and return their self-respect to them instead of making them beggars for no fault of theirs.

The example cited above is just one of the many where no steps are taken to control polluting effluents. In 1995 MIDC launched a project to set up CET plants in 13 industrial estates. While a beginning was made by setting up 4 plants, the rest are yet to be set up. They were to be funded under a World Bank scheme. Only Rs. 2.5 crores out of Rs. 47 crores were utilized under the scheme. Due to the delay, MIDC has now lost the balance World Bank Fund as it has expired. For some reason or the other, the setting up of CETPs is being delayed with no indication of these being set up in the near future. Hence pollution at this industrial estate continues unabated.

The destruction of the environment has been going on at a fast pace for decades since independence. The suffering people, having gradually understood, the cause of their sufferings are to a large extent due to lack of efforts on the part of the Government to effectively ensure protection of the environment, have been able to make their voice heard at the highest level in India. A two day conference of environment and forest ministers was held at Delhi about 5 years ago. The then Prime Minister, Shri Atal Bihari Vajpayee, inaugurated the conference and cautioned at the excesses resulting from flawed development strategies which merely looked at cost benefit analysis and short term gains. He also stressed the need for human development to be linked to protecting environmental resources from consumption and destruction. Some of the areas brought into focus during the conference are indicated briefly below:

(i) Rivers – the need for a holistic approach to tackle the pollution load at one go. Hence instead of tackling the problem of 14 towns, the efforts were to be focused on 7 towns to begin with. Incidentally it may be noted that a couple of years ago, hundreds of crores of rupees were spent on the Ganga action plan to prevent towns like Varanasi and a few other towns on the banks of the Ganga from discharging untreated sewage, industrial waste into the Ganga. The programme was discontinued as no improvement was noticed. (Incidentally no reference was made to the unsuccessful performance of this plan).

(ii) Polluting industries—the chairman of the Central Pollution Control Board (CPCB) made a number of suggestions, cited here:

  (a) prosecution of chief executive officers of industry for gross violation of pollution control norms.

  (b) adoption of ISO 14001.

  (c) streamlining of environmental audit system.

  (d) examine how implementation of system of obtaining bank guarantees can be uniformly implemented all over India as courts in Bihar have struck down this practice, while it continues in some states like Karnataka, Andhra Pradesh, etc.

  (e) Sewage treatment plants—the few plants set up in a number of plants are experiencing problems. In Delhi they are underutilized and hundreds of unauthorized colonies involving lakhs of people have no sewer system at all. In Bihar they are non-functional, UP is facing operational and maintenance problems, lack of funds is the reason for non-completion of such plants in J&K.

(iii) Vehicular pollution – need to enforce emission norms and also stop fuel adulteration.

(iv) The Chairman, CPCB, raised the issue of changes in the constitution of the pollution control boards and committees every few months resulting in lack of continuity and consequently affecting adversely the effectiveness of the authorities in implementing the norms.

But the lack of effective consideration of a few extremely vital aspects can be gauged from the fact that due attention was not focused on the forests and the rapidly depleting forest cover even in the catchment areas of dams resulting in rapid silting and fast depleting reservoir capacities even in a special 2 day conference on environment and forests chaired by the Minister in charge and inaugurated by the Prime Minister.

World Environment Days (June 5) come and go, conferences are held, but the consequent practical benefits in preservation of ecology and environment are rarely seen. The Central Government is very much aware of the need to strengthen the laws and policies governing the environment. In some cases, even after 12 years, the efforts to strengthen the laws have not resulted in any action. The Indian Forest Act 1927 admittedly needs amendments and the Government has been working on it for more than 12 years and is still in the stage of hoping to be ready soon with a uniform law to conserve and develop forests and shift the management of forests to the affected communities. But the Indian Forest Act needs to be entirely recast and 15 ministries need to clear the amendments.

Apart from the Indian Forests Act, the Wildlife (Protection) Act and the Environment (Protection) Act are also said to be in need for review. But degradation of environment goes on all over the country. A few more instances are given here:

The Maharashtra Government set up the Tarapore Industrial belt about 60 kms from Mumbai on the seacoast. The Government took credit for setting up the Industrial Estate and provide jobs to thousands of workers. But the negative aspect is completely ignored by the Government. There are more than

1000 industrial units, including about 400 chemical units. The resultant uprooting of thousands of villagers and destroying their traditional way of life and making them economically destitute and more importantly adversely affecting their health. There were hundreds of wells here which met the needs of the 30 villages in that area. Now the well waters are polluted and the water unfit for any use, least of all for drinking. Even groundwater has been highly contaminated by minerals, thus ruining agricultural lands. The Pollution Control Board (PCB) of Maharashtra is fully aware of the state of affairs but no effective action has been taken to control or improve the situation. As regards contamination of well water and subsoil water, the PCB officials plead their helplessness as according to them, there are no pollution control standards for chemical dyes prescribed under the law.

For generations, the needs of the thousands of residents of that area were used to obtaining their entire requirements water from hundreds of wells in that area. After the protest by the locals for adequate water, consequent on the contamination of the entire well, the State Government arranged to supply drinking water about 10 years ago by means of public taps. But this supply is not only inadequate but irregular and quite often red colored. The water supplied by the Government through the taps is also contaminated. The reason for this contamination being laying of effluent and drinking water pipes close to each other, and these pipes have sprung leaks. One would expect the State Government to take steps, to ensure supply of safe and adequate drinking water. But the agony of the locals continues. MPCB officials state that drinking water will continue to remain unfit for drinking. Even CETP will be of no help in removing the red dyes from the water.

But apart from pollution of water, the atmosphere is also polluted. Skin problems, dysentery, bronchitis are widely prevalent here. According to locals, at times the entire area is covered in thick smog, with irritation of eyes and results in breathlessness. Despite the existence of more than 350 chemical industrial units, the sole CETP can handle the waste of less than half the small units. Apart from contaminated water, polluted atmosphere, surface contamination due to dumping of solid wastes like chemical powders in nullahs outside the industrial area, MIDC and MPCB claim that common disposal sites are now being identified for dumping such waste and also taking steps to set up waste treatment and disposal plant.

The sea is also tinged with red. Hundreds of fishermen have lost their traditional means of livelihood as the once abundant fishing ground has been completely choked. Fishing is possible now only in the deep sea away from the sea shore. The fishermen who could easily earn about Rs. 100 a day by fishing in the creek or near the shore line are the worst affected, as now they can survive only if they can get any odd job and earn anything from Rs. 10 to Rs. 25 in a day.

From the seacoast near Tarapore, one looks at the "development" in the Himalayas. One would expect any country to maintain the pristine purity of a region full of natural beauty and untainted by atmospheric pollution. But a cement manufacturing plant has been set up in the Himalayan state of Himachal Pradesh. Setting up a cement plant naturally involves mining operations on a big scale. One plant is located about 60 kms from Mandi on the Kullu-Manali road. The mining of about 8,000 MT of limestone everyday for at least 16 years has blanketed the nearby town, open fields with brown cement dust. About 5,000 people in the immediate vicinity suffer from chronic asthma, in addition to throat and bronchial infections. Children and employees of the plant are the worst sufferers according to local doctors. But the actual mining process and the cement plant are not the only source of pollution. The plant is situated in the beautiful hilly region of Himachal Pradesh and dependent entirely on road transport. About 1500 trucks traverse the hilly roads everyday aggravating the atmospheric pollution with their noxious emissions.

Since the last few years, HP State Pollution Board (HPSPB) has issued 4 notices to the company to control emissions from their cement plant and coal mills. Some years ago the company had installed about 2 dozen electrostatic precipitators to control emissions and pollution. But reportedly they are seldom operated. The company claims that power fluctuations result in frequent tripping of the equipment while the activists allege the high cost of operating them is the principal reason for not operating them.

The company has set up another plant nearby. This unit is the only plant operated by the company in the hills anywhere in India. The unit in the hills of HP is the largest one with production of almost 3 million tonnes per annum. The mining operations and cement plant are expected to continue for another quarter of a century, by which time they would have exhausted all the limestone from the hill which stood more than 900 metres high. The lease expired in 1999 and the company is functioning with permission from the Director of Industries. The Zilla Parishad passed a resolution asking the Government not to renew the lease.

At Medak, Andhra Pradesh, Greenpeace sent an SOS "Save people from toxic death" people in Patancheru in grip of dangerous health problem due to industrial pollution – nervous, digestive and respiratory systems of people damaged and congenital malfunction rampant because people exposed to cocktail of chemical poisons for over 2 decades. Medak, once famous for lakes thriving with fish, irrigating vast areas of land and providing drinking water, now reduced to dead water and people becoming unemployed. The Government had to order the closure of the Hindustan Insecticide's DDT manufacturing factory at Eloorv, Kerala after Greenpeace submitted a detailed report giving the extremely adverse effects of the working of the factory over the course of decades.

In Haryana the textile dyeing industry has pushed the city of Panipat to the brink of environmental disaster. The colored water has now seeped into the ground and the only way to save the underground water from being further polluted, is to shift the dyeing industry to some other site. More than 500 units discharge more than 6 million litres per day of effluents containing nitrates, fluorides, heavy metals like manganese, lead, iron, etc. well beyond the permissible limits. A senior hydrologist has described the situation as slow poisoning of Panipat.

The need for a well thought-out and planned scheme is a

prime necessity for development. In some villages near Jind and Rohtak (Haryana), it is reported that the authorities provided piped water to all the houses. Previously all of the villagers depended on the village well which was adequate for their needs. But one very important factor which they reportedly overlooked was the need for adequate drainage. No drainage was provided. So every one had access to their own homes but the waste water flowed from the homes into the streets and formed puddles of stagnant dirty water – a source of disease. Skin diseases became common. Besides, there was an adverse psychological effect on the women. As there was water in the house, there was no need for them to go to the well, which used to be their meeting place and exchange gossip. This is an example of lack of adequate planning leading to more problems rather than resulting in development.

Some of the policies of the Government directly encourage pollution of the soil and underground water. One of the leading causes of ecological pollution (almost an irreversible disaster) is the: (i) excessive use of chemical fertilizers, (ii) digging deeper wells for water. Consumption of chemical fertilizers (as against organic fertilizers) is encouraged by subsidizing chemical fertilizers and encouraging farmers to use more fertilizers. The benefits are reaped by the bigger farmers, the fertilizer manufacturers and the traders. The chemical fertilizers run off during the rains and pollute the land as also the underground water. It also enters the food chain and all the agriculture products are thus affected by harmful chemical. The world is becoming more health conscious and avoiding chemical fertilizers.

Besides, the farmers are encouraged to waste water by supplying them with free electricity and/or diesel at subsidized prices. This again benefits the bigger farmers and those growing cash crops. Now Rayalseema district, Andhra Pradesh is a drought prone region. But even here sugar cane and rice crops are encouraged. Both are water guzzlers and are cash crops and not food crops, so water is being pumped out from underground with the help of subsidized power for the bigger farmers to grow cash crops.

But the development plans leave much to be desired. India

has enormous underground stocks of high grade coal in Dhanbad/ Jharia coal belt. It is reported that underground fires have been raging for more than 50 years in the belt with high grade steel grade coking coal which has very low ash content. At present India has to import huge quantities. The fire is spreading horizontally and vertically. Extracting this coal would not only benefit the Bharat Coking Coal Ltd (BCCL) to the extent of hundreds of crores of rupees, but also help reduce Indian steel industry to reduce cost of steel making and reduce dependence on expensive imported coal. A contract had been awarded after inviting tenders for extinguishing the fires and extracting the coal. But it is said that a single MP has prevented the contractor from starting work. In the meanwhile precious high quality coal continues to be turned to worthless ashes and the Indian steel industry continue to have to import expensive coal from abroad.

There are a large number of factories in India making Chemical dyes. This industry has wiped out our ancient vegetable dyes and communities of dyers and weavers who excel at the art of manufacturing dyes and also dyeing fabrics. But it is ironic that the Westerners who started manufacturing chemical dyes about a century ago and killed the natural vegetable dye manufacturing in India are themselves now banning chemical dyes. European Union (EU) has recently banned the import of Indian clothing using chemical dyes. But the Indian Government has not yet started reviving the ancient art of vegetable dyes. This can be a powerful tool to regenerate local flora. Natural dye producing communities can effectively manage the local soil, water and plant growth. There are a few tribal and rural areas where communities still use natural dyes. It may be recalled that India freely allowed import of synthetic dyes at the cost of our natural indigo and other vegetable dyes.

There is a widespread impression that development of a nation necessarily refers only to the growth of the industrial sector it ignores the non-industrial sector particularly the rural sector. There is also a tendency to consider the possession of technical knowledge as the monopoly of the highly educated urban elite. But a few examples are given here to show the scientific and technical talent found even in the uneducated/ semiliterate rural areas, and more importantly the efforts being made by dedicated individuals to unearth and nurture such talent.

Dr. R.A. Mashelkar, Director General, Council for Social and Industrial Research (CSIR) is also the Chairman of National Innovation Foundation (NIF) started in 1980. It identifies grass roots innovations, documents their work, adds value to it, protects intellectual property rights and incubates technology till their commercial release. Money is a serious problem. Most of the innovations are need based. A few examples are cited here.

SOME RURAL INNOVATIONS

But while on one hand there are thousands of examples of low cost non-polluting technology developed by Indians all over India, yet the recognition of the fact of their vital contribution to the development of the nation is not only ignored but attempts at implementation are often actively discouraged at all levels. Even in the simple techniques of putting water power to use of water mills are discouraged, though such water mills were used for centuries.

A village farmer from U.P. developed a low cost machine which pumps water from a stream or river upto a distance of 2 kms or at a height of 100 feet. The most remarkable feature is that it does not require any diesel or petrol to run it, and hence ideal for use in remote areas having adequate surface water. The cost of this machine is only about Rs 1.5 lakhs with an output of about 125 litres per minute. The machine has a shaft coupled to a gear box, the output shaft can be attached to a centrifugal pump or to a variety of farm implements like thresher, chaff cutter, oil expeller, etc. It can be installed near any small stream or low cost check dams.

Now this machine has been acclaimed by Indian Council of Agriculture Research (ICAR) and granted a patent. The ICAR has tested it and certified that an excellent wheat crop could be grown in the Rabi season. The ICAR scientists are certain of it being especially useful in growing crops in the wastelands. The development and technology demonstration was supported by the National Fund for Rural Development (NFRD) and Centre for Advancement of Peoples Action and Rural Technology (CAPART). The farmer inventor has received the Ashoka Fellowship from the Fellowship Resource Centre based in Virginia, USA.

Considering the tremendous advantages of using this locally developed and officially tested machine, it would be but natural to assume that there would be official recognition of the worth of this machine and Government would naturally encourage the wide spread use of this low cost non-polluting machine using non-conventional energy. But the Ministry of Non-Conventional Energy itself is reported to have ignored this machine and preferred to import Australian machines costing about Rs. 4 lakhs with an output of 3 to 4 litres per minute.

Another example of the lackadaisical approach to local ingenuity in harnessing the age old time tested techniques can be seen in the Government approach to modernizing watermills in the northern hill regions. For centuries watermills have been used in the hill regions for grinding grains into flour. Though there are hundreds of small waterfalls, each adequate for running watermills in tiny rural areas, so far the possibility of enhancing the utility of such mills has apparently not occurred to any official agency. Now the hill regions suffer from acute shortage of electricity. The basic principles behind large hydroelectric generators and these watermills is the same. So, up-gradation of these more than 5 lakhs watermills with appropriate technology could be used for non-polluting, eco friendly, renewable source of electricity for the remote mountain hamlets. Dr. Joshi of the Himalayan Environmental Conservation Organization (HESCO) is busy trying to upgrade the technology. It is felt that the up-gradation of these lakhs of watermills could revolutionize the economy of the poor hill people. As a matter of fact, their calculations show a potential of generating more than 2000 MW. This is an uphill task. Most of the water millers belong to the poorest people in the most backward regions of the hills. But Dr. Joshi toured the entire hill areas and managed to organize these people into an association and for the first time more than a hundred water millers from the hill states attended the convention at Delhi.

Big hydroelectric schemes involve investments running into hundreds of crores of rupees for each scheme, and pose a serious danger in the earthquake prone region. But these mills would not pose any such danger being very small. Upgrading these mills would also generate direct employment for the local educated youth in the watermills themselves, apart from the boost to the local economy.

The CAPART has already adopted technology intervention in mountain eco-system as one of the important thrust areas for the advancement of rural technology schemes. A few watermills have already been upgraded and tested and are being promoted by CAPART in the Himalayas. But for full exploitation of the immense potential of the eco-friendly scheme, the utmost co-operation of all the authorities is a vital necessity. Specific steps to make this scheme a success needs to be taken soon.

But this would be incomplete without narrating the actual story of one such watermill. Pushkar Singh, a resident of Rudraprayag district, by making an investment of only Rs. 2,000 has been generating 5 MW of electricity. He designed his own simple turbine without any technical help and today supplies electricity to his tiny hamlet. He has provided one bulb per house in each of the 51 houses in the hamlet. For the first time in history, the villagers get the benefit of electricity. He has shown that using watermills and generating electricity for the benefit of the village can be done without any technical expertise and at a very nominal cost. Most importantly, there is no need to depend on Government agencies.

An example of the innovative spirit of an Indian villager has just been described where a simple villager without any technical assistance could modify his watermill in the hills of Himachal Pradesh to provide electricity to each of the 51 villagers in the hamlet. This only shows that there is no dearth of rural based technological innovations. In Gujarat alone, a professor at the Indian Institute of Management (IIM) has built a data bank of more than 2,000 such innovations. A few such are given below: (i) a three wheel tractor cutting fuel consumption, (ii) use of local plant for pest control, (iii) indigenous technique for storing fresh water in saline areas of Kutch, (iv) tilting 4 wheel cart enabling spread of manure evenly and (v) locally devised gear box enabling production of 50 rpm of mechanical power with the help of a pair of bullocks—the gear box through transmission shaft can help run a shredder machine and similar attachments. It can also run a generator to produce electricity.

Shri. Madan Singh, a graduate from a small village in UP, has been very active in finding substitutes for chemical pesticides and weedicides. Some of his practical tested remedies are briefly indicated below. His basic approach is to persuade local farmers to use natural antidotes to fight pesticides instead of chemical pesticides. The use of urea can be reduced to 80 kg per acre from the present 3 quintals. Simple solutions to pressing problems are his forte. For instance, the monkey can be kept away from crops by spraying neem leafdust over the field; the hordes of wild animals coming to devour crops at night can be kept away by keeping a burning lamp in a perforated tin at night.

Agricultural Technology Management Agency (ATMA), a project funded by the World Bank, is engaged in improving the lot of the agriculturists in UP. Recently an epidemic took a heavy toll of cattle in neighboring Haryana but thanks to the vaccination drive launched with the assistance of ATMA, the cattle in Saharanpur were saved. The farmers who grew only potatoes in their small plots are now growing strawberries as a cash crop.

Patel from Nandurbar, a backward district of Maharashtra, developed matchsticks from jute - potential to revolutionize matchstick making industry which is entirely dependent on wood. Nripen Kalita, 47, Kamrup district, Assam always wondered how to get electricity to his village to help children study after dark – developed hydro-turbine capable of generating 2 MW and practically maintenance free—costing about Rs. 8,000 only against micro hydel plant costing Rs. 40,000 was given State award.

So it can be seen that there is no dearth of talent in the rural sector to solve their problems and develop in their own fashion without disturbing the ecological balance, yet neither the

Government nor industries have exhibited any interest in commercially exploiting the rural based technologies. Even the smokeless chula and biogas plants have not been put into common and widespread use, though they are eco-friendly and easy to build and operate. Needless to say, the increasing use of such eco-friendly devices based on rural technologies, would be a major factor in improving health of the rural sector without investing in costly health schemes. They would also give a boost to income generating schemes and reduce the drift to urban centres.

STATE GOVERNMENT'S ANTI-ECOLOGY ACTIONS

On the one hand it has been seen that rural people and non-Government organizations, as also individuals have been taking an active part in encouraging development of the nation by eco-friendly measures; on the other hand various authorities all over India give an impression of not making the slightest effort to preserve the ecology. Just two examples are given here of such an attitude.

About three years ago, the then Prime Minister of India, Shri Devegowda was to visit a small town near Gurgaon. In the interest of "security" of the Prime Minister, more than 300 trees carefully nurtured by students and faculty of a local college were cut down within a few hours. The trees cut down included: (i) 120-year-old sheesham tree, (ii) two 60-year-old neem trees, (iii) eighty number 10-year-old sheeshams, (iv) 80 eucalyptus trees, (v) 40 cacia semia, (vi) 15 arjuns and (vii) 25 jamuns and a list of other trees. The soil in the campus is highly alkaline and it was the effort of the staff and students with the financial aid from the students' fund that these trees had been nurtured all these years. The Principal maintains that there was no need to cut down a single tree, as in 1993, a helipad was built in the campus for the Chief Minister of Haryana without cutting a single tree. Besides, there is a civil aviation club barely 16 km away. Naturally this wanton destruction infuriated the college authorities and the students who had nurtured these trees all these years gladly spending their time money and energy. This only goes to show the attitude of the authorities in completely destroying such a large number of trees merely for a fleeting visit by a politician.

The above was just a local incident where more than 300 trees were cut down in one stroke merely to construct a helipad for a brief visit by a politician. But is this an aberration or betrays the attitude of the present day politicians to environmental conservation? It is a fact that no politician has taken a firm stand in favor of environmental conservation during the last few decades. After the passing away of Rajiv Gandhi, no PM or CM has taken any interest in protection of environment or wildlife. Rajiv Gandhi's keen interest was a big help in passing of the Forest Policy and the Environment Protection Act. As a matter of fact, the keen interest taken by Indira Gandhi and subsequently by Rajiv Gandhi was responsible for a number of important measures to be taken. A few of the important results due to their interest are given below. The setting up of the Ministry of Forests, giving Central Government concurrent powers for Forest & Wildlife by amending the Constitution, Wildlife Preservation Act, Project tiger, etc. are some of the important measures taken by them but the passing away of Indira Gandhi and Rajiv Gandhi saw a sea change in the attitude of the politicians.

Maharashtra has cleared proportionally the largest area for commercial plantation. It has transferred the best forests to the Forest Development Corporation and abolished a number of posts in the Wildlife Dept. Karnataka is insisting on partly denotifying a National Park to increase the area already utilized by the Kundremukh Mining Project. Rajasthan and some other states have decided not to set up any more national parks. Madhya Pradesh has one fifth of the total forest area in the country. It has now suggested that the annual diversion of forest land permitted by the Forest Conservation Act to 23,000 hectares should be drastically diluted. In other words, diversion of more forestland to other uses should be permitted, thus reducing further forest land. Some of their recommendations insist it should not apply to villages in forests and encroachments prior to 1980. It should permit harvesting of minerals from treeless forest lands. Besides it should apply only to forest lands notified under the Forest Act 1927 and not to other Government and private forests. But other states are also keen on de-notification of protected areas.

PROTECTING FORESTS AND ENVIRONMENT

But does this mean that with the Government Central as well as the states losing the will to protect the forests and on the contrary making efforts to denotify existing forests, and thereby damaging the environment, there is no hope of saving the environment from further degradation? Luckily for the nation, and the preservation of the environment, a number of individuals and NGOs are in their own manner making an important contribution towards the preservation of the environment. In Madhya Pradesh (MP), the illiterate tribals combined together and fought successfully for the preservation of their forests.

There are many ways of profiting from illegal cutting down of forests. In Chilghat village of Damoh district, MP, the timber mafia used an unusual method. They would cut down the trees and inform the police of illegal tree felling. The police would come and arrest a number of innocent tribals and confiscate the felled timber, which would then be auctioned for a nominal amount to the very mafia cutting down the trees. In the meanwhile, the tribals would be released, and as a result the mafia would get the timber legally for a pittance and the tribals would be set free, after withdrawing the false First Information Reports (FIR) filed with the police against the tribals. At last the tribals decided to fight back. About 70 families began community cultivation after forming the Navrachna Samaj Seva Sans then (NSSS). The land chosen was degraded forest land and they decided to regenerate the land by planting indigenous trees. The police arrested some of them and took them away to a far off police station. But the women went and gheraod the police station and forced the police to release the arrested tribals.The tribals now take care of the forest through their NSSS and the illegal felling of trees has stopped.

Central India is rich in forests of teak, barra, etc. Some years ago the tribals in some of these areas realized that the forest department officials were conniving in felling these tree to the timber mafia. The tribals viz, the Baigas, one of the most primitive tribes decided it was upto them to take action against these illegal activities. So the tribals of about half dozen villages joined together and decided on a course of action to stop the illegal destruction of the forest. A Chipko style movement, made famous by Sunderlal Bahuguna, came into existence. When the forest department staff came to cut down the trees, the women from the surrounding villages clung to the trees and warned them that only after cutting them down would the forest officials be able to cut down the trees. The officials threatened the tribals with severe action for obstructing Government employees from performing their duty. But the Chipko movement continued for a number of days and ultimately the police gave in. This encouraged the tribals from other nearby villages also to adopt the same tactics and thereby saved the trees.

DIVERSION OF GOVERNMENT FUNDS

But the systematic looting of funds meant for development activities has been probably the main reason for continuing poverty and lack of real development in India. After looking at a number of success stories, it is time to be reminded of the deep rooted corruption in India where money is diverted to the pockets of a few instead of being utilized for the development and betterment of the tribals. The International Fund for Agricultural Development (IFAD) had provided through the Central Government Rs. 60 crores exclusively for the all round development of the starving Hashipur block, Orissa. The funds were to be utilized through the Orissa Tribal Development Project (OTDP) the main objective was to develop degraded farm lands, forests, barren hills, provide roads, etc. and thereby increase the income of the tribals over the period 1988-1997. Now with assured availability of funds, it should have been reasonable to expect a noticeable improvement in the local conditions. But on completion of the period, it was found that the number of families living below the poverty line increased from 15,471 in 1992 to 25,000 in 1997. An official enquiry report found that the project has created a large number of contractors and suppliers who have made easy money without doing any work. No trace of saplings having been planted was found. Payments were made without any verification for non-existent works. The officials selected the contractors and awarded contracts without calling for tenders. The report goes to catalogue a number of irregularities. A huge amount of Rs. 5 crores was recorded as spent on 31 December 1997, the last day of the project. The report pointed out the impossibility of completing projects aggregating to such a huge amount on a single day. Even about 700 acres of tribal lands had been usurped by one non-tribal with the help of the authorities. But a new Collector, Mr. Sethi, managed to return 500 acres to the original tribal owners.

There are innumerable instances of individuals making every attempt to develop the nation, while simultaneously preserving the ecology. They are fully aware that development and preservation of ecology are not mutually opposed but on the contrary are complementary. Development at the cost of destruction of ecology can only lead to disaster.

Numerous examples can be found all over India of sincere, dedicated individuals and organizations devoting themselves wholeheartedly for the preservation of the environment and ensuring development with a human face. At present it is an uphill task, but the visible encouraging results from the efforts of such persons and organizations give hope for the development of the nation without destroying the environment. The most important factor giving rise to such optimism is the fact that such efforts are undertaken by highly educated and experienced persons as also the most backward tribals and their operations are not confined to any particular geographical area or state, but are observable scattered, at present, all over India.

BHOPAL—WORLD'S BIGGEST ENVIRONMENTAL DISASTER

On the night of 2 Dec 1984, the world's greatest environmental disaster struck a thickly populated area in Bhopal, capital of Madhya Pradesh.

Union Carbide Company, an industrial giant from USA, was permitted to set up an industrial plant in densely populated area of Bhopal to manufacture pesticides. One of the chemicals involved in the manufacturing process was methyl isocynate, an extremely poisonous and lethal chemical. The built up capacity was said to be almost double that of the expected demand. This naturally resulted in storage of large quantities of lethal chemicals.

Union Carbide India Ltd (UCIL) closed down the plant in 1983 as it was said to be losing money. But huge quantities of lethal chemicals including methyl isocynate continued to be stored in the plant. There was a leakage of about 41 metric tonnes of deadly methyl isocynate (MCI) gas from the storage tanks of the inoperative plant. The poor people living in the crowded bustees adjacent to the plant were the first to be affected. According to the MP Gas Relief and Rehabilitation Dept (MPGRRD), over 15,000 died and over half a million (570,000) suffered serious injury from inhaling the deadly gases.

The claims for compensation were filed in the Supreme Court of India. The Government of India quickly revised its claim against Union Carbide downwards from $ 3.3 billion to a pittance of $ 470 million (Rs. 715 crores) in 1989. The Indian Government assumed the role of parents of the victims and assured the Supreme Court (SC) it would make good any shortfall in compensation amount whenever needed. In court, the Indian Government is reported to have agreed to casualties' figure of 3,000 dead and 30,000 wounded. The SC (Chief Justice Ahmedi) and the lawyer of the Government of India felt that the hasty decision in 1989 to accept a pittance of $ 470 million as full and final settlement as compensation for 3,000 dead and 30,000 wounded by inhalation of poisonous gases was quite fair as otherwise the case would have dragged on for years.

It is also not clear the basis on which the pittance of $ 470 million was awarded nor the basis on which the Government of India arrived at the figure of 3,000 dead and 30,000 wounded. Subsequently claims were invited under the Bhopal Gas Leak Disaster (Registration and Processing Claims) scheme 1985. The number of claims filed was 10,29,000 out whom 5,72,000 were awarded compensation. So it was obvious that the figure of dead and wounded had no basis on facts. Large numbers of claims were rejected as no proof could be produced for sufferings caused by inhalation of toxic gases from the gas leakage. Almost all the victims were poor, illiterate and helpless. According to the court and the Government of India, dependents of each victim would get the sum of Rs. 25,000. It is reported that noted lawyer Indira Jaising has challenged the 'parents' of the victims, viz. the Government of India, to pay at least five times more than $ 470 million as Government had categorically stated it does not shut the door on revision.

But the SC not only granted a measly compensation of $ 470 million but also absolved UCIL and parent company UCC of criminal liability. It appointed Indian Government as the sole representative of the victims thus ruling out individuals or class suit against UCIL/UCC. The world's greatest environmental tragedy was inevitable as documents produced in court in New York in 2004 show that: (i) in 1972, the UCC officials had themselves noted that "design poses danger of polluting subsurface water supplies in Bhopal area", (ii) in 1982, UCIL had telexed UCC, USA "Continued leakage from evaporation pond causing great concern" and (iii) UCC's own study reported "majority of liquid samples contained napthol/ sevian in quantities far more than permitted – all samples caused mortality to fish".

All the above points were brought out in 2004 in a New York court. In addition a UCIL employee stated in this court that more than 1,000 mt chemical toxic wastes were dumped in and around UCIL factory between 1969 and 1984.

Numerous studies have shown groundwater highly contaminated due to large scale dumping of chemicals and made water unfit for drinking. Even the MP Government Public Health Engg. Dept has found water only in the factory area to be highly contaminated. But there was no way to tackle such contamination. They further stated use of water from this source to be stopped immediately. But water supply by tanker started in 2004.

More than a thousand people, all poor enfeebled by diseases, reportedly live on 2 to 5 litres of water every day- that too after fighting among themselves for this meager quantity of water. This was one of the issues, NGOs had been rising continuously for almost 20 years. Water from hand-pumps declared unfit for drinking but residents of 18 gas affected areas continue to consume highly contaminated water. Despite large quantities of toxic waste still lying in the factory closed since 1984, the M.P. Government took back the site from UCIL on 19 July 1998, though the original lease deed clearly specified land to be returned in original condition, thus absolving UCIL of responsibility and liability of the large quantity of deadly chemicals still lying in the factory area.

Official figures from the office of the Welfare Commissioner, Bhopal states that 60% of 15, 180 death claims were converted into injury claims and even 6,328 admitted death claims awarded not more than Rs. one lakh each. On an average each of the 560,000 admitted injury claims settled for as little as Rs. 26,000 after waiting for about 15 years with no interest or costs. Interim relief, lawyers'/middleman's fees to be deducted from final figure. All victims are poor, mostly illiterate and whose health has been shattered and incapable of doing any work.

But apart from the pittance granted as compensation, the entire system is bogged down by harassing these poor, illiterate and suffering victims according to the Bhopal Gas Pidit Mahila Udyog Sangathan, the NGO which had taken the case to SC. The harassment has reached such an extent that the NGO has threatened to take the Gas Claims and Welfare Commissioner to SC. For instance, 572,000 victims were identified when first round of compensations paid. But the department wants the poor suffering victims, with no money to go through the entire procedure of identification again. The NGO suggested that victims be identified from photos in the record of claims court or amounts be paid directly to banks. But such practical suggestions were ignored.

Some of the victims have got a meager compensation of Rs. 200 per month though no authority has clarified the basis on which this amount has been arrived at. In 1988, the Government started a scheme to provide free housing for about 3,000 widows and orphans. The scheme was incomplete even after 20 years but it is reported that the quality of construction is extremely poor with roofs leaking, latrines and drains choked and no water. The allotees are widows and orphans with impaired health and are supposed to get a destitute pension of Rs. 150 per month. But this has not prevented the authorities from demanding property tax of Rs. 180 or face eviction.

The Controller and Auditor General (CAG) has reported that the major part of Rs. 400 crores spent on social and economic rehabilitation of gas victims has been swindled. The death toll continues to mount and the authorities have failed to take any steps for the economic and social rehabilitation of the victims even after 20 years.

More than a lakh of people have been completely enfeebled due to cancer and lung related health problems and are unable to earn a living. They need constant medical attention. But the Government claims having compensated all the victims and nothing further needs to be done for the survivors.

UCC has been taken over by Dow Chemicals, USA, who have disclaimed all liability. A case study prepared by the Harvard Law School, USA, pinpoints the lack of enforcement of industrial safety and environmental laws and hence enabled UCIL to operate its deteriorating plant in Bhopal. And this according to them led to the biggest industrial tragedy the world has ever witnessed.

So, lakhs of victims continue to suffer from contamination of underground water and dangerous chemicals stored in the factory which is closed for over 20 years. The unbelievable callous response of the authorities to the world's biggest environmental disaster is an indication of the industrialist/ politicians/ bureaucrats/ citizens lack of regard to the sufferings of their fellow citizens and human beings and also the preservation of the environment, no matter what the loss of life and human suffering it entails.

It remains to be seen whether any fresh legal attempts in the SC will succeed in ensuring adequate financial/ medical aid to the affected people and their dependents to live atleast the remaining part of their life in dignity and put an end to the needless suffering forced on them though no fault of theirs.

Democracy

27

Democracy consists of three arms, viz. Legislature, Judiciary and Executive:

A. Legislature

India became independent in Aug 1947 and declared itself a Sovereign Democratic Republic in Jan 1950. It meant that India was now a democracy where all citizens are equal and a Government by the People, of the People and for the People, would run the nation.

At that time the Constituent Assembly formed before holding the first general elections consisted of highly educated professionals with a profound regard for Democracy and a burning desire to ensure that real Democracy flourished in India in the years to come. It is therefore only proper to reiterate here in brief their vision of the future of India.

Dr. B.R. Ambedkar, who played a major role in the drafting and framing of the Indian Constitution, had stated "Republics are created by the virtue, public spirit and intelligence of the citizens. They fall when the wise are banished from the public councils because they dare to be honest and the profligate are rewarded because they flatter the people in order to betray them ...I feel I ought to take this occasion to give expression of my reflections thereon...will Indians place the country above their creed or will they place creed before their country?... But this much is certain that if parties place their creed above country, our Independence will be in jeopardy a second time and be lost forever.... This eventuality, we must resolutely guard against ...The centerpiece of our constitutional system and a democratic system, is the periodic elections...movements divide, elections bring together".

Dr. Rajendra Prasad, President of the Constituent Assembly had stated, "Whatever the Constitution may or may not provide, the welfare of the country will depend on the way it is administered.... Though this will depend on the men who administer it...if the elected men are capable and men of character and integrity, they would be able to make the best even of defective constitution... if they are lacking in these, the constitution cannot help the country. After all the Constitution like a machine is a lifeless thing. It acquires life because of the men who control and operate it. India today needs nothing more than a set of honest men who will have the interest of the country before them. We have communal differences, caste differences, language differences, provincial differences and so forth...governance has to be of a standard from day to humdrum day... electoral system has to bring forth a set of men of strong character, men of vision, men who will not sacrifice the interests of the country at large for the sake of smaller groups and areas and who will rise above prejudices born of these differences". Dr Rajendra Prasad further went on to express regrets for (i) "for not simultaneous adoption of version of Indian Constitution in an Indian language and (ii) I would have liked to have some qualification laid down for members of the legislators. It is anomalous that we lay down high qualification for those who administer or help in administering the law but none for those who make it. A law giver requires intellectual equipment, but even more, capacity to take a balanced view of things, to act independently and above all to be true to these fundamental things of life... in one word to have Character". But ultimately adult franchise without any educational or property qualification was adopted.

Erudite men of character like Dr. Ambedkar, Dr. Rajendra Prasad and many others produced the Indian Constitution running into hundreds of pages. In 50 years it has been amended almost a hundred times. But it is not the fault of the Constitution. As Dr. Rajendra Prasad had pointed out more than 50 years ago, the Constitution is like a machine. It acquires life only because of men who operate it. Countries run successfully even without a written Constitution or with a very brief one. For instance, UK does not have a written constitution though it is considered as the mother of modern democracy and from which India derives its inspiration. USA has a Constitution of one page only, but it has been found to be adequate by the Americans and needing barely half a dozen amendment in about 250 years.

Multiplicity of political parties is a peculiar Indian phenomenon. Over 500 parties are registered with the Election Commission (EC) with allotment of election symbols but only about 50 political parties are registered for participating in elections. Hence coalitions are the order of the day. But each successful party and member of coalition claims its share in the running of the Government, resulting in dozens of Ministers with fragmented portfolios. UP has about 95 ministers. Mature democracies have very few recognized political parties and the proceedings of the legislature are conducted in the proper democratic manner through debates without resorting to violence. USA and UK have only two and three political parties respectively in their parliaments and conduct the business of democracy through debates. But in India, physical violence has erupted at times with mikes, chairs, tables, etc. being hurled at each other in the legislature with members taking shelter under the tables.

In India, under the present laws, persons of doubtful character and with dozens of criminal cases registered against them become Ministers and control the levers of power and hold charge of vital portfolios like Finance, Home, and Defence, etc. enabling them to wield power over all the departments of the Government.

This can be understood better by considering the stages in an election, viz:

(i) In mature democracies party selects candidate who has nursed his constituency properly, but in India caste, and religion play the leading role and ultimately the "winnability" is all that matters, no matter if the candidate is charged with dozens of criminal cases and he is referred to as "Mafia Don" by the media and also the people at large i.e the electorate – it is normally the Party Chief who selects the candidate and also the constituency from which he will contest – it indicates the lack of inner party democracy.

(ii) Lack of free and fair polls – in India, elections are held in large number of centers under heavy armed police/ Para military guard – this itself is a negation of democracy. But with all these precautions, repolls are frequently ordered. A noted Indian political commentator has observed, " If compliance with sensible rules can be secured only by intervention by Election Commission with the support of heavily armed police, how secure will democracy be in the long run?"

(iii) Choosing leader of legislature party after election results – even if party wins two thirds majority in the elections, there is frequently an intra party struggle and quite often the ultimate choice is left to the leader of he party – this also indicates lack of inner party democracy. Hence right from the first stage, the elected legislators and the members of most of the political pasties are used to lack of democracy within the party. Naturally the elected legislators follow the same mentality and disregard democratic principles in the conduct of the legislature and hence their disregard for the niceties of the Constitution. Horse trading and changing of parties – during and after elections is a common feature in India now. So, there is no sanctity now to a party manifesto – even if there is one, parties opposing each other bitterly in the elections join hands if needed to form a Government to share the fruits of power. Making opportunistic deals merely to share fruits of victory in elections is becoming quite common. Consequently, the Government so formed without a common ideology and merely to share the fruits of power results in nation suffering grievously from lack of stability and incapacity of such Governments to provide good governance.

But elected members need not join a coalition to form a Government. There is a new tendency to lend support from outside to a group forming a coalition Government but without joining the coalition. Thus, such a group lending support from outside can pressurize the Government for securing all the benefits for itself and influencing Government policies without accountability as it not a part of the Government. It can also disown Government actions/policies without withdrawing support. It remains to be seen in India how far such coalition Governments can provide good governance and develop and implement policies for the betterment of all sections of the vast and varied populace forming the sovereign democratic republic.

It is also worth noting that special constituencies are reserved for SC/ST (dalits) candidates. In an effort to redress the injustice of ages on dalits, generous privileges have been conferred on them by the Constitution. Positive discrimination like reserved seats in educational institutions, jobs in Government offices, easier access to loans, etc. has according to an official report created a vested interest in backwards. The number of dalit groups doubled between 1950 and 1960 with about 200 more wanting to be included.

The Constitutional privileges introduced in 1950 were meant to last only for 10 years but they continued. Babu Jagjivan Ram, a noted dalit leading the Freedom movement and senior member of the Union Government in the 1950s and 1960s, had apprehended that permanent privileges would make people think of dalits as a community of incompetent and inferior people; but felt that positive discrimination was needed for some time. The atrocities on dalits continue particularly in small towns and villages. To a large extent, lower level high caste officials have to share the blame. But it is felt that in the long run, economic revolution, particularly in the rural sector, with benefits of financial reform being reaped by the downtrodden castes along with social and political awareness brought about through proper education among the upper castes and others, is the only permanent solution to ameliorate the lot of the down trodden.

Though there is a vast bureaucratic set up known as Election Commission to keep a close watch on the conduct of elections all over the country yet the true democratic principles are missing. In genuine democracies all over the world, elections are held freely without fear and without the need for armed police. Elections held under heavy guard of armed police/ paramilitary forces negate the very concept of democracy.

But having gone through the expensive exercise of holding elections all over the country, do the elected members perform the minimum duty of attending Lok Sabha (LS) meetings? A comparison with the two major democracies, viz. UK and USA is instructive.

In UK (considered as the Mother of Parliaments and on whom most of our parliamentary conventions are based), their Parliament (House of Commons) normally meets for 170 days and average daily period of House Meeting is 9 hrs with quorum fixed at 10% of the House. In USA, quorum is fixed at 50% of the house. But LS requires only 55 members to form a quorum, but even this is not often available, with fewer working days and barely about 5 working hours on the average. Besides the LS adjourns for the day on the passing away of the sitting/ past member as a token of respect. But the MPs insist on a full payment of salary and perks including sitting allowance of Rs. 500 a day. In the organized sector, the principle of "no work, no pay" is generally applied and in the unorganized sector, the worker does not get paid without work. So it is the common honest tax-payer who bears all the burden of MPs abstaining from work.

The Constitution provides that MPs shall receive such salaries and allowances as Parliament may determine by law. In the original Act of 1954 , there was no provision for payment of pension. It was only during the emergency period in 1976, that a provision was made that former members who had completed 5 years of membership were eligible for non-contributory monthly pension from Sept. 1976 and provision was also made for Rs. 50 pm for each year's service over and above 5 years subject to total pension not exceeding Rs. 5,000 pm.

In 1981, the eligibility for pension extended to those former MPs whose service as MP fell short by 60 days or less. This amendment also made MPs (1950 – 52) eligible for pension even if they did not subsequently become MPs of either House.

In 1985, the minimum pension increased to Rs. 500 and upper limit removed.

In 1988, provision was made for payment of pension of Rs. 500 for 5 years to spouse or dependents of any member who died during the term of membership.

Recently, a joint session of both Houses of Parliament unanimously passed a Bill, *inter alia*, providing for payment of pension to every former MP even if he had put in only 1 year service in Parliament. This was naturally passed within minutes without any debate. But some citizens protested strongly and the President of India withheld his assent to the Bill. This was a unique example of the President withholding assent to a Bill passed unanimously without debate by both the Houses.

But the MPs did not take it lying down. They immediately passed similar bill but stating that any period even one day (earlier one year) is enough to make it a charge on the Consolidated Fund of India during the lifetime of the ex-member and also to take care of survivors through family pension. But apparently nobody including the media raised its voice against the Bill where even one days presence as an MP is adequate for a lifetime pension as also for dependents.

It appears that as things stand, all former MPs, members of the Provisional Parliament, Constituent Assembly, irrespective of period of membership, are entitled to a minimum pension of Rs 3,000- pm in addition to any other pension they may be getting. For every year of service after a term, an additional sum of Rs. 600 pm, shall be payable without any upper limit on the total limit on the total pension amount. Besides, provision for family pension also provided with 'family members "being liberally defined.

The total monthly payment to each MP in cash/kind in form of exemptions, immunities or facilities far exceeds Rs. 2 lakhs per month. All this is exclusive of Rs. 2 crore placed at disposal of each MP under the MP Local Area Development Scheme (MPLAD). Incidentally Mr. D. Pandian (MP –AIDMK) took his duties seriously when recently appointed Chairman of Joint Parliamentary Committee (JPC) for LAD scheme and insisted on monitoring the spending of such funds. He found numerous discrepancies in such disbursals. For instance, he found no evidence of Rs.1 crore spent on 150 kms of road in Bihar. But his efforts were futile as all MPs and bureaucrats were annoyed with him for raising such issues.

The MPs had given themselves a hike under the Salaries/ Allowances and Pension of MP Act 1954 in 2001. But they are now again demanding an increase in their perks and allowances.

The MLAs naturally follow the example of MPs in demanding hike in pay and allowances. In July 2005, MLAs of Maharashtra got their demands sanctioned, increasing the present pay and allowances increased by more than Rs. 10,000 per month to Rs. 45,000 pm putting an additional burden of about Rs. 4 crores on the cash strapped Government. Naturally the demand was passed in both Houses within minutes, the only MLA objecting to the increase was Narsayya Adam (CPM) who staged a walkout in protest but was ignored by all the other MLAs of all parties.

But with all the facilities enjoyed by MP/MLAs, a large number defaults in payments even of telephone and electricity bills have come to notice.

The contrast of the official remuneration/perquisites enjoyed by the MPs/MLAs representing the poor electorate and the non-payment of salaries to Government employees in Bihar is glaring. The MP from Bihar, Lalu Yadav is officially the Railway Minister at Delhi enjoying all the perquisites of that office. He was also the defacto Chief Minister of Bihar as he is the President of the RJD party when his wife was legally the Chief Minister of Bihar. Lalu Yadav was the Chief Minister (CM) of Bihar for almost 15 years at a stretch before becoming the Railway Minister. But over 40,000 employees of Bihar Government had not been paid their monthly salaries for 10 years, i.e. for 120 months. These include sweepers, clerks, typists officers doctors, etc. Some consider themselves lucky if they get paid at least a quarter of their dues after about 6 to 8 months—a period considered normal by the poor employees. It was only after a court order that the Government took some steps to pay the poor employees.

Meetings

The Parliament is meeting less and less frequently; 137 days in 1953, 102 in 1988 and 59 in 2004. From beginning of Sept 2004, working of both Houses adjourned without transacting any business. Lok Sabha session had commenced in June 2004 and by Sep 2004 had lost about 50% of the time. About a decade ago, the lost time in the comparable period was about 5%.

One of the most important functions of the opposition is to keep a watch on the performance of the Government in power by raising questions in Parliament. But in 2004, the opposition boycotted various Parliament committees, which scrutinize budgetary proposals including demands for grants. Parliament created history by approving without any discussion whatsoever the expenditure amounting over Rs. 478,000 crores proposed by the Government. It also passed annual grants without any scrutiny. Even the annual budget, which is the most important item, was passed without any scrutiny. Immediately thereafter the Parliament adjourned *sine die* about a week before the scheduled date. This not only created a record for passing various proposals including Annual Budget without any discussion but also losing almost half the time scheduled for the session. The budget for Parliament has gone up from Rs. 28 crores in 1991 to Rs. 174 crores in 2000-01.

It has been seen that the Lok Sabha (LS) members take scant interest at times in the performance of their duty in atleast attending the House and discussing the Bills. But in some of the states, the members attend the legislature, but fail to perform some of the Constitutional duties like attending to reports submitted by Controller and Auditor General (CAG).

A number of committees of legislators are charged with the duty of examining in detail the reports submitted by CAG and report their conclusions to the legislature after assessing the replies of the Government and undertakings in response to CAG report.

This duty is cast on the various committees of the legislature by the Constitution of India and hence the importance of performing the constitutional duty has to be understood by the State Government and the members of the legislature.

The most elementary duty cast by the constitution is to lay the CAG report on the table of the legislature. The CAG can finalize the report only after obtaining the necessary explanations from the concerned department/company. But for reasons not stated by the State Government, in a number of cases, the gap between the dates of placing of report in the West Bengal legislature extends even to decades. Some of the Government companies/undertakings like Oriental Gas Company or Government Sales Emporium have not even prepared accounts since 1960 and 1951 respectively. CAG has repeatedly drawn attention to the involvement of large amount of public funds involved and possibilities of serious financial irregularities remaining undetected for long periods.

Mr. Hashim A. Halim, Speaker of the West Bengal assembly for over 17 years as also Mr. A. Sinha (Congress) longest serving member cannot remember anyone ever being punished. The Speaker is reported to have stated "reports are not discussed in the House as there is no need because members of PAC do their job so completely that there is no need to discuss". He also reportedly said that nobody could be punished on the basis of a PAC report.

So, if even a state like West Bengal which has been ruled by the same political party for 25 years under one highly educated leader as Chief Minister, shows scant regard for the need to respect all the requirements of the Constitution of India in letter and in spirit, the future does not look bright for the future of democracy considering the large number of not very educated politicians with criminal charges getting elected to various legislatures.

But the laws appear to be suited to politicians charged with serious crimes. The levers of power are being wielded by persons of doubtful character with dozens of criminal cases registered against them. The present laws are a great help to such people. For Indian laws follow the Anglo-Saxon concept of a person being deemed innocent until proved guilty. In India, cases drag on for decades in court. So it is easy for such politicians to get cases (if any) filed against them adjourned repeatedly for decades. Even sec 8 (A) of Representation of Peoples Act provides that MP who gets convicted even of murder, shall be disqualified unless he files an appeal within 3 months. But such people can keep on getting adjournments from court and thus retain their membership of the legislature for years.

With more and more politicians with limited education and criminal backgrounds getting elected to the various legislatures, there is a general apprehension among some citizens that the entire judicial system may be subverted—after all law breakers will be the law makers.

But politicians exhibit their lack of regard for democracy even in petty matters like allotment of bungalow. A few examples are given here.

In Delhi, a bungalow had been allotted to Sis Ram Ola as Dy Speaker of Lok Sabha but Charanjit Singh Atwal reportedly took possession of the bungalow forcibly. Smt Vasundhara Raje Scindia had been allotted a bungalow as a Minister in New Delhi. She subsequently had to vacate it when she was elected as Chief Minister of Rajasthan. But she vacated it on condition that a bungalow, not a flat, was allotted to her son Dushyant, a first time MP (not entitled to a bungalow). Her argument was that her nephew Jyotiraditya also a first time MP continued to occupy the bungalow allotted to the late Madhavrao Scindia.

In Mumbai, two Ministers of the same Government fought for possession of a bungalow right in front of Mantralaya. Supporters of Minister of State Mr. Mhaske stormed the bungalow allotted to and occupied by Health Minister Smt Mundhada. They stormed the bungalow and also manhandled the husband of the Health Minister. In Maharashtra, R. Dutta, Naseem Khan, P. Awadi, erstwhile Ministers won election but not made Ministers again. They have refused to vacate these spacious bungalows in the most centrally located area opposite the Mantralaya. Even during April/May 2005 when Maharashtra was reeling under massive power cuts, the Ministers enjoyed the luxury of air conditioners working in their bungalows and running up individually electricity bills of Rs. 1,000 @ day on the average – with their constituencies facing daily power cuts of 8 to 10 hours.

A large number have been elected to the legislatures though charged with serous criminal offences. While charges of murder, rioting and dacoity are no doubt serious, yet some of the MPs are charged with offenses bordering on treason, threatening the safety and integrity of the nation.

Recently Special Task Force (STF) Commandos and Siwan district, Bihar police raided the ancestral house of Mohamed Shahabuddin (MP- RJD) on the basis of complaints received at the Janata Darbar held by the District Magistrate (DM) at Partappur. The main items seized include: (i) 2 semiautomatic rifles, (ii) 1 sohisticated foreign revolver, (iii) bulletproof jacket, (iv) 8 two wheelers, (v) 3 four wheeler, (vi) 1 VHF walkie talkie and (vii) 2 night vision devices. Now the last two items are supplied only to army and security forces.

The increasing political corruption and the increasing number of law breakers becoming law makers is extremely disquietening. It is well known that some elements in Pakistan are making every attempt to destroy the democratic nature of India and its stability and economic progress. But the politicians in India appear to be encouraging such attempts by anti-social elements. The Government has not been able to publish a white paper on ISI activities in India. It has expressed its inability to state the quantum of fake currency entering the country and all political parties preventing Central Bureau of Investigation (CBI) from becoming autonomous. It has also not been able to pass the Lok Pal Bill. But attempts seem to have been made to dilute the authority of the Vigilance Commission.

The passing of the IMDT Act for Assam and the strenuous efforts being made by the Government and its supporting parties to somehow negate the Supreme Court (SC) ruling and ensure the continuance of the Act , no matter if even the Census proves that districts of Bihar, Assam and West Bengal bordering Bangladesh have shown alarming increase in the number of illegal Bangladeshi immigrants and significantly changed the demographic nature in those areas.

Seen in totality, one would normally be inclined to consider these acts as being against the safety and integrity of the nation and wonder whether they could be considered treasonable. The actions of some political parties in power in considering such activities as not being inimical to the safety and integrity of the nation does not necessarily justify these actions. After all how far can a democracy where politicians charged with serious crimes not only get elected but also get control of important portfolios, be considered to be capable of looking after the interest of millions of law-abiding citizens. More than 50 years ago, important leaders like Dr. Ambedkar, Dr. Rajendra Prasad and others had expressed fears of power passing into the hands people not having the mental make up or character or the necessary vision and the possibility of failure of democracy and losing our independence a second time.

So, one cannot help being apprehensive, yet at the same time it is felt that the majority of the people who are silent or not active enough, will rise to the occasion and make a success in letter and spirit, of the greatest democracy in the world.

B. Judiciary

Democracy can survive and function successfully if all three arms of democracy, viz, Legislature, Judiciary and Executive function smoothly and efficiently. A shortcoming even in one of the arms will invariably result in unfortunate and undesirable effect on the working and continuance of democracy in India. A failure of democracy will have tragic consequences for the nation.

While the Legislature enacts legislation for the continuing growth of democracy, the Judiciary is concerned with interpreting the law and ensures giving justice, treating all citizens equally because in a democracy all citizens are equal in the eyes of law.

But justice must not only be done but also seen to be done. Is the justice system, as it exists today, capable of discharging its basic duty of providing justice to all quickly, efficiently and at a reasonable cost to all the citizens?

(a) Backlog in Courts

According to a former Chief Justice (CJ) of Mumbai High Court (HC), there were 2.7 million criminal cases pending in Mumbai HC as of 30 Aug 2004. 40% of the cases could have been quickly resolved by imposing fines on the guilty.

In 1999, there were more than 20,000 cases pending in the Supreme Court (SC), more than 32 lakhs (3 million) cases pending in High Courts and over 2 crore (20 million) in the lower courts. The large numbers of pending cases have not come about suddenly in a short time. It has increased gradually over the last 50 years and has now reached an alarming and almost unmanageable figure – with more cases being registered everyday.

Numerous efforts have been made by well intentioned people to ensure quicker disposal of cases particularly the backlogs but it appears that such efforts are not successful due to action of a section of the judiciary and lawyers.

About 5 years ago, 2000 fast track courts were set up by the Central Government to clear the backlogs. But the budget for 2005 does not make any provision for funding the functioning of these courts. So the SC extended the functioning of these courts for one year, hoping that the present Government will make adequate financial provision for the continued functioning of these courts to clear or atleast to reduce the backlog. But the sincerity of the Government to assist the judiciary to function effectively is open to doubt.

There has been an exchange between the President of India and the Chief Justice of India (CJ) stressing the importance for judicial reforms to reduce the backlog of cases and ensure quicker disposal in future. There have been debates at various fora on this issue. But no practical solution has emerged so far.

Some of the studies have thrown up some important points, viz:

(i) Government litigation accounts for about 60 % of litigation– efforts could be made to cut out unnecessary litigation and unnecessary laws.

(ii) It is reported that surprisingly Allahabad HC accounts for 25% of all pending HC cases and Kolkata and

Allahabad HCs together account for 50% of all pending civil cases listed for more than 7 years, indicating that causes of delay are not uniform and the existence of special factors at each HC leading to delays.

(iii) The courts and Governments have themselves weakened the mechanisms for alternative dispute resolution mechanisms.

According to some scholars the number of the judges at 2.7 per 100,000 is far below the international norm of 6.8. But some also feel that more important factor is the functioning of Indian judiciary without providing basic support to judges like well trained law clerks.

(b) Delayed Justice

A number of legal activists as also average citizens feel that a sense of urgency and sensitivity to the impact of delayed justice in people's lives is lacking in our courts. The general impression is that courts, including SC, are quick to deal with issues involving rich and the powerful but fail to realize the problems and the need for urgency in dealing with the average citizen. As human rights activist, Indira Jaisingh has stated— "The issues of the rich and powerful grab a disproportionate part of judiciary's time. Matters of big business houses or powerful politicians or customs or excise disputes are rarely delayed. But a plea that slums should not be demolished close to school and college exams may be ignored until it's too late".

A few cases involving inordinate delay are cited below:

(i) Relatives of 59 people who died in the Uphaar Cinema Hall, Delhi, still wait for justice. The President of the Association of Victims of Uphaar Tragedy (AVUT) formed for their united fight for justice stated, "While we are waiting for justice even after 8 years, the rich and the influential accused persons continue to resort to dilatory tactics filing frivolous petitions and revisions at each stage and keeping away from the court".

The Delhi High Court (HC) had responded to AVUT's plea for speeding the trial and had directed that the case be heard at least 10 days in a month and 110 days in a year. Despite this order, hearing has been possible only on 69 days in 2004 and progress sluggish due to delaying tactics by accused, according to AVUT. The Central Board of Investigation (CBI) had told the additional sessions judge holding trial , that many accused are "making a mockery of the trial" by securing exemption from personal appearance by filing "untruthful and frivolous petitions". CBI had urged the court not to entertain such petitions.

Many documents in the court records are missing and ink was smeared on others and some documents torn. A record keeper of the court was dismissed in 2004.

In April 2003, the HC ordered a total compensation of Rs. 25 crores for the families of the victims and those injured. But AVUT considers this a "partial victory "and will not rest till the guilty are punished.

So, even after 8 years the case drags on due to dilatory tactic of the rich and influential accused.

(ii) In 1985, Y C Pawar, then Assistant Commissioner of Police (ACP) Matunga, Mumbai, had crippled the infamous Don Varadarajan's gang activities, particularly hundreds of illicit liquor dens. Varadarajan was an extremely powerful gangster in those days and there were reports that Pawar was on the hit list.

On July 30, 1985, Pawar had noticed some boys waiting in a car outside Matunga police station. He chased the boys in his official police jeep. During the chase a car dashed against the rear of the police jeep. Later on it was found that this car belonged to Don's men.

Pawar managed to catch up with the car in which the boys were traveling and asked them to surrender. But they attacked the police with acid bulbs and stones. Pawar sustained injuries but managed to arrest five of the attackers who were booked for rioting, attempt to murder and preventing a Government servant from executing his duty. Thanks to Pawar the gang was finished.

Pawar, now retired as Inspector General of Police (IGP) was

present in the court but was not called to "depose in the session's court and identify the culprits. After 20 years, the court acquitted all the boys (already released on bail years ago) due to "lack of evidence". Comment is superfluous.

(iii) P. Haval was a superintendent in the Bombay City Survey Land Record Office and was accused of tampering with Government files to manipulate Free Space Index (FSI). The higher the FSI, the more space available for building and hence suits builders. In 1983, the Anti Corruption Branch (ACB) conducted raids against Haval for possessing assets disproportionate to his known income. Haval, his wife and son were chargesheeted by Inspector Dhoble in 1989, for possessing illegal assets worth Rs. 37 lakhs, subsequently arrested and released on bail. The case came up for hearing in 2001 in the session's court. In the meanwhile, Dhoble had been posted as a senior Inspector of a police station and found it difficult to take time off from his duties and attend court whenever required. But his persistence in following up the case during the last 20 years paid off, as Haval, his wife and son were sentenced by the court to 3 years jail and a fine of Rs. 15,000.

(iv) In 1987, Kojagri Papers had filed a case of cheating against M.K. Mehta for Rs. 2.69 lakhs. In Jan 2001, the court found Mehta guilty of cheating and sentenced him to one day's imprisonment till the rising of the court and a fine of Rs. 2,000 only. After 4 years the court fined Rs. 2,000 only for cheating to the extent of Rs. 2.69 lakhs.

(v) In 1991, a ward boy at the Sion Hospital, Mumbai, allegedly raped a 12-year-old girl in her house when she was alone. The parents of the girl immediately lodged a case with the police. The case came up for hearing after 13 years in 2004, but the ward boy was acquitted as the doctor who had examined the rape victim 13 years ago was "unavailable" as a witness and the medical papers registered at that time were also not traceable.

It is felt that in such rape cases the courts should play a more proactive role rather than wait for the case to come up.

(vi) An acid attack on girls by jilted lover is one of the most heinous crimes as it disfigures the girl for life. The case drags on for years even if acid thrower gets caught. But the punishment awarded by the court is mild compared to the enormity of the crime in destroying a young girl's life. For instance, in such a case recently, the victim is battling for the last 5 years and after 15 operations plus pints of blood. But the courts apparently goby the letter of the law which states that "if victim has suffered injuries to vital part of body, the perpetrator can be charged with attempt to murder, a non-bailable offence-," however at times the accused can be released on bail and case drags on for years.

But the courts must consider the young girls' fate where huge amounts have to be paid for medical expenses and cost of plastic surgery. If culprit is unable to pay, then the state must bear the expenses. The courts must now play an active role and not go strictly by the letter of the law without looking at the enormous life long price , financial and in suffering , the innocent victim has to pay.

(vii) In July 1995, the half burnt body of Naina Sharma,wife of the former Youth Congress President of Delhi was found in Central Delhi by a policeman on his rounds. It appeared to be an open and shut case, but it took 8 years for the case to be decided at the lower level. No new facts emerged during this period. But the final decision is yet to come. This is another instance where the politicians and influential can delay the case for years.

(viii) Justice delayed is justice denied. But judgments delayed can also be justice denied, particularly when justice is intentionally denied.

In 1961, the Patna High Court had expressed deep anguish at a magistrate delaying pronouncement of judgement by nine months, by stating "the magistrate who cannot find time to write the judgement within a reasonable time after hearing argument should not do any judicial work at all".

But it cannot be denied that individual judgements are voluminous and quite often run into hundreds of pages. For instance, a Supreme Court judgement in 2002 regarding NCERT Textbook ran into hundreds of pages. Numerous detailed extraneous remarks on the tolerant nature of Indian tradition were included in the voluminous judgement.

The SC judgement in the Mandal Commission case also ran into hundreds of pages but made only two significant observations, viz. (i) creamy layer among Backward Classes should not benefit from reservation and (ii) standing committee to be set up at Centre and States to review progress.

In most of the other countries, judgements are brief and to the point. For instance in USA , the notable judgement of Brown v/s Dept of Education (1954) is not even five pages long, yet it is a landmark judgement in the history of American jurisprudence. This is the basis on which many cases have been tried in America over the years – ranging from segregation in schools to affirmative action. Some other judgements even in the law of courts too are precise and draw attention to points of law. But even modern emerging democracies in Asia like Malaysia also believe in and try to practice brevity in expressing their judgements which are brief and to the point.

(c) Undertrials

There are innumerable instances of proceedings in court dragging on for years and even at times, to decades. But what is more alarming is the large number of people being kept in jail for years and sometimes decades, without being brought to trial. This is a negation of justice and democracy and portrays a state insensitive to the fundamental right of every citizen. It also proves the failure of the judiciary to enforce the rule of law and safeguard an individual's right to freedom. Out of the thousands of such cases, only a few are cited here. Such delays quite often help the perpetrators to escape the law:

(i) Child abuse charges were filed against Waters and

Grant who had established children's homes in Mumbai. Both fled the country but both were extradited with the help of Interpol and brought back to Mumbai in 2004. But the state of Maharashtra has not been able to find a special prosecutor to represent the four abused children in the fast track court. The session's judge at Mumbai has written to the Law Ministry at Delhi over its persistent failure to find a special prosecutor for over 6 months in a child abuse case. It is indeed curious that a lawyer cannot be found for more than 6 months in Mumbai in a child abuse case where Waters and Grant have been extradited and brought to Mumbai with the help of Interpol.

This case highlights the delay by law enforcement authorities in taking action even in cases relating to the basic rights of children guaranteed by the Constitution of India.

But the callousness of the people entrusted with administration of justice can be seen from a few cases cited here.

(ii) Ajay Kumar Ghosh was arrested in 1962 on charge of murdering his brother. He died after spending 38 (thirty eight) years in jail - but his case never came up for hearing in all these 38 years.

There are said to be about 2 crore (20 million) undertrial prisoners in jails all over India. Most of them are poor. A number of them have been in jail as undertials for more time than the maximum time they could be imprisoned even if found guilty. In UP, more than 80% are likely to be released as innocent. Only about one lakh convicted prisoners are in jail. In UP, presently the ratio of undertrial to convicts is 7:1 as against 1:2 in 1947. Many jails in India, particularly in UP and Bihar are heavily overcrowded. But the rich and the powerful, if perforce they land up in jail, are lodged in separate air-conditioned rooms with all facilities like TV, etc.

(d) Some Unusual Judgements by Supreme Court

(i) In October 2004, SC ordered issuance of non-bailable warrant for arrest of N P Mishra convicted and sentenced in a murder case twenty years ago. Nothing is unusual in action taken by SC apparently. But Mishra is now aged about 112 years (one hundred and twelve years) and has been lying in a comatose condition for years. He is now in a hospital in a comatose condition unaware of his surroundings. He is guarded constantly by a policeman who finds the duty embarrassing. Supreme Court judges are supposed to be exceptionally intelligent. Do they feel proud having spent time, money and energy in ordering the arrest of this semi-comatose man aged 112 years?

(ii) Another unusual case dealt with by SC is given here. A milkman in Haryana was charged in 1988 for mixing milk and water. One would be tempted to say that it's such common place practice in India, that most do not consider it an offence. In July 1989, the milkman Dayanand was convicted under the Prevention of Food Adulteration Act and was sentenced to 6 months jail and a fine of Rs 1,000. He had no previous conviction or any adverse comments on his character. He had three small children to support. The Punjab & Haryana High Court (P&H) gave him the benefit of the doubt. But the Haryana Government went in appeal to the SC against the HC judgement. Supreme Court Judges N.S. Hegde, S.B. Sinha and A.K. Mathur set aside the HC order and sentenced him to 6 months jail and a fine of Rs 1,000. What was so vital for the state of Haryana to appeal against the order of HC ? What was the need for a 3 member bench of the Supreme Court to hear the matter? Adulteration of milk with water is a commonplace occurrence and not as dangerous as adulteration of drugs or manufacture of "synthetic milk", yet one does not find Supreme Court convicting such criminals even when they can *suo moto* take up such cases. No wonder SC and HC are burdened with cases and important cases cannot be heard for years.

(d) Quality of Judiciary

Where the standards of public morality appear to be going down, it is natural that the judiciary cannot remain unaffected.

This was amply proved by a sting operation conducted in 2004 by Zee TV, where a metropolitan magistrate in Ahmedabad, Gujarat, accepted Rs. 40,000 to issue warrants of arrest against: (i) the President of India, A.P.J. Abdul Kalam, (ii) V. K. Khare, Chief Justice of India and (iii) R.K. Jain, President Bar Council of India. These warrants were issued without a scrap of paper as evidence and without any verification or scrutiny of identities.

In Gujarat, one Makwana jumped parole in 1996 but was rearrested in 2003, but went missing after being granted parole. The police had conveyed their strong objection to the session's court, when their opinion on parole was sought. But, despite vehement objections by the police, the Government granted parole. The Government contended that minister's decision is final. The police had succeeded in getting Makwana convicted in an old murder case. Could the judiciary have played a more proactive role?

But in a number of cases the judiciary has taken an active role. In 1999 *Time* magazine of USA published an article describing a unique association of Dead People in UP, India. It appears that in 1975, one Lalbehari discovered he had been declared dead by his uncle merely to acquire his property. Lalbehari tried various methods to prove that he was alive, like: (i) tried to stand for election to Parliament, (ii) wrote pamphlets, (iii) organized his own funeral, (iv) demanded widow's pension for his wife, (v) wrote "deceased" after his name, etc. But nothing worked. He found a number of such cases and formed an association of Dead People. The authorities continued to treat him as dead.

Ultimately Justice Dhawan and Justice Dikshit took *suo moto* notice of the article *Time* magazine and directed district administration to pool information about such living dead and place it before Chief Judicial Magistrate by September 1999. 80 such cases were detected in Azamgarh, UP. 30 of them were declared alive and rehabilitated but only 4 got their land back. 16 revenue officers were identified as guilty but not a single one was punished.

(e) Equality in Law

There is a common perception that the rich and powerful are above the law in India. No rich person or politician appears to have been prosecuted in India, for that matter even charges are rarely framed against such people. But in a true democracy all citizens are equal before the law.

In UK, there are a number of cases where the children of present and past Prime Ministers were charged with offences. In atleast one case the Prime Minister had to appear in court for offences committed by his minor children.

In USA, 24-year-old daughter of George W. Bush , President of USA, was charged with prescription fraud when she tried to obtain anti anxiety drug " Xamax" from a pharmacy in the small town of Tallahasee. She was jailed for failing to follow court that ordered treatment for her addiction to tranquilizers.

In Indonesia, the prosecutors have asked court to jail Tommy Soharto for 15 years for murder and firearm offences – both offences carry maximum death penalty. Tommy Soharto is the youngest son of Soharto, former Dictator of Indonesia for 15 years.

In a democracy, no one is above the law. In USA, Bill Clinton, President of USA was accused of perjury. In UK, Jeffrey Archer, millionaire author and Member of the House of Lords was convicted of perjury. He was sentenced to 4 years in jail and a fine of Pounds 175,000 in 2001. In India no one is punished for perjury, least of all a politician or a Government employee, though India is considered as the world's largest democracy.

CONCLUSION

It is for the Judiciary to explore ways and means to provide speedy justice to the poorest of the poor at an affordable cost. Today recourse to the courts is not only expensive but also subject to delays extending over decades. Consequently the services of antisocials who can provide rough and ready justice at a price, is increasingly in demand, thereby striking at the very roots of democracy and a free and fair society.

But a lot of questions regarding the judiciary still needs to be debated. For instance, what is the constitutional liability of Head of State for mass deaths/killings like the Delhi riots of 1984 or the Bhopal Gas tragedy? Who was actually responsible for the Bhopal Gas tragedy—Union Carbide or Government for failing to monitor safety standards? Did the Supreme Court merely permit itself to be a mediator between the demands of the Indian Government and the offer for settlement by Union Carbide without considering the enormity of the world's greatest industrial disaster? Should the Supreme Court as court of last resort in India have taken a searching look into all the aspects, legal and otherwise to ensure justice to half a million who suffered from the Gas tragedy ? Did the legal system live upto the expectations in a democracy as the steel frame of accountability in the Delhi riots of 1984, the Bhopal Gas tragedy and other similar tragedies?

The failure of the judiciary to uphold the rule of law is encouraging antisocials to flout the law openly without the slightest fear and thereby endangering the very foundation of society based on the rule of law.

Pappu Yadav (Rajesh Ranjan) threw a party in Beur High Security Jail. The Patna High Court (HC) ordered First Information Report (FIR) to be registered against him for throwing such a party. But within a month, he hosted a party for 50 of his cronies in high security restricted area of Beur Jail. This area is extremely high security where even pass holders are not allowed. No entry was made in jail register of such visitors. The Inspector General of Police (IGP) demanded explanation from the jail superintendent. But Pappu Yadav telephoned the Jail Minister from the jail itself. The Minister ordered IGP not to take any action. Pappu Yadav is in jail being accused of murdering Ajit Sarkar (CPM – MLA) in 1988. The trial has not commenced even after 6 years. The Patna HC had already ordered transfer of Beur Jail Supdt after similar charges had been made earlier. But the orders of the HC continue to be flouted with impunity and the jail supdt continues in his post despite HC orders. Even HC orders are not enforceable in Bihar.

This is nothing unusual in UP or Bihar. Amarmani Tripathi,

former Minister and Samajwadi party legislator is in Lucknow jail since Oct 2004 for the murder of Madhumita Shukla and enjoying VVIP facilities ever since.

In Feb 2005, he hosted a party in the jail premises to celebrate the wedding anniversary of Prakash Chand Pandey, fellow inmate in the jail and main accused in the murder of Madhumita Shukla. Preparation for the party was on for two days in the jail. Liquor flowed freely. The invitees included other inmates and also guests from outside included Shiv Pal, younger brother of Mulayam Singh Yadav, Chief Minister of UP. The CBI had raised objections at the special court to Amarmani enjoying free movement within and outside the jail. But things continue as before.

Mulayam Singh Government and his Samjwadi party colleagues see nothing wrong in having such parties in jail. Azam Khan, Parliamentary Affairs Minister, UP insisted that no rules were broken. He went onto state there was no violation of jail manual. Beni Prasad Verma, Samajwadi party MP, and father of UP's Minister of Prisons, Rakesh Verma, sees nothing wrong or new in entertainment within jail premises. According to him, it happens all the time in all the jails. This appears to be a normal practice in UP. In Dec 2004, Raja Ram Pande, one of Mulayam Singh's Ministers, is reported to have organized a mushaira inside Partapgarh jail in honor of Raja Bhaiyya lodged under POTA. In the mushaira, poets sang praises of Raja Bhaiyya. The District Magistrate (DM) and the Senior Supdt of Police (SSP) are reported to have enjoyed the mushaira and the sumptuous feast.

So, the judiciary appears to be unable to enforce the rule of law even within the jails. The judiciary encourages class distinction even among criminals lodged in jail. In Andhra Pradesh (AP), the rules officially provide for such distinction. The Andhra Pradesh Prison Rules 1979 provide for differential treatment of prisoners based on their social status, education and way of life. This enables prisoners to be classified as "A", "B" or "C" category. So an "A" class prisoner can have all the privileges of food of your choice, laundry facilities, etc. Jails have no servants, so such menial services are provided by "C" class prisoners. The classification is ultimately dependent on money and muscle power.

M. V. Krishna, IG (Prisons) is said to have agreed that such classification of prisoners is against the fundamental rights guaranteed by the constitution but no action had been taken.

Justice Pandurang Rao commission of enquiry report also felt that categorization of prisoners was against the provisions of the right to equality as envisaged in the constitution.

But there is strong opposition from the Congress leader Y S Rajasekhar Reddy to the proposed abolition of such categorization. A large number of MPs/MLAs all over India have criminal charges filed against them. As such one cannot expect them to support abolition of such distinction and ensure fundamental right guaranteed by the constitution. Perhaps future elections may throw up MPs/MLAs more interested in enforcement of guarantees provided by the Constitution, yet in the meantime, it is felt that it is the duty of the judiciary to take an active role and ensure abolishment of such unconstitutional practices.

In conclusion, one wish is that the judiciary, at all levels play a more active role in providing justice in an efficient and economical manner to all strata of society. As things stand today, people have little faith in the legislature or in the executive but so far have retained faith in the judiciary.

C. Executive

The executive is concerned with the implementation of the policies/enactments laid down by the legislature. The successful implementation depends on the efficiency with which the executives function at all levels – right from the seniormost Secretaries in the Union Government at Delhi to the junior most Government functionary at the village level. Some of these executives like the IAS, IPS, IRS, and IFS, etc. are chosen after undergoing a strict written exam and subsequent interview by the Public Service Commission. This is to ensure that the best possible talent is selected for the service of the nation. They are renumerated handsomely and enjoy a number of perquisites—perhaps the most important being permanency in service till retirement. Having selected the best candidates as administrators, one expects the nation to progress rapidly in the laid down policies. Besides they are expected to provide carefully considered advice to the Ministers as the administrators are far more educationally qualified than the politicians.

Prior to 1947, the administration depended essentially on the Indian Civil Service (ICS), who are considered to have discharged their responsibilities successfully. After Independence, the Indian Administrative Service (IAS) was constituted in place of the ICS. Besides various All India services like IPS, IRS, etc. were also set up. There is a widespread feeling that the administrators, whether they be IAS, IPS, IRS, IFS, etc. have generally failed the people of India in providing in recent years, citizen friendly administrative structure, as they seem to have become politicized and lost their independence.

Even a number of Public Service Selection Boards have been corrupted as can be seen from reports appearing in the media. The chances of upright candidates being selected seem to be diminishing – but not extinguished. A candidate who has to pay bribe just to get selected is going to start his administrative career by stooping to corrupt means to recover his investment and in the process lose his capacity for honest and fair play.

Gradually, the honest and conscientious officers start losing interest in being just and fair in their dealings with the people – and it is the nation that suffers. But even today a number of such sincere, honest officers carry on performing their duties, no matter what the obstacles.

Old time civil servants feel that the present day civil servants lack the vital concept of public service but more concerned with non-accountability and self preservation, no matter what the cost to the nation. In the 1980s, during the Prime Ministership of Rajiv Gandhi, a directive was issued that no action could be taken against any Government officer of the rank of Joint Secy. or above (JS) without the prior permission of the Government. In 2005, the Chief Vigilance Commissioner, P. Shankar, put up on the CVC website (www.cvc.nic.in) a list of 70 officials against whom sanction has been delayed for more than a year.

CBI had made a case against two former IAS officers in 1993, but sanction is not forthcoming.

It has to be realized that IAS officers are generalist and today's socio-economic climate needs a number of specialists at various posts. But it appears that the efforts are more to ensure that only IAS officers are selected for very senior posts requiring high degree of special qualifications.

After decades of desultory actions, India is making every effort to improve oil exploration, transport, refining, storage, etc. Special companies are also being set up in this regard. For instance Petronet LNG is a professionally managed company set up to build terminals for importing natural gas in ships. It is run by Board consisting of representatives of the promoters viz, ONGC, IOC, BPCL & GAIL (all owned by Govt of India), French consultant Gaz de France and the Asian Development Bank. A professional Chief Executive Officer (CEO) chosen through interviews heads the company. The Secy, Petroleum Ministry, Government of India is the ex-officio Chairman of the company. It is reported that a group of IAS officers is trying hard to force the company to change the norms for the selection as CEO of the new company. The idea is to ensure that an IAS officer of the rank of Joint Secy is made the CEO. Such posts go to specialists in the field (professional, not generalists like IAS) with commensurate pay packets and perks. But need to have the best specialist talent for such a post does not appear to weigh with some of the IAS officers who only want a generalist IAS officer to occupy the post. The need of the country for the best available talent does not appear to matter to such IAS officers, for whom ensuring the post carrying generous perks (comparable to international norms) seems to be more important than national interest.

It is interesting to note the comments of the Chief Minister , Maharashatra, made in Nov 2004. He admitted that there were too many IAS officers at senior level with the largest number of additional chief secy/principal secy. He further went on to add that principal secy deals with files which were formerly dealt with by section officers (very junior officers). It shows the wastage of talent in using IAS officers for such work. Senior IAS officers draw very generous pay and perquisites. It raises the question as to why the taxpayers' money is used in such a wasteful manner.

But does this large number of highly educated IAS officers who have been selected from lakhs of candidates help the state in providing efficient service to the people at large. The number of pending files is an important indicator of the efficiency with which such senior officers' work. Recently data obtained by a leading newspaper under the right to information act, gives the factual position regarding the cost of maintaining over 7,000 officials and employees in Mantralaya (headquarters of Maharashtra Government).

The table below gives data pertaining to the salary paid to officials (from desk officer upwards), the files cleared and the average cost per file.

Table 1

Dept.	Salary for Dec 2004-Rs	Files cleared number	Average cost per file-Rs.
General Administration	1.77 crores	524	33,806
Home	58.36 lakhs	511	2,324
Public Works	64.72 lakhs	733	8,830
Finance	57.78 lakhs	2,677	2,158
Irrigation	5.43 lakhs	1,078	6,870
Revenue & Forest	63.29 lakhs	1,204	5,257

Table 2: Period for which files pending

Dept.	upto Dec 2004	more than 2 years
Agriculture	8,198	1,035
Co-op Marketing, textiles	10,817	937
Home	16,397	1,621
Higher & Technical	10,630	1,377

Contd...

PWD	7,646	928
Revenue & forest	28,098	7,076
Rural	13,428	2,626
Urban	9,508	2,829
Water resources	15,077	2,808
School edu. & sports	9,375	1,509

As per reports, Mantralaya staffs were paid Rs. 106 crores as salary for 2004, though they kept 190,000 files pending. Some of the departments like GAD managed to dispose of 525 files out of more than 5600 pending files. The average output per staffer is about 1 file per month.

But one cannot blame a normal person from asking himself "How do these babus keep themselves busy?"

In 1999, Arun Shourie was made a Minister in the Central Government and was given charge of 4 high sounding departments, viz. (i) planning (DP), (ii) administrative reforms (DAR), (iii) programme implementation (DPI) and (iv) statistics (DS). The DAR was divided into 5 groups to build chronologies of files with details of dates, names and designations of officers commenting on the subject and the action taken. This matrix enabled the Minister to make a series of case studies in bureaucratic file pushing. A few such examples are given here which can explain the inordinate delay in the action taken by the Government in most of the cases.

Case-1: On 16 July 1997, a file was opened with a simple question "Should Mr. Singh (S), Dy Adviser in Programme Evaluation Organisation (PEO) of the Planning Commission (PC) be allowed to attend a training course at the Indian Institute of Public Administration (IIPA) in Delhi?"

On SEPT 1997, Advisor, (Evaluation) Mr. P. wrote to Mr. A Jt. Secy. Training, seeking content of training course. No reply was received. Mr. P. wrote on the file that he had discussed the matter with Member (Evaluation) and had written to National Institute of Rural Development (NIRD) Hyderabad, so that PEO officers could be trained there. On 26 Nov 1997,

Dy Secy, GAD, Mr. R states orders have been issued for in-service training programmes at the NIRD.

On 9 Dec 97, Jt Secy, Training , Mr. A is back in the picture saying there is "no specific relevant course" anywhere but it may be worthwhile to "consider" the Institute of Economic Growth, Delhi. Two days later, on 11 Dec 97, a note is written with regard to above for "considering" the Institute of Economic Growth.

On 23 Feb 1998, Mr. C, Director General of NIRD wrote offering 2 programmes, one for 3 weeks and the other for 4 weeks costing Rs. 3,500 per participant per week with minimum number of 20. All was quiet for 5 months when suddenly on 28 July 98, it was noted that Institute of Economic Growth would not be a bad idea after all. On 28 Oct 1998, Advisor, Evaluation, Mr. P, wrote back saying it would not be possible to send a batch of 20 officers for training for more than 2 weeks at a stretch, so the period of training should be less than 2 weeks. On 16 March 1999, the Principal Advisor wanted to know what had happened to the IIPA proposal of July 1997. Next day, Advisor, Evaluation, Mr P, pens a note that IIMA would take Indian Economic Service (IES) members only and that it would not be charging less than NIRD.

At last, on 23 Aug 1999, (two years after initiation of the file) and the 48th note by Dy Secy, GAD, Mr Amar Singh and 19 others are cleared to go to Hyderabad for the 10 day course in programme evaluation from 20 Dec to 31 Dec 1999. But this is not the end. On 31 Dec 1999, there is 52nd noting that the accounts branch of the Commission had not released Rs. 140,000 being the fee for the course.

The above is only one incident merely to indicate how the babus keep themselves busy.

Case-2: The Ministry of Steel forwards a "profound" query to the DAR as to which color of ink – green or red – is permissible for Government work. After several notings , reference is made to Bureau of Indian Standards. It cites a 1962 order that for a ball pen red or green is permissible but for a fountain pen it must be blue black. But such "profound" matters cannot be allowed to rest so early. At this stage, Secy, Personnel enters the picture and involves the Defence Ministry by asking them if they have a "uniform ink color-code". The Defence Ministry states that the three Service Chiefs are authorized to use red ink, while principal staff officers can use green but not red. The rest must use blue black. One year later the matter was still being pondered over.

Case-3: But even major projects get entangled in the bureaucratic procedure and are delayed. Joint Commissioner, Mr. B wanted a proposed National Project on Cattle Development, estimated at Rs. 402 crores, to be reframed as a Central Sector scheme by clubbing 3 ongoing schemes viz, Extension of Frozen Semen Technology, National Wool Production Programm and Assistance to Military Farms stating that the "objective of the scheme is to bring all the breedable cattle and buffaloes under artificial insemination or natural service, to arrange doorstep delivery of artificial insemination (AI) and to produce progeny tested bulls".

It had to do rounds in Yojana Bhavan as it included re-categorization as a Central scheme. It shuttled between 4 rooms in the same building within a minute's walk of each other. Each officer had his own views. One of them noted that it would require approval of full Planning Commission to be treated as a centrally sponsored scheme.

On 15 Sept 99, the Dy. Chairman, Planning Commission, clears the draft note for approval of full Commission. But even after 5 months the project for making frozen Cattle semen delivered at the farmers' doorstep is pending approval of one member.

ANNUAL CONFIDENTIAL REPORT

But there is a system of annual confidential report (ACR) on each bureaucrat. So does the ACR not help in separating the efficient and the inefficient ? Till about 1980, the ACR of two pages used by the British all these years was in use. It consisted of about one and half page for factual data and about 4 inch space for overall performance and grading. It was found adequate for decades and by and large the performance of the

Civil Service was satisfactory. Some of the comments in the ACR were quite pithy and to the point, e.g. Mr. A is a handsome officer 6 feet tall and that is saying it all.

It appears that since the last three decades, the politicians have devised a system of tempting bureaucrats with lucrative postings, and sinecures after retirement; on the other hand transfers used as a weapon to force unwilling bureaucrats to fall in line with the wishes of politicians. But with the generous salary and perks with security of service and without any fear of prosecution of almost any offence, it is indeed surprising that so many bureaucrats seem to be falling in line with the desires of the politicians. One cannot help feeling that the fall in standards of administration can be blamed on the lack of moral fibre in the absence of any other obvious factor.

But the senior officials will not accept any blame for this state of affairs as can be seen from the non-answering of questions in the assembly. In July 2005, the Chief Minster, Maharashtra was furious for leaving some starred questions unanswered though more than 30 days notice was given by MLAs. The Chief Minister issued notices to all departmental officers with clear instructions that firm action will henceforth be taken on any such delay or lapse.

But responsibility for preparing the reply for such questions has been fixed on subordinate officials. No action will be taken against any IAS officer. The blame has been put squarely on the section officer and will be suspended, the undersecretary will be let with a minor punishment, the deputy secy, will be given a written warning but no action whatsoever will be taken on the senior most official, viz. the Secretary in-charge of the concerned department.

GRASS ROOT LEVEL

In the final analysis the success of any organization depends on the ability of its leaders to motivate the rank and file, and the creation of appropriate atmosphere for the subordinates to function to the best of their ability

How far are the senior most IAS, IPS, IFS, IRS and other all India services successful in building an efficient organization in all spheres? For instance, the security of a nation ultimately depends on the sincerity and integrity of the ordinary policeman. But does the State provide with at least the basic necessities like shelter, decent pay and perquisites, working hours, etc. to such policemen?

The ordinary Mumbai constable puts in atleast 12 hours work everyday with each shift of twelve hours. Very few are provided with residential quarters . Most of them are compelled to stay in slums with quite often criminals as their neighbours. The State Government is under an obligation to provide free accommodation. Yet most of the almost 40,000 cops have to make their own arrangements.

But the Government forces him to lead a life without dignity, yet expects him to perform his duty (12 hour shift) efficiently and honestly. For instance, it is common to find cops-even senior cops with 20 years service – living in a slum through which flows an open drain. His home consists of only one room where his entire family lives, including teen aged children and at times dependents also.

The Police in Mumbai work in 2 shifts of 12 hours. But during festivals and VVIP bandobast duty, they quite often put in upto 36 hours at a stretch. No wonder the numbers of cops in Mumbai crack under this unnatural life and commit suicide. Sometimes they enter into a suicide pact with their family so as to save their family the hardships after their death. Yet no Government has taken any steps to ameliorate their working or living conditions. The state budget provides only Rs. 500 crores for the Mumbai police whereas the budget for the Delhi police is said to be Rs. 1,000 crores for far fewer number of policemen.

A Head constable with 20 years service in Mumbai can get a maximum pay of about Rs. 150,000 per annum, gross inclusive of all benefits. Lately the Maharashtra Government is talking a lot of making Mumbai into another Shanghai. But Shanghai pays its new recruits Yuan 3,000 per month (over Rs. 15,000 per month). In New York, the lowest recruit earns about Rs. 20,00,000 per annum – but even after adjusting for Purchasing Power Parity, it still comes to about Rs. 5 lakhs per annum.

The MLAs and the IAS (and all India service officers like IPS, etc.) get generous salary allowance and perks, though they are very miserly when giving bare minimum payment to the ordinary constable. Even the miserly payments are delayed at times for months.

Recently the Home Dept (Maharashtra) had promised to double the refreshment allowance for constables and police sub inspectors from existing Rs. 15 a day to Rs. 30 a day. But it will be paid for only a maximum of 200 days in a year and not for the actual number of days even when normally it amounts to more than 300 days. The Government's excuse for putting a 200 day limit is to prevent undue claims for allowance made by the police—who are also poorly paid and not even provided quarters as the Government is required to do. In contrast, the MLAs and the IAS, IPS officers feel nothing wrong in hiking individual MLAs salary by Rs. 10,000 per month. Some of the Ministers have more than one air conditioner in each room of their bungalow and Government foots the bill of an average of Rs. 1,000 per day for such privileged persons. An average constable's salary is about Rs. 6,000 per month with no perks like accommodation, etc.

Even rewards promised by the Government of Maharashtra are rarely honored. In 1993, a 10 member police team had made a record haul of 1,500 kg of RDX (A deadly explosive) from Mumbra, suburb of Mumbai after the serial bomb blast in 1993, and was promised a reward. Despite repeated reminders, neither the Home Dept nor senior police officials took any initiative to give the promised award to the team. Ultimately the media reported the sad delay in rewarding the team for the record haul. The issue of non-payment was raised in the Legislative Council by some member. This forced the State Government to issue order for immediate payment of the long delayed (over 12 years) award.

In contrast, the Tamil Nadu Government is reported to have paid immediately the cash reward of Rs. 50 lakhs and promotion to the special task force and the police personnel involved in killing of the notorious Veerappan. Even the Gujarat police were honored and rewarded immediately after they arrested the

5 terrorists who planned to eliminate the then Dy. Prime Minister, L.K. Advani, more than a year ago.

The police department is treated shabbily, giving an impression that it is not considered important enough to merit attention. The ordinary constable and the non-IPS officers like sub inspectors are paid poorly whereas the IPS officers, being an all India cadre, get recompensed handsomely during their service period as also in retirement.

The Government has failed to provide accommodation to most of the poorly paid constables. But even their efforts to form a co-operative housing society and develop housing for themselves have failed. The State Government had promised to alleviate the acute housing problem of policemen. Several societies were inaugurated in Mumbai, but the Government has not sanctioned even a single plot for the police societies. Consequently about 5,000 policemen who had registered societies after paying the charges have been left high and dry. For instance, a plot at Worli (south Mumbai) meant for policemen has now been allotted to MLAs. In the last few years, a number of such plots have been allotted to MPs, MLAs, etc. but none to policemen.

While on the one hand the state of Maharashtra, one of the most prosperous states, is unable to provide even basic facilities to enable cops to lead a life of dignity, it admits providing security cover to about 800 people for supposedly facing threat to their lives. This involves about 2,000 policemen including 100 officers. These policemen are withdrawn from regular duties of providing security to the common citizen. The Government admits it loses Rs. 180 crores a year and is a drain on the finances of the state.

While almost Rs. 200 crores are spent on providing security cover for such people, the Government is so cash strapped that even telephone lines of some police stations are cut off for non-payment of bills. It may be noted that telephone/electricity supply of MLAs/MPs are not cut off even if individual bills of lakhs of rupees remain unpaid.

While some citizens are provided special posse of policemen

to guard them, it cannot safeguard an ordinary citizen. Even a simple thing like continuous patrolling a small stretch of road about 10 km from the Mumbai airport (within the city limits) to the heart of the city cannot be kept under continuous patrolling for about 4 hours at night. Ordinary citizens work abroad and return with their hard earned money. On this small stretch of road in the heart of the city, the police themselves admit that on an average 2 robberies of passengers returning from abroad, take place every month.

All over India, policemen used as private security guards for politicians and favored few at the cost of the honest tax-payer. For instance, after demitting office, ex-Prime Ministers get protection from special protection group (SPG) — (a) Narsimha Rao – 162 SPG and 24 SPG cars at Delhi and 71 SPG and 25 SPG cars protect Rao's offspring at Hyderabad, (b) H.D. Devegowda , 159 SPG and 24 cars at Delhi plus 60 SPG and 60 cars at Bangalore, (c) Inder Gujral, 167 SPG Plus 25 SPG cars. Besides they get additional police force from local police when they travel. In addition, Central Reserve Police Force (CRPF) are also posted outside ex-PM's homes. 7 SPG men also accompany ex-PMs on every flight. If this is democracy, then why is this burden on the honest tax-payer?

But despite all these handicaps, like extremely poor salaries, no career path or promotional avenues, miserable working and living conditions, by and large the ordinary cop not only resists temptation in the performance of his duties, but tries his best to give a better life to his children. But honesty does not guarantee a better life for his dependents. On the contrary it quite often leads to suicide. There have been many such instances in Mumbai.

As can be seen, the ordinary people of India, including cops want a better life, at least for their children. A shining example for the betterment of the Policemen's children is given here. With the assistance of the police Commissioner, Thane, about 4,000 policemen have pooled in nearly Rs. 3 lakhs to renovate a building with new furniture, etc. so that about 100 kids – all children of policemen can have good education in good surroundings. Two sets of uniform have been given to each child from the police welfare fund. The children are enthusiastic about the renovated school and started taking keen interest in their studies and also in new educational cum play activities in school.

Similarly, a number of IAS officers are taking interest in improving the lot of the people. Just one instance is given here. In Bihar, an honest and upright IAS couple perform their duties despite setbacks.

Amit Khare did his Management degree from IIM Ahmedabad and then entered IAS. As Deputy Commissioner, Singhbhum, Jharkhand, he uncovered the Fodder scam which allegedly involves the then Chief Minister, Lalu Yadav. As District Magistrate (DM) Patna, he conducted a raid on High Security Beur jail and recovered 50 TV sets, a number of mobile phones, music systems, numerous knives, generators, etc. His wife is also an IAS officer. When posted as Sub Divisional Officer (SDO) Seraikela, Bihar, she fought against witchcraft, launched a successful literacy drive and promoted tribal culture like Chau dance and Madhubani paintings.

Looking at bureaucratic delays and inefficiencies at all levels one cannot be blamed for thinking that ordinary Indians are completely lacking in management or organizational skills. It is the normal practice in India to look to graduates of AIIMS or IITs or IAS officers or foreign consultants to solve organizational problems. There is a tendency particularly at the Government level to look down upon our traditional skills in all spheres. A few such examples are given here to show that great organizational skills are possessed by ordinary people.

Case-1: Kumbh Mela—Allahabad (UP) 2001

It is held on the banks of the river Ganga at Allahabad and extends over 41 days. One particular day is considered particularly auspicious. In this case it was 24 Jan 2001 when about 2.5 crore people (25 million people) took a dip in the restricted area. The arrangements for the Kumbh Mela start about a year in advance. The Government estimates of all possible requirements as also the budget is made a year in advance by the UP Government.

Shri Jeevesh Nandan, an officer of the UP Government was specially appointed as the Mela officer. In just about 2 months, he created a township on the banks of the river Ganga. A township (Kumbhnagar) with basic amenities for an expected 7 crore (seventy million) visitors, all of whom come to have a dip in the holy Ganga. The temporary township was built to accommodate seventy million people, i.e. over twice the size of greater London.

The entire mela site was the handiwork of Government workforce of about 20,000 people with a little voluntary help who essentially helped in sanitation, cleanliness, as life guards and crowd management. Under the conditions prevailing, safety of such vast numbers over a period of 41 days was a major concern. Not only was a record number of police personnel employed but even the help of the army was taken.

The actual work of setting up the Kumbhnagar began towards the end of September, but in some spots the river was flowing till October.

The logistics were overwhelming – a tent township was set up on 5,000 hectares on the banks of the river. About 500,000 (half a million) tents were set up for common devotees, space was allotted to more than 1000 religious and cultural organizations for their own shamianas and tents. A hospital, 20 clinics, 28 police stations and 35 police posts were set up along with 17,000 toilets, 5000 temporary phone connections and 16,000 street lamps, 20 big tube wells, 145kms of pipelines as also 150 telephone booths.

The mela site was divided into 4 zones and 15 sectors with thousands of police including mounted police. In Oct, i.e. 3 months before the mela, the entire area came under heavy surveillance. A dozen anti-sabotage teams with mine detection and bomb squads with sniffer dogs were pressed into service, besides terrorist spotters from the army. The safety measures were extremely thorough, they also included river police, CCTV and infra-red night vision cameras, etc.

Because of the religious nature of the mela, consumption of alcohol, and non-veg food was forbidden. No attempt was made to commercialize the mela by attracting or permitting advertisements.

The entire mela attracted about 3 crore (thirty million) devotees with about 10 lakhs (1 million) staying over a month in the temporary township. The mela went of smoothly without a hitch, even without any health problems.

Shri K.R. Narayanan, the then President of India was all praise for the officials in conducting the mela involving millions, without any mishap.

Case-2: Kumbh Mela, Nashik (Maharashtra) 2003

In August 2003, a Kumbh Mela was held on the banks of the river Godavari, Nashik. More than 250,000 sadhus came for the mela. This is another example of extremely efficient organizational skills lying dormant among the ordinary Indian bureaucrats, particularly with the Municipal offices all over India.

The entire exercise was properly planned and flawlessly executed. To ensure cleanliness and avoid increasing the workload on existing staff, additional 800 cleaners were taken up on contract. Each one was paid Rs. 100 a day. They were provided with new yellow T shirts, rain coats, and boots.

Normally the city generates about 250 mt of garbage per day but quantity almost doubled during the mela period. Nashik already has an 87 acre compost plant to convert garbage into manure. The closed drains at Sadhugram were connected to the sewage treatment plant. For the first time, the Godavari river was free of sewage. Everyday about 80 million litres of treated water gushes into the river from 5 pumping stations. With the springing up of Sadhugram, about 350 million litres of water as against normal 220 million litres of water were supplied after treatment at 2 new filtration plants. 3,700 toilets and 800 bathrooms had been built with drains that did not leak and taps that worked. Though the city normally gets drinking water for 5 hours daily, Sadhugram was supplied for 24 hours.

Health measures were very strict. Uncovered food or overripe fruits were confiscated by the food inspectors. Nashik faces mosquito nuisance. All fever samples at mela were tested for malaria, but no case of malaria was reported. Common complaints were nothing more than flu or common cold.

With about 2.5 lakh sadhus from all over the country descending on Nashik, there was no rotting filth, no disease, no epidemic or any stampede. Everything went of smoothly, thanks to the management skills of the organizers and the efficiency in working at every level.

It can be seen that talent and capacity to deliver goods exists at every level but the appropriate opportunities and atmosphere is not being provided, as a rule, at the lower levels i.e. below the IAS and all India services level leading to frustration of capable people. With proper motivation and guidance, there is no reason why India cannot be a leader in every sphere.

The Summing-Up

28

In January 1950, India declared itself a Sovereign Democratic Republic and took over the reins of power. It was free to plan for the development of the nation so as to build a healthy prosperous nation based on a vibrant and newly emerging democracy where every citizen would be expected to play his role for the ongoing benefit of the newly formed republic.

It is therefore time to take an overview of the state of the Sovereign Democratic Republic of India 50 years after it came into existence. As clarified earlier, this book is not an empirical study and hence does not depend on economic or statistical data or parameters. It deals with the perception by the average citizen of India of the quality of life as enjoyed by him and the change effected during the last 50 years.

India had tremendous advantages as indicated in chapter 4. South Korea, Japan, China, Malaysia, Taiwan, etc. whose achievements have been briefly touched upon in the earlier chapters, passed through civil wars or suffered severe damage due to World War II. Yet all these countries are far ahead of India socio-economically – judged by any standards. An average citizen in any of these countries lives a life of simple dignity with no class or religious discrimination and takes for granted the unrestricted availability of necessities of life.

Has it built up a nation where even the poorest citizen can lead a life of simple dignity with atleast his basic needs being satisfied? Has it been able to provide adequate quantity of water to every citizen – whether in urban or rural sector? Has it ensured that not a single citizen, no matter whether he is an urban dweller or a tribal in the forests, remains hungry even for a day? Has it been able to provide residential accommodation on affordable rental basis to every citizen who needs shelter? Has it been able to provide public health care on affordable basis for the millions of citizens all over the country? Has it been able to ensure that every citizen has access to primary education and becomes literate? Has it been able to provide electricity on a continuous breakdown free 24 hour basis all over the country including the rural sector? And after more than 50 years, has it instilled the spirit of unity and oneness among the millions of citizens of diverse caste, creed, community, religion or province? Has it become one of the leading nations in atleast some sphere of industrial, scientific, consumer product manufacturing?

Unfortunately for India, the answer is in the negative as can be observed from the earlier chapters.

But it is felt that the failure to nurture the delicate plant of Democracy as also the lack of good governance , has resulted in all the shortcomings and failures.

As Dr. Ambedkar, Dr. Rajendra Prasad and all the members of the Constituent Assembly and members of the parliamentary session after the first general election had held high hopes for the success of Democracy, but they had also spelt out the need for men of character to be elected so as to ensure success of democracy. They had also specifically spelt out the dangers to the fledgling Indian nation in case of failure of democracy if men without vision and character were to be elected.

Their forebodings seem to be coming true, judging by the number of people charged with criminal offences and basing their election campaign on narrow religious or parochial grounds, getting elected to Lok Sabha or State legislatures.

This raises a very profound question with far reaching consequences viz, is democracy losing ground? Or will people of vision and character, as envisaged by Dr. Ambedkar, Dr. R. Prasad and others, be able to get elected despite the tremendous odds in fighting candidates with alleged criminal background?

If people charged with criminal offences like murder, dacoity, rioting can get elected, is it not possible for such candidates also charged with sedition or treason to get elected and form a

Government at the Centre? In such a case, will the President of India be bound by the Government's advice? A very frightening possibility to contemplate – that will be the end of Democracy and possibly the existence of India as Sovereign Democratic Republic.

But the concept of Democracy in India is a very recent one. For centuries there were hundreds of kings, maharajas, nawabs, etc. ruling the princely states, often fighting with each other and facilitating the conquering by the invaders, of the entire land mass then known as Hindustan.

In 1857, India (or Hindustan) became a part of the British Empire. The Indian National Congress (INC) was soon formed thereafter by Mr. David O Hume. In due course INC raised the demand for independence as a democratic country. But even INC gave great importance to Shri. Mohandas K Gandhi in the 1940s, when he was the guiding spirit, but not a member of the INC.

This could be considered an example of peculiar form of democracy in India when the INC deferred to the wishes of Mahatma Gandhi who was not even a member of the INC. He wielded moral authority but not legal authority.

Even to this day, very few parties exhibit inner party democracy – quite often members of a party are only too willing to leave ultimately all decisions to the Head of the Party. Some observers feel that this is due to the fact that the Indian mindset is still in a feudal state and has yet to grasp the fundamentals of democracy where all members are equal.

Another worrisome factor for the continued growth of democracy is the undue importance given to caste and religion, particularly where elections are considered – whether at the village panchayat level or the general elections for the Lok Sabha membership, irrespective of the merits of the candidate. Dalits continue to be oppressed despite the enactment of laws for their protection. Religion, unfortunately, plays an important role in almost all activities. The subcontinent was divided in 1947 on the basis of religion and the Muslims who desired a separate Muslim homeland got Pakistan. The majority preferred to stay in India. It is evident that politicians are encouraging factionalism and fissiparous tendencies among the Muslims and dalits only for the sake of votes. No attempt is being made by such politicians to ensure the unity and integrity of the nation by giving all citizens equality irrespective of religion, caste, creed or province. Socio-economic means to eradicate casteism are not implemented in earnest. This is an area where urgent rational steps are needed for ensuring the unity and integrity of the nation and the safety of every citizen of the country irrespective of caste, creed, color, religion or province. Even entire regions like the North Eastern states have started feeling alienated from the rest of the country for the socio-economic treatment meted out to them.

But people's expectations for a better life are rising – if not for themselves, then at least for their children.

The present bureaucracy at the highest level consisting of mainly highly educated people, selected after rigorous tests have been found wanting as a class though with honorable exceptions. There are hundreds of bureaucrats doing a wonderful job, no matter even if sincere work is not appreciated by their superiors. A few token examples have been mentioned in the earlier chapters. It has to be reiterated that India has the talent at all levels to tackle any job successfully, if only such people are left free to carry on their jobs without any extraneous pressures likely to affect their work adversely.

India as a nation is very lucky to have a diversity of talent in every sphere of activity – only it has not yet been harnessed properly for the progress of the nation and betterment of the citizens as a whole.

A few examples are given here to show the wide diversity of talent all over the country.

In 1890 (repeat 1890), there were very few hotels and restaurants in Bombay; but the officers, mainly British and Parsis, needed their lunch. This need was met by an organization set up by one Shri Mahadeo Bacche, a semiliterate from Junnar district, Maharashtra. He arranged a system whereby his men would collect the lunch (tiffin) from the residence and deliver at the office anywhere in Bombay city. Even today, after almost 115 years of existence, the organization is going strong. It is now a legendary dabba (tiffin) delivery system run by semiliterate people. It is a low tech network known for its clockwork precision and now being asked to give lectures on the basics of management and planning to corporate bosses. Daily they deliver 1,75,000 tiffins to the precise address. Some years back the leading US business magazine "Forbes" gave the Dabbawallahs a 6 Sigma performance rating – which means one error in 6 million transactions.

The low tech network known for its clockwork precision in delivering dabbas is giving tips to the management institutes and their high flying senior manager alumni on the basics of management and planning. Shri Raghunath Medge, Head of the Nutan Mumbai Tiffin Box Suppliers Charity Trust and Organization, recently, in a seminar held at Mumbai, explained their system to senior business executives. He told them that their simple system is based on teamwork with no owners and workers and no middlemen either. He was a special invitee, to speak about the network of 5,000 carriers, who deliver dabbas daily to about 1,75,000 people without a single mistake, all over Mumbai. He explained their simple coding system easily understood even by semiliterate workers, on every tiffin box which enables them to deliver the tiffin box without a single mistake. Prince Charles had personally invited the organization to his wedding in UK. The two representatives of the Dabbawalla Association who went to UK in response to the invitation personally extended by Prince Charles were overwhelmed by the graciousness with which they were treated at the reception.

Anyway, this is just one more example of the talent which awaits to be fully exploited for the benefit of the nation.

But it has to be reiterated that plenty of talent is waiting to be discovered and nurtured along proper lines. For instance, in 1960, a school was started by late Keshavrao Deshmukh with a donation of Rs. 1.5 lakhs plus 100 acres of land. The Sanskriti Samavardan Mandal is primarily for the under privileged children from rural areas in Nanded, Maharashtra. It has about 3,000 students out of whom 600 are orphans. Many children are sent by Juvenile Courts and some from disturbed families. More than 2,000 are taught free of charge.

A businessman from Mumbai recently volunteered to adopt 50 of the students and train them in athletics. 20 girls and 30 boys were handpicked and started training with National athlete Bhagwan Nagaroji being appointed as a full time coach. These kids are kept on a special diet to optimize their performance as they have to participate in the National Games, Asian Games, Commonwealth Games and the 2008 Olympics in Beijing as their final target.

At the 16th annual Varsha Marathon held at Thane (Maharashtra) in July 2004, 21 students from the school participated and 14 of them won prizes. These children were easy to identify in the Games as they were the only ones participating without shoes while all the others wore Nike or Reebok shoes.

From Sports to education, it is the same heartening story of grit and perseverance overcoming all obstacles.

Rajhans Night High School, Dombivli (near Mumbai, Maharashtra) is a one classroom school that produced three toppers getting 84.6 %, 80 % and 78 % marks at the Secondary School Certificate exam in 2005. Classes are usually held from 6.30 pm to 9.30 pm, but twice a week, classes are held from 2 pm to 5 pm because of no power due to load shedding. All the students come from families where money is hard to come by. The school had 45 students of whom more than 30 passed the SSC exam. Shri Pavan Singh, Principal of the school was proud of the performance of the students knowing the background and problems faced by the students. The teachers also teach at day schools and give personal attention to such students. With no infrastructure and irregular power due to load shedding for hours at a stretch, the school produced 3 toppers at SSC exam.

Nandurbar is a tribal dominated district in Maharashtra which shot into fame for its malnutrition related deaths of infants. But today, the youth of Nandurbar are exploring possibilities of higher education all over the world, thanks to interest taken by the Government and encouragement by the

Tribal Commissioner. But due to the spread of Information Technology, TV, computer, education is spreading rapidly in the backward district and children are finding wonderful options on the internet. Already Nikhil Valvi, a tribal boy from Nandurbar is now studying in Perth, Australia. Other students are trying to follow suit. The Government is also extending a helping hand with free scholarships for atleast 10 students to study abroad with preference to children of landless tribals.

Then there is the story of Rina, daughter of a leper begging in the streets of Raxaul (Bihar) who was lucky to be taken to UK. Rina learnt reading and writing skills at the Mission School in Raxaul. In 1994, she impressed Lady Patsy Putham who was touring Community projects in India. Lady Putham was impressed by Rina's desire to learn and arranged for her to get a scholarship at Gordonstoun Public School in Scotland, of which Prince Charles is an Alumnus. She has now graduated with 3 A- levels in Pharmacy and is now concentrating on the next challenge to join medical school. She hopes to return to India after qualifying as a doctor to help fight leprosy.

Rural violence appears to be increasing particularly in Bihar –the main reason being increasing socio-economic disparity and lack of Government support to the poor villagers to live peaceful lives and to fight violence.

Tiliya devi and America devi fought opposition from all quarters, including their homes to bring about a change in the lives of the poor and downtrodden, with peaceful methods, they have prevented the Maoists from spreading over more than 550 flood prone villages in Darbhanga, Saharsa, Madhubani, etc. districts of Bihar. These 2 illiterate dalit women are associated with "Lok Shakti Sangathan" and "Samajik Shaikshanik Vikas Samiti". So far no incident of Naxalite violence has been reported from these 550 villages.

These 2 women from Bihar now figure on the preliminary list of nominees for this year's Nobel Prize to be jointly given to 1,000 women from all over the world.

All these activities of such diverse people only go to show that the people of India, particularly the young and the women, urban and tribal, are no longer content with the present state of affairs. Thanks to the spread of TV, and Internet they have realized that life need not continue to be bleak. They see opportunity for a much better life, which they now believe is achievable, if not for this generation, atleast for their children. They have now started realizing prosperity, progress and peaceful life are their birthright like for any other citizen. In due course, the pace of progress will rapidly pick up momentum and only those politicians who can give them a better life will win elections. Even the bureaucrats, senior and junior, will realize that people's expectations are high and people will no longer tolerate bureaucratic hassles, corruption and procrastination, but will insist on results.

The present scenario looks dismal for the nation but considering the rapidity of the spread of information and knowledge thanks to Information Technology, TV and computers as also the efforts by young and old in pockets spread all over India in diverse fields, the dream of a united prosperous and healthy nation where real democracy with every citizen an equal partner in the continued growth of the nation is no longer a dream. India is slowly awakening from the sleep extending over almost half a century and should be taking its rightful place in the comity of nations.